PERSPECTIVES ON BRAZILIAN HISTORY

INSTITUTE OF LATIN AMERICAN STUDIES
COLUMBIA UNIVERSITY

PERSPECTIVES
ON BRAZILIAN HISTORY

Edited with an Introduction and
Bibliographical Essay

BY

E. BRADFORD BURNS

COLUMBIA UNIVERSITY PRESS
NEW YORK & LONDON
1967

E. Bradford Burns is the author of *The Unwritten Alliance: Rio-Branco and Brazilian-American Relations*. He
is Associate Professor of History at Columbia University.

Copyright © 1967 Columbia University Press

Library of Congress Catalog Card Number: 67–13779

Printed in the United States of America

THE INSTITUTE OF LATIN AMERICAN STUDIES OF COLUMBIA
UNIVERSITY was established in 1961 in response to a national, public, and educational need for a better understanding of the contemporary problems of the Latin
American nations and a more knowledgeable basis for
inter-American relations. The major objectives of the
Institute are to prepare a limited number of North
Americans for scholarly and professional careers in the
field of Latin American studies and to advance our
knowledge of Latin America and its problems through
an active program of research by faculty, by graduate
students, and by visiting scholars.

Some of the results of the research program, as well as
other research of direct interest to the program, are published in a series of the Institute of Latin American
Studies. The faculty of the Institute believes that these
publications will stimulate interest in and improve public and scholarly knowledge of Latin America and con-
tribute to the advancement of inter-American relations.
PERSPECTIVES ON BRAZILIAN HISTORY is the
third volume in the series.

The Institute of Latin American Studies is grateful
to the Ford Foundation for financial assistance which has
made this publication program possible.

To
Linda Musser
I remember.

PREFACE

It is my hope that this collection of essays on Brazilian historiography will achieve two purposes: first, to provide the American public interested in Brazil with some new insights into Brazilian history; and second, to make a modest contribution to a long-neglected field of study in the United States—Latin American historiography in general and Brazilian historiography in particular. Although the nine essays translated for this volume are by recognized experts in the field, they have not been published in English before.

The essays are all self-contained; and except for "Problems in Brazilian History and Historiography," by José Honório Rodrigues, they are presented in their entirety. To put the essays into sharper focus for a North American audience, I have added a general introduction, describing the colonial historiographical background, as well as a brief introduction to each essay. In the bibliographical essay which concludes the collection, I have indicated other sources the interested reader may consult in order to pursue this subject further. As much as possible I tried to standardize the notes, which varied widely in form in the original essays. Where necessary, I added explanatory notes. Portuguese spelling changes periodically, and these essays written at different periods reflected that variance; it was my intent to make the spelling of proper names consistent.

I personally do not subscribe to everything these seven authors have said. It is not surprising to find them occasionally contradicting one another. It is a little distressing, however, to find them in several instances contradicting themselves. I refrained at those points from making an editorial comment. The situation simply illustrates the complexity (and perversity) of Brazilian historiography, and should move others to take up the task of clarification. At any rate, those minor internal contradictions do not detract from the admirable major points made by the authors.

I am indebted to Diane Yap for making a first-draft translation of the Pedro Moacyr Campos essay and to Norris Lyle for the first-draft translations of the other essays. I thank Gregory Kurtz for his careful proofreading of the manuscript. I am grateful to Robert J. Tilley of Columbia University Press for the enthusiastic encouragement he gave me to prepare this historiographic study.

A research grant from the University of California at Los Angeles helped to facilitate and expedite the work on this book.

E. BRADFORD BURNS

Muscatine, Iowa
January, 1967

Contents

PERSPECTIVES ON BRAZILIAN HISTORY

E. BRADFORD BURNS

Introduction

Americans have been reticent to recognize the importance of Brazil, the fifth largest, eighth most populous, and potentially one of the richest, of the nations in the world. As a consequence, they have been slow in studying their South American neighbor in depth and, hence, slow in understanding its development and aspirations. Some excellent travel accounts and a few general introductions constituted for many decades the only American contributions to the study of Brazil. Not until 1942, when Alexander Marchant published his *From Barter to Slavery: The Economic Relations of Portuguese and Indians in the Settlement of Brazil, 1500–1580,* did the first monograph on Brazilian history appear in the United States. Even today, although studies of the Brazilian past are being published with increasing frequency, there is still no satisfactory history of that land in English. In fact, there is only one history in our language which attempts to cover the entire sweep of the Brazilian past, João Pandiá Calógeras's unimaginative and expository study, *A History of Brazil,* translated by Percy Alvin Martin. First published in 1939, this translation was reprinted in 1963. There is at present an urgent need for a penetrating history which will discuss the patterns and meanings of Brazilian development for the educated American public.

With the hope of providing some greater depth to the study of Brazil's past, the following essays have been collected from diverse sources and translated into English for the first time. With the exception of Karl Friedrich Philipp von Martius, who wrote the learned and incisive article "How the History of Brazil Should Be Written," the authors are all Brazilians. These historiographical essays were selected because they met one or more of four criteria. First, they tend to be to a greater or lesser extent interpretive studies concerned with understanding and explaining the past. Second, they provide a wider perspective of the past through the insights and reflections of some of the most challenging intellects active in the writing of history. Third, they serve as critical and selective guides to some of the best historical literature concerning Brazil. Fourth, most of them discuss some of the major problems posed by the study of the evolution of Brazil: What, for example, have been the significant influences at work on the formation of Brazil; or what are the major periods into which Brazilian history can be divided; or what are the principal themes pervading the history? These and similar questions have received increasing attention from the twentieth-century Brazilian historians who have become less expository and more interpretive in their approach. Vianna Moog, author of *Bandeirantes and Pioneers,* expressed that attitude when he wrote, "The truth is that not only do the facts not speak for themselves but in order to make sense they perforce have to be interpreted." José Honório Rodrigues, the contemporary historian who has contributed more than anyone else to the study of Brazilian historiography, also has expressed the need for interpretive history. According to him, "The variability of interpretive opinion and the inalterability of the facts are the two poles of historical studies. But, in order to distinguish the shadows and the darkness, theories are indispensable." Both Moog and Rodrigues concur then with the eminent British historian, Edward Hallett Carr: "Interpretation . . . is the life-blood of history." The essays in this collection reveal various aspects of interpretive historiographical thought.

As with the histories of all the republics of this hemisphere, the basic division of Brazilian history has been into the colonial and national periods. For Brazil, the political division between these periods came on September 7, 1822, when Prince Pedro gave the cry of Ipiranga: "Independence or Death!" Although the essays which follow are concerned with the totality of Brazilian history, they place emphasis on historians and historiographical tendencies since independence, the most active period for studying and writing about the past. For that reason a short discussion is in order now of some of the men who wrote history during the colonial period and what they wrote.

Colonial Brazilian historiography is divided into two periods. The chroniclers dominate the first; the historians, the second. Such a division rests upon the obvious historiographical differentiation. The chronicles were written by observant, literate men on the scene, witnesses to the events described. Those chroniclers kept a simple record of facts and events, arranged in order of time, as observations and judgments on their own present. They did not seek to recreate the past. Their story was a drama of flesh and blood, undisturbed by the sterile compilation of documents, and uninterested in analysis or interpretation. Consequently they were not preoccupied with the definition, concepts, or theories of history. What was direct reporting of current events for one generation, however, became historical narrative for those which followed. The passage of time transforms the chronicles into histories of a past age.

It was the historian, with his concern to recreate the past, who dominated the last century of the colonial era. He not only recorded chronologically but explained and interpreted Brazil's development. In his effort to accomplish those goals, he used documents, letters, reports, and of course chronicles. Based upon those primary sources, supplemented by previously published histories, oral interviews, and some hearsay, he reconstructed the past as best he could. The better his source material, the more successful were the results of his efforts. Unlike his predecessors in Brazilian historiography, the colonial historian lacked the drama and excitement of active participation which remain as the major charm and attraction of the chroniclers.

The chroniclers made their appearance very early in Brazilian history and in one form or another remained throughout the colonial period. However, they were most active during the sixteenth and seventeenth centuries. With two important exceptions, they held a monopoly during the years from 1500 to 1730. Their works began to appear as soon as the Portuguese set foot in the New World.

Pero Vaz de Caminha, a governmental scribe accompanying Pedro Alvares Cabral to the East, witnessed the discovery of Brazil and was the first to write about the new land. In a letter dated May 1, 1500, and addressed to King Manoel, he described the discovery and painted a verbal picture of the shore the Portuguese first visited.[1] The letter testified to the beauty of the land. It spoke of the inhabitants as "good and of pure simplicity." In its rhapsodic passages on the Indians, it exemplifies the early romantic attitudes toward them. Those attitudes disappeared within a few decades, not to reappear again until José de Alencar and his followers set pen to paper in the mid-nineteenth century. Caminha's charming letter, the first Brazilian chronicle, sounded a note of optimism which nearly all the chroniclers and historians of the colonial period echoed. Here was a land of unmeasured extent, rich in vegetation, alluring to both the eye and the imagination, and inhabited by an attractive new race.

If Pero Vaz de Caminha related the excitement of the discovery, it was Pero Lopes de Sousa (150[?]–1539) in his *Diário da Navegação* who recorded the first efforts at colonization, 1531–1532. After exploring much of the east coast of South America, Martím Afonso de Sousa, brother of the chronicler, founded São Vicente (near the present-day Santos) and a short time later Piratininga, the humble ancestor of São Paulo. The *Diário* is written in a difficult style. Its brusque manner lacks the pleasantness of most of the chronicles, but the information it contains concerning the foundation of Portuguese America is invaluable.

The historiography of the first century of settlement owes much to the Jesuits.[2] Those indefatigable correspondents began to write as soon as they arrived in 1549; their rambling and garrulous letters and reports span the remaining half-century. The Jesuit letters fall into three series. The first, written by Padre Manoel da Nóbrega (1517–1570), covers the period 1549–

1561.[3] The second, the miscellaneous or "random" letters, bridge the years 1550–1568.[4] These sixty-three letters were written by twenty-four different Jesuits. The third series contains the letters and reports of Padre José de Anchieta (1534–1597) from 1554 through 1594.[5] Taken together the one-hundred-and-twenty-four letters and three reports in these series are primary sources par excellence for the researcher who seeks both the events and the flavor of that century. They vividly depict life in sixteenth-century Brazil. Afrânio Peixoto has observed that in those letters one sees the birth and growth of Brazil.[6] They are considerably more than historical documents. They vibrate with emotion, since they were written by men who actively participated in the events.

The Jesuit letters contain material of interest for a wide range of scholars: theologians, anthropologists, botanists, linguists, historians, economists, *et al.* As their letters demonstrate, the padres were curious observers, fascinated by their novel surroundings. They traveled up and down the three-thousand-mile coastline, where they had access to the highest governmental office and to the humblest Indian hut. Relating their experiences in numerous and often long letters, they discussed or mentioned every conceivable topic. The subjects most frequently treated were religious matters, Portuguese-Indian relations, Indian life, Indian-Church relations, the *aldeia* system, expansion, the French (and to a lesser degree other foreigners) in Brazil, agriculture, and descriptions of the new land and of colonists and officials.

As a group, the Jesuits displayed enthusiasm for their new surroundings. They worked to dispel the derogatory opinions held in Portugal about the American colony. Typical of the high regard they felt for their new home is this passage from a letter written in Bahia in 1560:

And for the love of Christ, I ask you to lose the bad opinion which you have of Brazil, because I tell you truly that if there is paradise here on earth, I would say that it is in Brazil. And if I feel this way, I do not know anyone here who does not. . . . There is no healthier place in the world—fresh air, pleasant countryside—another like it cannot be found;

the foods I think are better than those in Portugal, or at least that is my opinion, and truly I never even have a desire for any of the food there. If there are chickens in Portugal, here there are more and they are cheaper; if there is livestock in Portugal, here there are so many animals which are hunted in the forest, and they have such delicious meat, that I laugh to think of those in Portugal. If there is wine in Portugal, here there is delicious water everywhere which I find superior to the wines there. . . . Anyone who elects to live in a terrestrial paradise must come to live in Brazil; at least that is my opinion. And whoever does not believe me, let him come here and try it for himself.[7]

Most of the colonial writers on Brazil shared these exalted opinions of the New World.

The arrival of the Jesuits and the establishment of a central government in 1549 indicated the crown's intention to establish an agricultural colony in the New World. Sugar became the staple crop and sold well on the European market. Increasing profits attracted more colonists and capital. With their interest in Brazil aroused, the Portuguese desired to learn more about their overseas possession.

Pero de Magalhães de Gândavo, who came to the New World shortly before 1570, informed his compatriots of the opportunities awaiting them. In his two works, *Tratado da Terra do Brazil* and *História da Província de Santa Cruz*,[8] he pictured Brazil as a land of abundance. Indeed, conveying such an impression was his real purpose in writing the two accounts. He thought that the poor of Portugal should be encouraged to migrate to Brazil in order to raise their standard of living and phrased that objective as follows: "So that here in the kingdom its [Brazil's] fertility might be divulged and many poor persons might be induced to go live in the Province." [9] Then he revealed the formula for success in Brazil:

The first thing they obtain is slaves to work the farms; and anyone who succeeds in obtaining two pairs or a half-dozen of them (although he may not have another earthly possession) has the means to sustain his family in a respectable way; for one fishes for him, another hunts for him, and the rest cultivate and till his fields, and consequently there is no expense for the maintenance of his slaves or his household.[10]

In such a fashion he was one of the most convincing of the
early propagandists for Brazil.

As a matter of fact, the *História* and *Tratado* together gave
the first complete description of Brazil. The two chronicles devote most of their attention to the land and the Indians, to the
flora and the fauna, and to the growing number of settlements
scattered along several thousand miles of coast. The romantic
notions about the Indians had disappeared by this time. In
contrast to Caminha, Gândavo wrote of the Indians as "un-
grateful, inhuman, cruel, inclined to fight and extremely vin-
dictive. . . . They are very dishonest and given to sensuality,
giving themselves up to their vices as though they were without
human reason." [11] He devotes about a fifth of both works to
the *brasis* and their customs. Their ceremony of greeting visi-
tors with a weeping committee fascinated him. His description
of that custom is well written as well as amusing. Their cannibalistic practices scandalized him, as they did all other chroniclers. In his treatment of indigenous foods, he called special
attention to manioc, maize, sweet potatoes, bananas, Brazil nuts,
pineapples, and cashews. The pineapple, bearing its poetical,
indigenous name, *abacaxi*, particularly delighted him. He mentioned that some had been shipped to the motherland.

The *História* is better written and organized than the *Tratado*. Carefully polished, the *História* stands as a fine example
of the literary style of the period. The Academia Real das
Ciências of Lisbon cited Gândavo in 1793 as one of the Portuguese authors whose works were worthy of study and emula-
tion. That august body thereby set the seal of approval on him
as a man of letters. Writing the first prose penned in Brazil,
Gândavo, like his successors, contributed significantly to the
birth of Brazilian literature. He has been remembered for his
style as well as for making Brazil better known to the sixteenth-
century Portuguese.

Padre Fernão Cardim (1540–1625), who arrived in Brazil in
1583, continued the tradition established by Gândavo. His
three descriptive works have been brought together under the
title *Tratados da Terra e Gente do Brasil*. Like other chroni-

clers and correspondents of the century, Cardim emphasized
natural history and the beauty of the land with its exotic plants
and animals. There was still little history to record, but there
was considerable information to add to the general fund of
knowledge of geography, linguistics, biology, botany, and ethnography. He, too, found himself fascinated by the Indians, and
he discussed their habits at length. Finally, as a witness to the
formation of Brazilian society, he recorded the conditions in
the colony during its infancy.

The *Tratado Descritivo do Brasil em 1587* by Gabriel Soares
de Sousa (1540–1591) is the last of the important sixteenth-
century chronicles. Its wealth of details makes it an extremely
valuable account. In fact, José Honório Rodrigues considers it
the most important of all the sixteenth-century chronicles.[12]
Soares de Sousa arrived in Brazil in 1569. He owned a sugar mill
which made him wealthy before he returned to Portugal in
1586. Back in Lisbon, he gathered together the notes he had
taken while overseas. The chronicle consists of his observations
of life in the colony, especially Bahia where he resided. His
work followed the established pattern: accounts of the flora and
the fauna and the Indians, and descriptions of the various captaincies, with the emphasis on the colonial capital and its en-
virons. Optimistic about the future of Brazil, he prophesied,
"This land is capable of becoming a great empire." [13] Livestock, fish, cotton, sugar, and dyewood were riches the colony
could already boast of. The extensive coastline indented with
safe ports gave entry to a fertile land of healthy climate. The
interior, which the chronicler was certain possessed wealth and
mineral riches, promised to be the key to the future. Because
of present wealth and future potential, Brazil attracted the
covetous eyes of several European nations. Soares de Sousa ad-
vised Portugal to construct coastal defenses to keep foreigners
away.

Those chroniclers of the sixteenth century, with the exception of Gândavo, boasted little or no style—and style remained
alien to most of their successors as well. Because they contain
many errors, they must be read with caution. All of them wrote

of monsters and myths. They people the little-known hinterlands with grotesque and impossible inhabitants. To disregard
the chroniclers, however, would be to bypass one of the principal sources of information about the colonial past. A comparison of the chronicles with each other as well as with the
documents of the period indicates which aspects can be trusted
and which must be disregarded.

Optimism was perhaps the chief characteristic shared by all
these chroniclers. The new land favorably impressed them. It
reminded not a few of them of what they had thought the terrestrial paradise would be like. This theme of a vision of paradise
would reecho throughout Brazilian literature. The chroniclers
seem to have been following well-established medieval traditions.[14] After all, respected maps in the Middle Ages often
referred to some terrestrial paradise, and books discussed the
lost Garden of Eden. A typical description is this anonymous
Portuguese account from the end of the fourteenth century:
"The earthly paradise is another delight where there are all
manner of beautiful trees which give fruits. There one finds
the tree of life. It is neither hot nor cold, and the air is always
pleasant." [15] Having been thus prepared by European thought
to find an earthly paradise, the new arrivals saw Brazil as the
promised land. Impressive, for example, is the number of times
the Jesuits employed the words "terrestrial paradise" in their
letters. They, like the others, commented at length on the
pleasant climate, neither hot nor cold, on the evergreen countryside, where the trees did not lose their leaves, and on the
abundance of nature, which provided a variety of fruits, fish,
and animals. One correspondent, concluding a rhapsodic description of the land, exhorted, "Anyone who elects to live in
a terrestrial paradise must come to live in Brazil. . . ." [16] Such
agreeable impressions prompted the chroniclers to want to make
Brazil better known in Portugal, and to that end they began to
write.

The seventeenth century witnessed the appearance of an increased nativistic character in the chronicles. Many of the authors of that century were *mazombos,* men born in the New

World of European lineage. As native sons, they displayed an intense love of and devotion to the land of their birth, without necessarily being antagonistic toward Portugal. Their ardent pride in Brazil contrasts with the more detached enthusiasm of their sixteenth-century predecessors.

The foremost chronicle of the seventeenth century, *Os Diálogos das Grandezas do Brasil,* aptly illustrates that new pride. It appears that the author, Ambrósio Fernandes Brandão, a resident of the Northeast, was born in Portugal. However, as a New Christian, he found Brazil to be a haven from possible persecution and repaid the benign attitude of the colony with his loyalty and dedication, as evidenced in this work. He frequently spoke of "our Brazil." Obviously a man of considerable education, he knew Latin, had read the classical authors, had studied history and geography, and demonstrated a command of a wide range of factual knowledge.

As the title of the work suggests, *Os Diálogos* is a conversation. The two participants are Brandônio and Alviano. The latter has recently arrived in Brazil, and complains bitterly about his new environment. Brandônio, who knows Portuguese America well, loves and praises the land, attempting to convince his friend of its values and virtues. The conversations between the two, one attacking, and the other defending Brazil, are six in number and encompass the following topics: 1) a general description of the land and each captaincy; 2) the climate and man's adaptability to the tropics; 3) the riches of the land, principally brazilwood, sugar, and cotton; 4) the flora; 5) the fauna; and 6) the Indians. Before the convincing arguments of Brandônio, the hostility of Alviano toward Portuguese America gradually breaks down. By the end of their last conversation, he declares himself persuaded by Brandônio and promises, "You have convinced me so thoroughly that wherever I go hereafter I shall boast of Brazil and its greatness, giving it the praise it deserves." [17]

Os Diálogos was an admirable contribution to colonial historiography and to the growing body of prose literature on Brazil. At times the style becomes involved and complex but it is always colorful and moving. The organization is clear and logical. The information conveyed is invaluable for an understanding of seventeenth-century Brazil. The primary significance of the chronicle lies in the fact that it was the first time a "Brazilian" attempted to define his identity and that of his land. The Brazilian traditionally suffered from an inferiority complex. He was on the defensive before the *reinóis*, those born in Portugal, and other Europeans. To counteract that feeling, Brandão indulged in some self-assurance. Brazil, he claimed, was inferior to no land—quite the contrary. To reach that conclusion the author had had to question himself and his environment. The answers he found were favorable to his cause but by no means definitive. They did not put to final rest the ingrained feeling of inferiority. Accordingly, one of the principal characteristics of Brazilian literature thereafter has been a search for national identity, meaning, and values.

The work of Brandão is a high point in the writing of chronicles. No one surpassed his skill in the seventeenth century.[18] The many other chroniclers of that century continued in the more pedestrian fashion set by their sixteenth-century counterparts; they wrote contemporary descriptions of the land and its inhabitants. Worthy of consultation are the anonymous *Rezão do Estado do Brasil* prepared at the opening of the second decade of the century; *La Discripción de Mil y Treinta y Ocho Leguas de Tierra del Estado del Brasil, Conquista del Marañón y Gran Pará* by Pedro Cadena de Villasante, printed in Madrid in 1634 to invite the king's attention to the wealth of Brazil and the need to protect it; the anonymous *Relação das Capitanias do Brasil*, written during the second or third decade; and the most complete of the chronicles, the anonymous *Informação do Estado do Brasil e de Suas Capitanias*, written after 1680, and descriptive of everything between the Amazon and the Prata.

The chronicles of the seventeenth century reflect the territorial expansion of Brazil. The Luso-Brazilians moved in every direction. They incorporated the mouth of the Amazon into their territory and then ascended that "river-sea" and its tributaries. Their attention shifted away from the coast to focus on the beckoning *sertão* with its still unfulfilled promises of quick wealth. Waves of exploration swept westward. From Belém, São Luiz, Recife, Bahia, Rio de Janeiro, and São Paulo, men marched inland to conquer the unknown. Expeditions crept southward along the coast. Then suddenly, in 1680, jumping over hundreds of miles, the Luso-Brazilians founded Colônia do Sacramento on the left bank of the Rio da Prata directly opposite Buenos Aires. These adventures called forth chroniclers, such as Antônio de Araújo (1566–1632) and João de Sotomaior (1623–1656), to inform the world of the new achievements. From south, west, and north came accounts (most of them lamentably brief) of the new territories. These contributions enriched colonial historiography.

The final chronicler who merits special mention is André João Antonil (João Antônio Andreoni, 1650–1716). His book, *Cultura e Opulência do Brasil,* was confiscated by the Portuguese government as soon as it appeared in 1711. The Lisbon authorities considered the work far too revealing. His lavish praise of Brazil might reawaken the covetous desires of other European states—better to ban the book than to risk another invasion of foreign interlopers.

The Jesuit father divided the book into four studies, each dedicated to one of the main industries of the colony: sugar, tobacco, mining, and cattle. Abundant in detail, the book gave a precise economic picture of Portuguese America at the opening of the eighteenth century. Antonil cogently pointed out the fortune Brazil annually provided Portugal. *Cultura* contains less of the defensive explanation found in *Os Diálogos* and more boasting. It represents the psychological change brought about in the Brazilians by their defeat of the Dutch and conquest of the interior. It set the stage for the swelling feeling of nativism which overcame the eighteenth-century Brazilian literati. In fact, Antonil concluded with a convincing plea for a more favored treatment of Brazil:

From what has been said up to now, there is no one who can doubt that today Brazil is the best and most useful conquest, for the royal treasury as well as for the common welfare, of the many made by the Kingdom of

Portugal. This is proven by the great quantity of goods that each year leaves these ports that are virtual mines of wealth and abundantly profitable. And if it is thus, who doubts that so great and continuous a source of wealth justly merits the favor of Your Majesty and of all your ministers, in the quick dispatch of the petitions they make and in the acceptance of the suggestions, for the relief and convenience of the inhabitants, humbly proposed by their own councils? If the owners of the sugar mills, and the sugar and tobacco plantation owners, are the ones who most promote this esteemed profit, it seems that they deserve more than others to be preferred in your favor and to find in all the courts prompt expedition of their business. . . .[19]

The Brazilians were becoming sufficiently bold to make suggestions for changes in administrative policies. Before the century ended, Portugal's continued neglect of those suggestions would turn colonial minds to thinking in terms of independence.

The book is replete with vital factual material and statistics. The organization is excellent; the style, clear and simple. It was the last outstanding chronicle of the colonial period. Some chronicles continued to appear throughout the remainder of the colonial period, but the attention of indigenous writers began to shift from the chronicle to history.

Frei Vicente do Salvador (1564–1636/39) had been the first to write a history of Brazil. Born in Bahia, he visited the metropolis in order to study at Coimbra University. Returning to Brazil, he later entered the Franciscan order. His religious duties took him to Olinda in the north and to Rio de Janeiro in the south, travels which acquainted him with the most important cultural, economic, and political centers of the colony. In 1627 he completed his *História do Brasil*, which described events from the discovery to the struggle against the Dutch. The book is divided into five sections. In the first he depicted the land and related the story of the discovery; the second treated the captaincy period; the third was devoted to the foundation of the *governo geral* and its development until 1580; the fourth gave the history of the North down to 1606 and of the South down to 1609; and the final section discussed the conquest of Maranhão and the struggle against the Dutch in Bahia. The history covered the whole of Brazil but it concentrated on Bahia and Pernambuco where most of the important events of the period occurred.

Frei Vicente escaped the elaborate and suffocating Gongorism characteristic of the literature of his century. He wrote in a simple and natural style, a quality contributing to the ease with which the book can be read. Since he did not burden himself with archival research, he did not base his *História* on documents. Instead he interviewed people who had participated in the events he described or who had spoken to others who had participated. It was this use of an oral tradition that gave to the *História* "an anecdotal, folklore character." [20]

Clearly discernible in the work is a pride in Brazil. In the first place Frei Vicente used a Portuguese which revealed Brazilian modifications. In the developing dialect of the New World, he boasted of Brazil's favorable position, its gigantic size, the wealth of its sugar industry, and the potential population it could support. Such was the variety of its products and resources that, he assured his readers, Brazil could exist satisfactorily without contact with the outside world. He was one of the first to suggest that if Portugal were ever invaded the crown would find Brazil the logical and desirable place from which to rule. In the optimistic tradition of the chroniclers, Frei Vicente prophesied, "This will be a great kingdom." [21] The *História do Brasil* remained the only history of Brazil for over a century. Frei Vicente was one exception to the trend of his century, which favored the writing of chronicles.

Another exception was Simão de Vasconcelos (1597–1671), who wrote primarily about the sixteenth century. By means of three biographies he told the story of the Jesuits in Brazil and secondarily, as a corollary, the history of the colony. His *Chrónica da Companhia de Jesu do Estado do Brasil* covered the years 1549–1570 and was principally concerned with the life of Manoel da Nóbrega. The *Vida do Venerável Padre Joseph de Anchieta* continued the history of the Jesuits through the biography of the indefatigable Anchieta, and the *Vida do P. João d'Almeida* recounted the life of Anchieta's foremost disciple, who died in 1653. Throughout the three works, Vasconcelos exalted Brazil. In his *Chrónica* he even defended the thesis that the New World was the spot where God had created an earthly paradise.

Both Vasconcelos and Salvador were seventeenth-century heralds of the trends which would dominate eighteenth-century historiography. They revealed a growing preoccupation with the past. The foundation of historical and scientific academies in Europe in the eighteenth century found an echo among the intellectual elite of Brazil's two great ports, Rio de Janeiro and Bahia. When João V established the Academia Real de História Portuguêsa in Lisbon in 1720, an impetus was given to historical study throughout the realm, and Brazil did not delay in imitating the trend.

The Vicerei do Brasil, Vasco Fernando César de Menezes, the Conde de Sabugosa, organized the first colonial academy, the Academia Brasílica dos Esquecidos.[22] It met in Bahia for the first time in 1724 and held eighteen sessions during that year and the next. In the following decades Rio de Janeiro and Bahia witnessed the establishment and demise of a series of such ephemeral academies: the Academia dos Felizes (Rio, 1736–1740), the Academia dos Selectos (Rio, 1751), the Academia Brasílica dos Renacidos (Bahia, 1759), the Academia Scientífica (Rio, 1771), and the Sociedade Literária (Rio, 1786).[23] These organizations provided an opportunity for the local intellectuals to meet together and to exchange ideas. The spiritual conviviality of these meetings apparently encouraged men like Sebastião da Rocha Pita and José de Mirales. In the best physiocrat tradition the academicians interested themselves in better understanding their surroundings; they tried to comprehend Brazil more fully. Two of the groups, the Esquecidos and the Renacidos, had as their principal objective to write a history of Brazil. To use the phraseology of the Renacidos, their aim was to write "an ecclesiastic and secular, geographical and nat-

ural, political and military history—in short, a universal history
of all Portuguese America." [24] A bibliography of all the books
on Brazil was to accompany their work. Such a goal focused the
attention of the academicians on their native land and made
those academies centers of nativistic sentiment. Their encouragement, overtly or covertly, of patriotic feelings can help to
explain why the Lisbon authorities, if they were not hostile to
them, were at best unfriendly and unsympathetic.

The Academia dos Esquecidos produced one of the foremost
eighteenth-century historians: Sebastião da Rocha Pita (1660–
1738). He was born in Bahia and studied at Coimbra. Family
wealth and the leisurely pace of the plantation allowed him
much time to read and to write. Association with the Academia
dos Esquecidos encouraged him to prepare his *História da
América Portuguêsa,* published in Lisbon in 1730. The ten
books into which the history is divided cover events from the
discovery through 1724.

Accuracy does not characterize this history. Like many of the
early colonial historians Rocha Pita was deficient in archival
research, and lacked a critical spirit in examining the evidence.
The history is further handicapped by overly florid and excessively ornate language. Sílvio Romero considers the book more
a "historical novel" than a true history.[25]

Rocha Pita's optimism, his exaggeration in favor of Brazil,
his praise of the land, reveal a strong devotion to the New
World. One of the most frequently quoted passages from his
history conveys his pride and patriotism:

In no other region are the skies more serene, nor does the dawn come
more fair; in no other hemisphere does the sun have rays more golden,
nor are its nocturnal reflections more brilliant; the stars are kindlier, and
always shine gaily; the horizons, whether the sun be rising or sinking, are
always clear; the waters, whether they be taken from springs in the country
or from the aqueducts of the cities, are always of the purest. In short,
Brazil is the earthly paradise regained, where the greatest of rivers rise
and have their course; a salubrious climate prevails; the influence of the
stars is benign; and the gentlest of breezes blow, making the land fertile,
and permitting innumerable inhabitants to dwell therein.[26]

Such descriptions follow the pattern established earlier by the Jesuit correspondents and intensified by each succeeding generation.

The eighteenth-century writers, both the poets and the historians, took their cues as well from Antonil and Salvador. A well-defined nativism was emerging which would form the basis for later nationalism.[27] Generally speaking, nationalism first appears, in underdeveloped areas, as a cultural movement encouraged by the literati who praise local traditions. They compensate for their inferiority complex by zealously and defensively lauding their surroundings.[28] The academicians and historians of the eighteenth century demonstrate that such a generality is applicable to Brazil.

Another academy which apparently exerted influence over the study of history in the colony was the Renacidos. It was consciously organized along the lines of the Academia Real da História Portuguêsa. Among its members were Lt. Col. José Mirales, author of *História Militar do Brasil* and a former member of the Esquecidos, and Frei Antônio de Santa Maria Jaboatão (1695–1764?) author of *Novo Orbe Seráphico Brasílico ou Chrónica dos Frades Menores da Província do Brasil*. Enrolled as associate members were Gaspar da Madre de Deus (1715–1800), author of *Memórias para a História da Capitania de São Vicente* and other works; Antônio José Vitorino Borges da Fonseca (1718–1786) of Pernambuco, who wrote *Nobiliarquia Pernambucana;* and Domingos do Loreto Conto, another Pernambucan, author of *Desagravos do Brasil a Glórias de Pernambuco.*

As a group, these historians displayed strong nativistic tendencies. Loreto Conto praised the Indian. His vision of the noble savage foreshadowed the Indian romanticism of the following century. The *Desagravos* frankly sought to call attention to the achievements of the colony. Borges da Fonseca produced four manuscript volumes of biographies of Pernambucans, who emerge in his pages as heroes turning the wilderness into prosperity. Mirales recounted the feats of arms of the Luso-Brazilians from 1549 to 1762, in a none-too-modest fashion. Jaboatão wrote a primarily religious history but the narrations wandered over the entire course of Brazil's development. He was particularly informative about studies pursued in the convents and education in general in the colony.

These eighteenth-century historians also displayed an increasing concern with the use of documentation. Mirales's work, for example, may be excessively dry and dull but one can only commend him for his prompt citation of sources. These sources included documents as well as some histories and monographs which had been published earlier and were by that time regarded as authoritative. Rocha Pita already was recognized as an important source, and references to his history were frequent.

Both Frei Gaspar da Madre de Deus and his fellow Paulista Pedro Taques de Almeida Paes Leme (1714–1777) are best remembered in colonial Brazilian historiography for their command and use of source material. (Alan K. Manchester considered them to be the outstanding historians of the colonial period.[29]) Both were absorbed in writing the history of their own area of Brazil. They thus turned away from the coast to tell the dramatic story of the opening of the interior, which is not "Portuguese America," but truly Brazil.[30]

Born in São Paulo, Madre de Deus went to Bahia in 1731 to pursue his studies as a novitiate in the Benedictine Order. In that colonial capital, by then the second city of the empire, he met Rocha Pita as well as other intellectuals who had been members of the Academia dos Esquecidos. From them and from his association with the Renacidos, he apparently gained a profound respect for documentation. Consequently, in the preparation of his histories, he visited public, private, and ecclesiastical archives. His works number four: *Memórias para a História da Capitania de S. Vicente, Notícia dos Annos em que se Descobriu o Brasil e das Entradas das Religiões e Suas Fundações, Relação dos Capitães Locotenentes da Capitania de S. Vicente,* and *Notas Avulsas sôbre a História de São Paulo.*

The *Memórias,* published in 1789 by the Academia Real das Ciências, was his most important historical contribution and reads well. The style is unadorned and lucid. Most of his sources were documents, which he not only consulted but cited, too. He also made extensive use of the chroniclers. Throughout the text he confronted and argued many historical questions with the intention of resolving the facts in dispute. First, he presented the different views and the basis for each of them. Then, he put forth his own view or conclusion, carefully stating the reason for his position. For the time and the place, his use of historical methods was advanced.

The other Paulista historian, Pedro Taques de Almeida Paes Leme, was not associated with the academy movements in Brazil. However, he was well acquainted with Madre de Deus, and on a visit to Portugal from 1755 to 1757, he met various Portuguese intellectuals, including the well-known bibliographer, Diogo Barbosa Machado. These associations coupled with his own extensive reading apparently formed his historical thought and helped to establish his methodology. Like his contemporary Madre de Deus, with whom he carried on long consultations and correspondence, Pedro Taques acquired a devotion to documentation. He conducted research in the archives of Lisbon, São Paulo, and São Vicente. Although he wrote a number of histories, he is most remembered for two: *História da Capitania de S. Vicente desde a Sua Fundação em 1531* and *Nobiliarchia Paulistana ou Genealogia dos Principaes Famílias de S. Paulo*. The first mentioned is inferior to the similar work of Madre de Deus, lacking, for example, much of his detail. However, the attention to documentation is noticeable at once. Several documents are reproduced *in toto* or at great length.

The *Nobiliarchia Paulistana* is Pedro Taques's principal contribution to Brazilian historiography. In it, he made a salutary innovation in colonial historiography. Unlike the other chroniclers and historians, who told of kings, bishops, and governors, he wrote about the people. The *Nobiliarchia Paulistana,* the labor of fifty years, is in essence a social history.[31] Crammed with facts, it recounts the daily lives of the colonials, especially the leading families of São Paulo. Some of his biographies cover a few lines; others consume many pages. This entire wealth of information is carefully documented.

The biographical data on the Paulistas includes information about the leading *bandeirantes*, the seemingly indefatigable explorers and conquerors of the West. The hinterlands, or *sertão*, through which the *bandeirantes* tramped exerted a non-European influence on them, and, in fact, helped to create the "Brazilian." [32] Pedro Taques introduced the idea of the *sertão* as a new factor shaping the development of the colony. For that reason, the literary critic Sílvio Romero was able to describe the book as "an indigenous history, a history with our own characteristics, created by our deeds and by the hand of our men." [33]

These historians, as well as the chroniclers, displayed a great devotion to the land about which they wrote. The chroniclers described what they saw in an instantaneous verbal snapshot of their surroundings, however, while the historians attempted both to describe the growth of the colony and to explain the cause and origin of the major events contributing to that growth. The first saw the land from a contemporary point of view, the second from a historical vantage point. Both offered to future historians an abundance of information and data, which would help later generations in deciphering and understanding Brazil's colonial past and national origins. Both set the course for future historical studies.

The nationalism clearly manifested in the creation of an independent Brazilian Empire in 1822 animated Brazilian intellectuals to dedicate greater study to the past in an effort to understand and define the present. Historical activity increased accordingly in the nineteenth century and soon far surpassed the activity of the colonial period. Historical organizations and journals were founded, and flourished. In each passing decade increased attention was focused on the writing of history; Clio was summoned to defend the position of the sprawling nation.

The essays which follow discuss the activities of the historians and historical associations during the national period, as well as the tendencies and objectives of national historiography in Brazil.

KARL FRIEDRICH PHILIPP
von MARTIUS

How the History
of Brazil Should Be Written

THIS perceptive essay, written in 1843 by the German
scientist Karl Friedrich Philipp von Martius (1794–1868),
reveals an insight into Brazilian national formation and
character which few Brazilians possessed in the nineteenth century. Martius was introduced to Brazil when
he was selected to accompany Archduchess Leopoldina to
Rio de Janeiro, where she would take her place as the
Princess of Brazil beside the young and dashing Prince
Pedro. Martius spent only three years in Brazil (1817–
1820), but he traveled extensively, visiting not only the
easily accessible coastal cities but the farthest reaches of
the interior as well in his search for botanical specimens.
How carefully he observed the country and its inhabitants
is shown at once in this essay.

One of the primary goals of the Instituto Histórico e
Geográfico Brasileiro, founded in 1838, was to encourage
the writing of a national history. The members at once
confronted the basic historiographic problem involved:
How should such a history be written? To obtain the best
answer to their question, they sponsored a contest.
Martius, a corresponding member of the Instituto, submitted the most convincing reply—and an excellent reply it was. It displayed a remarkably clear vision of the
uniqueness of Brazil. He saw the amalgamation of the
three racial groups—Indians, Europeans, and Africans—

This essay is translated from the Portuguese "Como se Deve Escrever a História
do Brasil," in the *Revista do Instituto Histórico e Geográfico Brasileiro*, VI
(1844), 381–403.

and their contributions to a single civilization, as the key to understanding Brazil. In many respects his views were far ahead of their time. The essay shows that its author had overcome many widely held prejudices of the period to qualify as a true son of the Enlightenment. Martius spoke loudly and unmistakably in favor of "the perfectibility of mankind." No one seriously followed his suggested plan until nearly a century later, when Gilberto Freyre took up the theme of racial amalgamation and popularized it in his brilliant study *Casa Grande e Senzala* (*The Masters and the Slaves*), first published in 1934.

In addition to the theme of racial and cultural fusion, Martius also discussed the phenomenon of unity and diversity in Brazilian development, one of the most perplexing themes—or problems—in Brazilian history. A vast nation remained united despite alluring centrifugal temptations. Within that union there was a kaleidoscope of variety, sirens perpetually singing hymns of regionalism. The balance of diversity and unity, which Martius saw and understood, has characterized the genius of Brazilian development. His essay still makes fascinating reading, and the student of Brazilian history continues to learn from it.

I t was a great pleasure for me to read in the excellent *Revista Trimensal*[1] (Supplement to Volume II, page 72) that the Instituto Histórico e Geográfico Brasileiro had set as a goal the composition of a history of Brazil. The *Revista* requested its readers to communicate ideas that might help this useful and laudable plan.

I am too far away to know how many Brazilian men of letters are qualified to accomplish the project of the Instituto. But even so, I do not want to let this occasion go without manifesting my interest in the association's worthy plan and communicating to it some ideas on this matter, ideas that are recommended to the kind attention of the Instituto.

GENERAL IDEAS
ABOUT THE HISTORY OF BRAZIL

Anyone who undertakes to write the history of Brazil, a country which promises so much, should never lose sight of the elements which contributed to the development of man there. These diverse elements come from the three races, namely: the copper-colored, or American; the white, or Caucasian; and the black, or Ethiopian. Because of the reciprocal and changing relations of the three races, the present population consists of a novel mixture, whose history therefore has a very particular stamp.

Each human race competes, in a historical movement, according to its innate propensity and the circumstances under which it lives and develops. Therefore, we see a new people, born and developing from the union and contact of these very different races. I propose that its history will evolve according to a special law for these converging forces.

Each physical and moral peculiarity characterizing the different races offers a special force in this development of a new people. The more energy, number, and dignity that characterize the race, the more will be its influence on the common development. Thus it necessarily follows that the Portuguese, as discoverers, conquerors, and masters, greatly influenced this development; and because the Portuguese created the conditions and the physical and moral guarantees for an independent kingdom, they emerge as the most powerful and vital force. However, it certainly would be a great error for the principles of a pragmatic historiography if we disregarded the force of the natives and the imported Negroes, who likewise contributed to the physical, moral, and civic development of the whole population. The natives as well as the Negroes resisted the dominant race.

I know very well that there will be whites who will charge that such a linking of these races disparages their ancestry. But, I am also certain they will not be found among those seeking to write a philosophic history of Brazil. On the contrary, the most enlightened people will discover from this investigation that the Indian and Ethiopian races have been and still are involved in the historic development of the Brazilian people. This investigation will be a new stimulus for the profound and humane historian.

The history of peoples, as much as that of individuals, shows us that the genius of world history, which leads mankind in directions whose wisdom we should always recognize, frequently resorts to mixing the races to obtain the world order's most sublime ends. Who can deny that the English nation owes its energy, resoluteness, and perseverance to the mixture of the Celtic, Danish, Roman, Anglo-Saxon, and Norman peoples?

Perhaps even more important, the genius of history proposes the blending of peoples of the same race with races so entirely different in their individualities, moral character, and physique in order to form a new and marvelously organized nation.

We will never be permitted to doubt that providential will predestined this mixture for Brazil. The powerful river of Portuguese blood ought to absorb the small tributaries of the Indian and Ethiopian races. This mixture has taken place in the lower classes. As in all countries, the upper class is developed from elements of the lower class, vitalized and strengthened by them. Thus the highest class of the Brazilian population is made from this mixture. For centuries this mixture has had a powerful influence on the elevated classes and transmitted to them that historical activity for which the Brazilian Empire is noted.

I believe that the philosophic writer, comprehending the doctrines of true humanity and enlightened Christianity, will find nothing in this opinion that could offend the Brazilians' sensitivities. The current *conditio sine qua non* for the true historian is to appreciate man according to his true value, as the Creator's most sublime work, and to disassociate this from his color and background. This transcendent humanitarianism —which appreciates man in any situation in which he discovers him, as an instrument to work for and to serve—knows the infinity of the world's order and is the animating spirit of the true historian. Thus I consider the Brazilians' personal relations, which allow the Negro and the Indian to influence the development of the Brazilian nationality, to be a benefit for the destiny of the country. I can contrast this with attitudes in other areas of the New World, where these two inferior races are excluded from the general development as unworthy by birth or because their small number in comparison to whites makes them of little importance.

The reflective historian's essential task should be to show that the conditions were established during Brazil's development for the improving of the three races, which are placed next to each other in a manner previously unknown in history, and that they should help each other in every way.

This reciprocity in the history of the development of the Brazilian people offers a picture of an organic life. The task of a truly human legislation will be the proper appreciation of this. The historian can judge the future from what has been done for the Negroes' and the Indians' moral and civic education so far. From this history, he can become a sibyl prophesying the future, and he can offer some useful projects, etc. The stronger his defense of the interests of these unprotected peoples, the greater will be the merit of his work. It will have the stamp of noble humanitarianism that our century requires of the historian. The historian who doubts the perfectibility of mankind allows the reader to suspect that he does not know how to rise above odious and partial opinions.

THE INDIANS AND THEIR HISTORY AS A PART OF THE HISTORY OF BRAZIL

If the above-mentioned general ideas deserve the approval of the Brazilian historian, he ought to undertake the meticulous investigation of the American aborigines' life and the history of their development.[2] He should extend his investigation beyond the time of the conquest, and scrutinize the history of the primitive inhabitants of Brazil. Their history presently is not divided into distinct periods, nor does it highlight important events. It is still wrapped in obscurity. For this very reason, it excites our curiosity.

Who were the peoples found in the Land of Santa Cruz[3] when the Portuguese extended the discovery of Cabral? Where did they come from? What caused them to be reduced to this state of moral dissolution so that we do not even recognize them as ruins of people? The answer to this and other similar questions should precede the examination of later relations. Only with an accurate analysis of the primitive nature of the native Brazilians can one explain the development of their relations with the immigrants and the influence the Portuguese laws, commerce, and communications exerted over them, as well as the influence they exerted on the Portuguese.

Until recently, the generally accepted opinion was that the American Indians issued forth directly from the Creator's hand. The Brazilian aborigines were considered as an example of the development possible in man deprived of any divine revelation, and directed only by his innate reason to follow the path of his needs and physical inclinations. As seen by this mistaken philosophy, this was man's primitive state, from which he tried to derive the most extraordinary organs of public law, religion, and history. The more profound investigations have proved for the unbiased person that he was not dealing with man's primitive state. On the contrary, the sad picture offered by the present-day Brazilian Indian is that he is a remnant of a very ancient, though lost, history.

As soon as we have understood this concept, the difficult but interesting task remains to use it to illuminate the obscure past of the American race. The path that the historian should follow is, first, to consider the physical being of the Brazilian and to compare it with that of neighboring peoples of the same race. The next step will lead us to their soul and intelligence. This is connected with the investigation of their spiritual activity and how this is manifested in historical documents.

The Indian languages should be the most general and significant document. One cannot overemphasize the need for research in this rarely studied field. The American languages are found to be fusing increasingly, and some of them are becoming extinct. There is much to say on this subject, but I suppose few Brazilian historians will interest themselves with linguistic studies. I take this occasion to express my desire that the Instituto Histórico e Geográfico Brasileiro select some linguists to edit grammars and dictionaries for these languages. These scholars should be in contact with the native speakers. I would especially recommend the investigation of the roots of the Tupi language and its dialects, from the Guaraní on the banks of the Rio da Prata to those of the Amazon. The vocabulary that the Empress Catherine[4] ordered made for the Asiatic languages would be a good model for such a Brazilian dictionary. The most important vocabulary to collect should refer to natural objects, legal definitions, and social relations.

The principal language of the past spoken throughout the vast extent of Brazil was Tupi, or the *lingua geral* [universal language]. It is significant that a great number of Brazilian tribes understand this language. As in Peru with Quechua and Aymará, Tupi extended over the vast Brazilian territory. There is no doubt that all the tribes that used it belong to a unique and great people which possessed its own history and its own civilization, which declined to the present state of degradation and dissolution, the same as occurred in western South America among the Incas. It should not pass unnoticed that the Caribs in the Guianas and the Antilles spoke a language related in syntax and vocabulary to Tupi. This fact is made more interesting when one realizes that the Caribs were pirates who extended themselves from Florida and Bermuda to South America. In this way studies of the language of the Brazilian aborigines assume a wider importance, leading to ethnographical investigations and an understanding of a large part of the New World.

Language ought to be linked to studies of the mythology, theogony, and geogony of the Brazilian races. A philosophical observer will not fail to discover still extant in the remnants of the myths and in the poetic gibberish some very significant vestiges of a lost natural philosophy and of a still enigmatic religion. A superficial look at the contemporary religion of the Brazilian Indians tempts one to consider it as a fetishism or witchcraft; but such an explanation will not satisfy a philosophical historian, who sees in the present examples of religious ideas and ceremonies purer antecedents and forms of an ancient religion, of which the human sacrifice of prisoners, cannibalism, and numerous customs and domestic habits can be considered a brutal degeneration and only in this way explicable. Such researches will lead us necessarily to those phenomena related to superstition, to the curative powers of Indian magic, witch doctors, and mystics, and from these we will continue on to investigations concerning the wisdom of the Indians in relation to natural phenomena and the position of the priest class among them and the relations of the *Pagé* [priest], the witch doctor, and the chief toward the social community.

We will be confronted with the vestiges and symbols of traditions of law, and we can undertake a general investigation concerning the social and juridical relations of these men as members of a single tribe, as well as those which exist between diverse tribes. This completes the circle of ethnographic investigations that the historian should make.

It is undeniable that the picture will be much better and richer as a result of historical and philosophical studies when a bold historian carefully examines the American aborigines and compares his Brazilian materials with those on other peoples of the New World.[5]

An ethnographic and philosophical historian's most pleasing task would be to coordinate all of the American aborigines' myths, customs, legal usages, geogonies, theogonies, and traditions of universal deluges and natural catastrophes. If a history of Brazil offered only this, it would be enthusiastically received by all literary men. Since Lafitau's work,[6] the material has grown at an astonishing rate. This abundant material requires severe criticism because of the multitude of extravagant allegations and entirely false facts (as, for example, the scandalous work spread by M. de Pau). This ought to be excluded once and for all, and the real value of this ethnographic material of the American peoples should be established.

The most exciting subject for ethnographic research is the discovery of ancient American archaeological monuments. The Brazilian historian should study the ruins of Paupatla, Mexico, Uxmal, Copán, Quito, Tiaguanaro, etc., to understand the American past. Vestiges of similar ancient ruins have not been discovered in Brazil (at least not that I know of). The manuscript notes copied in the *Revista Trimensal* (Vol. I, No. 3 [1839], p. 181) induced Senhor Benigno José de Carvalho e Cunha (*Ibid.*, Vol. III, No. 9 [1841], p. 197) to suspect that a great ancient city existed on the south side of the Serra do Sincorá on the Sincorá's left branch. These are the only Brazilian ruins that might resemble the grandeur of those of Mexico, Cundinamarca, and Bolivia. Just because none have been discovered in Brazil is not enough evidence to cause one to doubt that there also reigned in Brazil in very remote times a superior civilization similar to that of the above-mentioned countries. Past experience indicates that vestiges of superior American civilizations are found in mountainous countries. This does not necessarily mean that there is no possibility of finding one in Brazil. Certainly many members of the Instituto share with me the desire to support archaeological investigations, especially aiding travelers trying to discover these ruins. Considering that tall virgin forests rise above some locations of ancient ruins, such as Paupatla, it is not improbable that ruins might be discovered in similar Brazilian forests, which are largely unknown and inaccessible.

THE PORTUGUESE AND THEIR PART IN THE HISTORY OF BRAZIL

When the Portuguese discovered and settled Brazil, they found only a few primitive Indians.[7] Thus the Portuguese colonies developed and expanded almost without caring about

these Indians. Only when the Portuguese colonists were forced
by threat of hostile attacks did they create a defensive institution, the system of militias.

The militias were an important influence for two reasons:
First, they encouraged and maintained the spirit of adventure,
the voyages of discovery, and the extension of the Portuguese domain; secondly, they furthered the development of self-governing municipal institutions and helped to nurture a bold citizenry that took up arms to oppose the governing authorities
and the powerful religious orders. We also find that this was
the reason for the success of Portuguese arms against the in-
vasions of the French in Maranhão and Rio de Janeiro, and of
the Dutch along a great part of the northeastern coast.

Establishing himself in Brazil, the Portuguese abandoned
some of the rights he possessed in Portugal from the monarch,
because in place of a king he here had an overlord.[8] For this
reason as well, the colonists were constantly armed and always
ready to fight. Ever armed they continuously moved inland from
specific focal points on the coast, where European civilization
was first established. In the interior no one recognized any superior, and they either forcefully overcame the Indians and
made slaves of them or deceitfully induced them to serve the
invader.

The Portuguese colonist's warlike relationship with the Indians greatly contributed to the rapid exploration of the interior as well as the expansion of the Portuguese domain. Still
Brazil's particular nature, especially the abundance of gold, was
of no small moment. First came the plundering raids to enslave
the Indians, and then the journeys to discover mineral wealth.

We should not judge the Portuguese immigration to sixteenth-century Brazil, which laid the foundation for the present
Empire, by the principles which regulate today's colonization.
Today's colonization, with few exceptions, is a private undertaking made by the poor who want to improve their conditions.
These immigrants consist of farmers and artisans, almost never
the nobles and the rich. Such was not the case in the beginning
of the colonization of Brazil. It was a continuation of the bold

undertaking directed toward India and carried out by princes, nobles, and their followers. The Portuguese nation became very famous and rich from these enterprises. The desire to immigrate was not born out of religious crises as in England. It was a consequence of the great Portuguese discoveries and commercial undertakings along the west coast of Africa, the Cape, Mozambique, and India. The same powerful reasons that gave such a driving movement to Europe's smallest nation, causing it by itself to create a monumental epic within the flow of universal history, influenced the immigration to Brazil.

This period of the discovery and early colonization of Brazil can be understood only in relation to the Portuguese maritime, commercial, and military achievements. This period never can be considered as an isolated event in the history of the active Portuguese people. Brazil's importance to and relations with Europe are the same as those of the Portuguese expansion. As the Portuguese expansion had an important influence on European politics and commerce, so did it also affect Brazil.

These observations might seem to belittle the historiography of Brazil. But it should never be forgotten that the history of world commerce of the time formed a part of the history of the colonization of Brazil and its civil and legislative developments. Although the East Indies did not have the same commercial products as Brazil, still it would not be difficult to compare the commercial history of India and Brazil if we wanted to understand the European's motivation for immigrating to India or the New World. In the study of the history of Brazil, the historian must point out and deal with the different commercial routes—the use of the Red Sea or the rounding of the Cape of Good Hope—and the effect of these sea and land routes on the price of the commercial products.

The history of the discovery of Brazil is intimately connected with the commercial history of an India wood called "sapan wood," commonly known as "brazilwood," *legno brasilo, bresil,* etc. The main reason the Land of Santa Cruz received the name the "Land of Brazil" was because of brazilwood. The commercial history of the precious stones and metals is closely related to the history of Brazil. Finally, the useful tropical plants, known in Europe after the discovery of the New World, can never be treated apart from the colonization of Brazil.

Later we will discuss the great influence exerted on Brazil's development by the Portuguese voyages to Africa, Brazil's commercial relations with that part of the world, and Brazil's participation in the slave trade.

The Portuguese, who immigrated to Brazil in the beginning of the sixteenth century, brought the time's characteristic spirit and courage with them. Although exempt from the immediate effects of the Lutheran schism, the Portuguese colonist represented the period's peculiar temperament. Because of the numerous conflicts with Spain and the greater part of Europe, he was more accessible then, than later, to the great intellectual movement of that century. If the Brazilian historian intends to describe these men who came from across the ocean to found a new Portugal, he cannot avoid drawing his picture from the customs of the fifteenth century.

The historian should follow closely Portuguese legislative history and the Portuguese social conditions in order to be able to show the gradual development of the very liberal municipal institutions, their transplantation to Brazil, and what were the causes for their perfection in Brazil. A very interesting task for a historian, who sees this legislation as a mirror of the times, would be to show how immune the old Portuguese legislation of Dom Diniz[9] was from the influence of the Roman law propagated in Portugal by the Spanish kings.

At this point the historian should discuss the relations between the crown and the church. It is important to do so because the ecclesiastical orders often found themselves opposing the municipalities or the inhabitants and favoring the Indians, as they did also in Spanish America. According to my understanding of the ecclesiastical establishment in Brazil, its actions did not proceed solely from Brazilian decisions but were owed to decisions made in the metropolis or in Rome.

Of all the religious orders in Brazil, the Jesuits played the most important role.[10] Their buildings are the only monuments left from that remote time. Their institutions have not entirely disappeared nor lost their influence. Because of their missionary activities, the Jesuits obtained the most varied and important information on the Indian languages, civil and domestic life, etc. Many of these accounts still remain unused and lie buried in the various archives of the order or in the libraries which obtained them after the suppression of the order. Germany and Italy have taken the most advantage of the materials that the Jesuits collected in Brazil. It suffices to cite the voluminous work of Padre Stoeckler O. Welbote (*O Mensageiro Universal*) or the other works published in Italy by Hervas and Muratori. The German Jesuit missionaries in Brazil were less erudite than the more distinguished French Jesuits, but they were more capable than the French Jesuits of living with the barbarous neophytes. The German Jesuits' accounts of the moral and civil customs of the Indians were commended for their sincerity and accuracy.

Some of this literature is represented in French by the *Lettres Edificantes*. Without any doubt the Jesuit sources remain inadequately explored.[11] It should be easy for a historian of Brazil to obtain, by diplomatic intervention, extracts of the Jesuits' communications from their archives in Rome, Munich, Vienna, and Belgium. Other religious orders, such as the Franciscans, Capuchins, Augustinians, Carmelites, and Paulists, also had missions in Brazil. Their reports might disclose some important material on Indian ethnography as well as the history of the customs of the European settlers. The activity of these orders was not generally unfavorable for Brazil. Often they were the only carriers of civilization and education to a restless and turbulent people. At other times, they protected the oppressed from the powerful. Because of this, their numerous disputes with the city councils (illustrated in repeated references in [Bernardo Pereira de] Berredo's *Chrónica do Maranhão*) cannot be understood without reference to the clergy—mainly the orders—the foundation of their convents, asylums, missions in the interior of the country, and the mercantile speculations that they undertook. The colonists' opposition to these generally philanthropic orders resulted from their apparent conflict of interests.

The Portuguese government was vigilant toward the religious orders' influence on the population and suspiciously guarded the crown's prerogatives. The prohibition on founding convents in the province of Minas arose from this distrust of the orders. The history of the expulsion of the Jesuits was clearly related in Portugal to the Jesuits' political position in Pará; and in Spain, to the Jesuits' power in Paraguay. This kind of event, so important in the annals of universal history, is deeply rooted in the history of Brazil.

An interesting task for the pragmatic historian would be to study the establishment and development of the arts and sciences in Brazil as a reflection of European life. The historian should bring us into the colonists' homes, show us how they lived in the city and the country in various periods and developed their relationships with their neighbors, servants, slaves, and customers. He should depict church, school, and government for us and take us into the fields, the plantations, and the sugar mills. We should learn something of the rural economy, the agriculture, and the colonial commerce of Brazil. It would be interesting to learn how and where the colonists gradually introduced European plants and trees to Brazil. How did the present system of agriculture develop? What part was played by the Portuguese knowledge of naval construction, navigation, and the sea?

The historian who studies the Brazilian schools, their teaching methods, and the quality of the instruction must investigate the Portuguese educational system. Thus the Brazilian historian should analyze the progress of poetry, rhetoric, and the other sciences in Portugal; compare them with the rest of Europe; and show their influence on the scientific, moral, and social life of the Brazilians.

To complete this aspect of the Brazilian historical picture, many questions should be asked about the influence of Portuguese military life. What were the methods employed in military recruitment, education, command, and duty? Were the strategic concepts based on Brazilian experience, which is so much different from European conditions? There is no lack of data on the wars with the Dutch. The few written documents buried in various archives in Brazilian cities and towns should be sought out in order to describe little-known expeditions of discovery of the Paulista *mamelucos* into the Brazilian interior and their wars with the Spanish and the missionaries in Paraguay.

Most Brazilian chronicles relate the monotonous and routine events of the community, which have minimal significance. Therefore, the historian will be drawn to the variety of the narrations about the many expeditions and forays into the hinterland from the coast. These *entradas* were undertaken to procure gold and precious stones or to capture Indians and make slaves of them. The participants in the *entradas* had the energy, ingenuity, perseverance, and courage of a Cortés, a Balboa, or a Pizarro, and their adventures are worthy of posterity's admiration. One can seriously hope that rigorous research in municipal archives will furnish us with more documents similar to those that referred to the romantic adventures of Bueno da Silva, who discovered Goiás on September 19, 1740. His adventures were worthy enough to inspire an epic poet, as well as the more tranquil muse of the historian.

An exact description of these exploratory expeditions is very difficult because of the lack of geographical data that would determine the precise routes taken by these *entradas*. It is hard to believe that these expeditions covered many areas that are no longer visited or are forgotten by us, as for example the fabulous gold-rich Valley of the Martyrs. An exact description of these routes would be very interesting for geography, ethnography, and new explorations into these little-known regions for natural wealth.

A deeper investigation of these expeditions will acquaint the historian with the numerous fascinating legends about Brazil's subterranean wealth. These romantic legends gave the Brazilians a substitute for the many European tales of ghosts or chivalry which were such an inexhaustible source of European popular poetry. In evaluating the popular Brazilian superstitions found in these tales, the historian should not forget to consider the Negro's contribution. The Negro's love of talking, his African way of thinking, and his fetishism supplied him with different poetic thoughts about the supernatural, and miraculous events. The special orientation of the inhabitants of Minas, São Paulo, and Goiás can be discerned in the development of their complete set of fables about Pluto.

There are no vestiges of this in the Amazon region with its majority of Indians. The Amazonian fables revel in the fantastic monsters of the Indian's imagination, which is saddened by the jungle's dismal solitude and the terrors of a menacing Nature. Everywhere one encounters the horrible monsters, satyrs, and mythical animals which the European first learned from the extravagant accounts of Sir Walter Raleigh and his companions.

The historian who is familiar with these popular myths certainly will not disregard them. He will give them the particular importance they merit as a key to understanding the daily life of the inhabitants, as well as the extent of their intellectual achievements in general. The diversity of the origins of these tales offers the historian a chance for many observations, both historic and ethnographic.

The African Race and Its Relation to the History of Brazil

There is no doubt that Brazil would have developed differently without the Negro slaves.[12] The historian will resolve the problem of whether it was for the better or the worse after considering the influence the African slaves exerted on the civil, moral, and political development of the contemporary Brazilian population.

If we want to show the Negro's influence on Brazil, it is important to investigate the Negro's background, customs, civil attitudes, natural discernment, preconceptions, superstitions, and his race's particular defects and virtues. As the Portuguese had visited Africa before the discovery of Brazil and had extracted great commercial advantages from that continent, Africa doubtless had already influenced the customs and political development of Portugal.[13] We should analyze the conditions in the Portuguese African colonies, which all sent slaves to Brazil. This analysis should indicate the slave trade's influence on the industry, agriculture, and commerce of both the African colonies and Brazil.

The primitive Portuguese trading posts on the coast and in the interior of Africa, and the organization of the slave trade, make fascinating subjects and are almost unknown in Europe. Some recently published English material presents one side without adequately clarifying the management and conduct of the slave trade in the interior of Africa. On the other hand, the Portuguese literature tells us little about the history of the world slave trade. (Luiz Antônio de Oliveira Mendes wrote a valuable study, based on personal experience, on the diseases of the Negroes, published in *Memórias Econômicas de Real Academia de Lisboa*, IV, 1–64. The Visconde de Cairu [José da Silva Lisboa] wrote another study of the Negroes.)

An important service would be rendered to the history of Brazil by the author who makes a thorough study of the slave trade. His work would be even more interesting if he compared the Negro's character, customs, and practices with the Indian's. It would be advisable for him to indicate the influence that the various phases of the slave trade had on the metropolitan Portuguese character.

The Brazilian historian must never forget that his task is larger than simply to describe the development of one people; Brazil's crises and experiences are a part of the larger scope of world history. Furthermore, Brazil is still in the process of change and development. He must not consider Brazil's unique fusion of different elements as unfavorable, but rather see them as a fortunate and important union. The history of Brazil will always be primarily a history of a branch of the Portuguese. However, if Brazilian history is to be complete and to deserve

the name history, it can never exclude the roles played by the
Ethiopian and Indian races.

SOME OBSERVATIONS ON THE FORM
OF A HISTORY OF BRAZIL

The works published up until now on the separate provinces
are of inestimable value. They abound with important facts
and minutely examine many events. Nevertheless, they do not
satisfy the requirements of real historiography, which demands
more than mere chronicles. These historical works monoto-
nously repeat many insignificant facts and certain information
of slight historical importance. All this lessens the work's interest and bewilders the reader about the point of the work.
What is gained by repeating each provincial governor's acts and
omissions, or by relating unimportant facts about the administration of cities, or bishoprics, etc., or by a scrupulous list of
citations and records of dubious historical authenticity? My
opinion is that all this should be excluded.

The vast extent of Brazilian territory presents the historian
with a difficult problem, for he is surrounded by an immensely
varied natural setting and by a population composed of very
different elements with different customs and practices. As Pará
has an entirely different climate from Rio Grande do Sul, different soil, natural products, agriculture, industry, customs,
and necessities, the same is true for Bahia, Pernambuco, and
Minas. In one province the white descendants of the Portuguese
predominate; in another an Indian mixture has the majority;
in a third, the African race manifests its importance; and each
of these exerts a special influence on the state of civilization in
general. The author who does not see this broad interplay of
forces risks the chance of writing, not a history of Brazil, but
only a series of special histories of each province. Another historian who does not give these peculiarities the necessary attention runs the risk of not discovering the special local temperament that is indispensable when he is trying to rouse the

reader's interest, to give vitality to his description, and to impress the reader with the ardor that we so much admire in the great historians.

In order to avoid these difficulties, it seems necessary to begin by describing the general state of the whole country in well-chosen epochs, including relevant relations with the mother country and the rest of the world. Passing on to those parts of Brazil that are basically different, only those provinces that have a real historical significance should be emphasized. By proceeding in this manner, it will not be necessary to start from the beginning in each province, and all the repetitious material can be omitted. Those parts of Brazil that are similar in physical conditions and belong with each other can be treated together. Thus, the history of São Paulo, Minas, Goiás, and Mato Grosso converge into one; Maranhão and Pará can be treated as one; Ceará, Rio Grande do Norte, and Paraíba form a natural group influenced by Pernambuco; and finally, the history of Sergipe, Alagoas, and Pôrto Seguro will be the same as Bahia's.

For such a work, it seems indispensable for the historian to visit these provincial areas and to penetrate the peculiarities of nature and population with his own eyes. Only in this manner will he be able to evaluate properly all the historical events that have taken place in whatever part of the empire, explain them by the particularities pertaining only to inhabitants of the place where it occurred, and connect them with other events in the area. How different Pará is from Minas! They possess divergent natural conditions, different men, different needs and passions, and consequently are influenced by different historical forces.

This diversity is not sufficiently recognized in Brazil. Because few Brazilians have visited all of the country, many erroneous ideas have been developed about local conditions. Without any doubt, this fact contributed to the length of time it took to extinguish the political turmoils in some provinces. Since the officials in Rio de Janeiro could not recognize the true causes of these vexing situations in the distant provinces, they did not administer the appropriate remedies. If the historian thoroughly acquaints himself with these local peculiarities, and presents them exactly, the administration will often ask him for his useful counsel.

If the reader is not acquainted with the details of the local natural setting, he will neither be interested in nor be able to develop an intimate knowledge of Brazil. Following the system of Herodotus, the "father of history," the historian will find many opportunities to include enchanting pictures of Nature. He will make his work attractive to the inhabitants of Brazil's different regions, for the reader will be able to recognize his own home in these descriptions and identify himself with the greater Brazilian scene. The European reader will be especially interested in such a rich and varied book.

In conclusion, I ought to add an observation about the position of a Brazilian historian toward his country. History is the master of the present and the future. It can spread noble patriotic sentiments among contemporaries. A history of Brazil ought to stimulate the love of country, courage, constancy, industry, fidelity, prudence—in a word, all the civic virtues—in its Brazilian readers. Brazil suffers from a politically immature population. There we see republicans of all complexions and of all types of ideologies. It is precisely among them that many people will be discovered with an interest in the history of their homeland. A book should be written just for them, to correctly convince them of the impracticability of their utopian plans, of the impropriety of licentious discussions about public business, of the undesirability of an unrestrained press, and of the necessity of a monarchy in a country where there is a large number of slaves.

Brazil has just begun to feel that it is united. Many provincial prejudices still prevail; they ought to be removed by judicious education. Each part of the empire should turn its face toward the others. They ought to attempt to prove that such a vast, rich country as Brazil with so many varied sources of good fortune and prosperity will attain its most favorable development when its inhabitants firmly support the monarchy and establish a wise organization of reciprocal relations among all the provinces. Often foreigners have tried to sow discord among the different parts of Brazil, and by the principle of "divide and rule" obtain an important influence in the state's affairs. The patriotic historian ought to take advantage of every occasion to show that the provinces belong together by organic law and that their progress can be guaranteed only by a closer union among them.

Brazil's greatness and power are based on its very vastness, the variety of its products, and also on its inhabitants, who are sons of the same land, with the same historical background and the same future aspirations. In order to render his fatherland a real service, the historian should write as a constitutional monarchist, a real unitarian in the purest sense of the word. His work should not exceed one sizable volume, written in a popular though noble style. It should satisfy the intelligence as well as the heart, not be written in a pompous language, nor be overburdened with a heap of sterile citations. It should avoid taking on the character of a mere chronicle or a dry, purely erudite historical investigation. As any history that deserves the name of history, it will be an epic! A really popular epic is written only when the people still believe in progressive development.

As Brazil is a country entering a phase that demands dynamic progress, it surely is a worthy subject for a popular history. Its author will find in the favorable development of the land a propitious stimulus to present in his work all his patriotic zeal and love, that poetic fire appropriate for youth, to which at the same time he can apply the depth of judgment and firmness of character belonging to a mature and virile age.

PEDRO MOACYR CAMPOS

An Outline of Brazilian Historiography in the Nineteenth and Twentieth Centuries

MR. CAMPOS, a professor at the University of São Paulo, presents in this essay a sweeping view of Brazilian historiography in the national period. National historiography began in Brazil with the important contributions of Karl Friedrich Philipp von Martius (see first essay) and another foreigner, Robert Southey. Mr. Campos emphasizes four subsequent stages in its development: 1) the foundation of the Instituto Histórico e Geográfico Brasileiro, 2) the work of Francisco Adolfo de Varnhagen, 3) the work of João Capistrano de Abreu, and 4) the establishment in the universities of faculties of philosophy with the responsibility for teaching history. Indeed, it is the introduction of history courses at the university level in the mid–nineteen-thirties which marks the creation of a historical profession in Brazil. Since that time the faculties of philosophy increasingly have become the centers of historical research and publication, diminishing the century-old monopoly that the historical institutes —centers of dilettantism—held over the field. As a consequence, Brazilian historiography at this moment is undergoing a profound alteration.

Little by little, in spite of the inevitable ups and downs in the phases of a consciousness of maturity, signs of a renaissance in the study of history in Brazil are appearing. For example, the

This essay is translated from the Portuguese "Esbôço da Historiografia Brasileira nos Séculos XIX e XX," a special appendix to Jean Glénisson, *Iniciação a Estudos Históricos* (São Paulo: Difusão Européia do Livro, 1961), pp. 250–93.

certainty that it is impossible to consider our country as something historically autonomous is now evident and is leading to an ever greater widening of horizons. In our case, Brazilian peculiarities are far from justifying isolation since several of them can be reasonably explained only by reference to outside influences. Development in other branches of study, principally in sociology, has helped to shed light on various problems, the examination of which leads to a new view of them in time and automatically results in an enrichment of historiographical knowledge. Experience which has been validated in other areas is now being applied in Brazilian historiography. It can be seen that political-geographical limitations do not provide an intelligent framework for history, which should be studied within incomparably broader limits. Brazil finds herself in that great complex commonly designated as Western civilization; her formative process can be understood only in connection with this larger entity.[1] We are not going to refer to the most obvious ties which link this country with Portugal, and from which originates the belief in the absolute necessity of studying Iberian history in order to understand Brazil. Of course, such a study does apply to the entire colonial period. Just the same, as someone has already said with respect to our undeniable relations with the Portuguese, it was Europe, and not Portugal alone, that supplied this nation with its most important fundamentals;[2] and it is only by turning our thoughts to all of western Europe that an approach to Brazilian history will be intelligent.

The integration of our past in space will have as its corollary integration in time; and it would be a fallacy to take the period of the great discoveries as the absolute starting point in our history. The new concepts dominating the subject emphasize not only that history appears in the concrete sense, but also that it is only the expression of processes arrived at through thought. Even with the qualification that the statement "all history is the history of thought"[3] is exaggerated, it is necessary today to take this concept into account for an examination of the Brazilian experience. By so doing, we will achieve two great results: a) the connection of the formation of Brazil with the Mid-

dle Ages in Europe not only through the transplantation or reflection of institutions, but also through many, many influences
on the development of Brazilian ideas, art, religion, and mentality which would lead us to the Middle Ages;[4] b) the direction
of attention toward an organic framework of our past in which,
without giving predominance to economics, politics, or any
other particular field, all would be viewed in constant interac-
tion, thereby giving us something that would be closer to a
reconstruction, on a higher level, of Brazilian life through time.
In this way, the field of study continually widens, becoming ever
more difficult in the numerous facets of its complexity. Only at
the cost of this widening, however, will it be possible to read-
just our history to the predominant tendencies in contemporary
Western thought and to give Brazil a definite position in the
framework of Western culture. The words of a modern French
author deserve to be remembered here: "The disagreeable
thing is that we have histories—of philosophy, the sciences, and
literature—that do not intertwine. And yet, everything is entangled. . . . Everything is entangled. It is not the single fact
which is important, but rather the interplay and interpretations
which have importance." [5] Strictly speaking, these last can be
seen only after the first; in this way the danger of neglecting
facts and the study of documents in favor of uncertain theses is
minimized. The historian worthy of his profession will never
expose himself to such a risk. What we intend to make clear,
then, is that the history of Brazil is also derived from an interrelationship of facts and events of all types, which leads to the
breakdown of a rigid geopolitical framework.

At times some of our historical themes lead far back into time
and demand from us constant examination of the history of the
entire Western world. In this respect, the panorama of Brazil's
historiography in the first half of the nineteenth century, in
which an Englishman, Robert Southey, and a German, Karl
Friedrich Philipp von Martius, stand out, seems symbolic for
us. The simple recall of these names is sufficient to corroborate
what we have just said, all the more because by using the work
of such authors as the source for the study of their epoch, we

will be directed to a projection of the image of Brazil onto the European intellectual panorama, which cannot fail to be a contribution—and one of the most genuine—to Brazilian history. And it is from a consideration of the importance of their ideas about our country's integration in the Western environment that we will take their period [the early nineteenth century] as the basis for our outline of Brazilian historiography. Still another fact confirms our choice: the foundation of the Instituto Histórico e Geográfico Brasileiro, an event which was contemporaneous with these authors.

In the beginning of the nineteenth century there existed only one general history of Brazil:[6] that by Sebastião da Rocha Pita (1660–1738), under the title of *História da América Portuguêsa,* which treated the period from the discovery until 1724 and was published in 1730. The critics consider it much more as a chronicle, a poem in prose, or even a historical tale,[7] than as a real history, such as we understand a history to be today, or even as it was understood to be in Europe in the middle of the eighteenth century. Rocha Pita's intention was decidedly to compose a hymn to his land, from which come famous passages in which nature especially was praised in all her splendor in a Gongoristic exaltation to the beauty and opulence of Brazil.[8] Another fundamental characteristic was also noted in his work: the desire to exhibit his knowledge, on any pretext, a desire which was in accordance with the then current style of the literary academies, one of which—Os Esquecidos ["the forgotten"]—Rocha Pita was associated with.[9] The classical element assumed considerable importance, allowing the author to judge Portuguese America as a rival of Italy and Greece in the production of ingenious sons; but besides this, much more came into play: "The origin of gunpowder, genealogies, horoscopes, theology—everything paraded through his pages, primarily to show the knowledge of the author, rather than to shed light on the matter." [10] However, beyond any doubt, Rocha Pita occupies a place of prominence in national historiography for the influence that he had in the further development of historiography. He was rejected by Southey, on one hand, and respected—when not followed—by the thinking prevalent among the founders of the Instituto Histórico e Geográfico. Furthermore, we find him expressly mentioned in the short preface of the British historian [Southey] as follows: "The only general history of Brazil that exists is the *América Portuguêsa* by Sebastião da Rocha Pita, a meagre and inaccurate work which has been accounted valuable merely because there was no other." [11] On another occasion, upon confirmation of the arrival of a document, Southey completes his judgment: "The manuscript has arrived, and it will be of great utility to me, inasmuch as Rocha Pita assumes a position opposite to mine in this matter and omits, as he habitually does, its major points." [12]

Such was the mission which Robert Southey took upon himself: to fill the lacunae already acknowledged. Several motives led him to do this. In the first place, we should remember the attraction exerted by a tropical region, a foreign landscape, upon the romantic imagination of "a poor, nervous being," impassioned by the sun, the luminous climate, the "delicacies of the south." [13]

The land was beautiful, and abounded with whatever the heart of man could desire: the splendid plumage of the birds delighted the Europeans; the trees diffused an inexpressible fragrance and distilled so many gums and juices, that they thought if their virtues were but rightly understood, there would be nothing to prevent man from enjoying vigorous health to extreme old age. If the terrestrial paradise were upon this round world, they fancied it could not be far from hence.[14]

The theme of Eden in the equatorial zone, revealed in England by the *Principal Navigations of Hakluyt*,[15] adjusted itself excellently to the dreams of Southey's generation, everything indicating that, through them, the image of Brazil was entering into British romanticism.[16] In spite of its similarity to the ideas of Rocha Pita, however, a passage like the preceding one is derived from a concept which is very different from the subject; and the first pages of the work suffice to convince us of this, since not everything is smiling and beautiful in Brazilian history, as one can see:

In perusing its annals, disgust and anger will oftener be felt than those
exalted feelings which it is more grateful for the historian to excite. I have
to speak of savages so inhuman that little sympathy can be felt for any
sufferings which they endured; and of colonists in whose triumphs no joy
will be taken, because they were not less cruel than the cannibals upon
whom they warred, and being avaricious as well as barbarous, perpetrated
the worst crimes for the vilest of motives. Even the few higher characters
which appear have obtained no renown beyond the limits of their own
religion, scarcely beyond those of their language.[17]

However, Southey stated all this based on abundant documentation, never incurring the defect "of giving some facts as true
which any minute examination or rational investigator would
declare false and even implausible." [18] Even the admirers of
Rocha Pita were forced to recognize that virtue in the Englishman. Indeed, Southey had at his disposal the library of his uncle,
the Reverend Herbert Hill, who had lived more than thirty
years in Portugal gathering a "collection of manuscripts, not
less extensive than curious, and which is not to be equalled in
England." [19]

The ease of access to this rich material certainly contributed
to his decision to compile the *History of Brazil,* a necessary
complement to the *History of Portugal* on which Southey also
worked. His interest in the subject is explained, moreover,
thanks to the comparative importance conferred upon Brazil
by the migration to the New World of the royal family [the
Braganzas] in 1807.[20] This is what led him to foresee a most
brilliant future for the country, in front of which even the importance of India in the plan of the Portuguese conquests would
pale,[21] and awakened in Southey the ambition of being remembered as the historian of a great nation.[22]

Still another aspect should be emphasized. Southey understood the necessity, at least, of associating the history of Brazil
with that of the adjoining Spanish colonies, and in this respect
he anticipated the reader and never failed to trace the history
of those colonies, since he judged it necessary for the clarification of the facts relating to the history of Brazil.

Finally, he proceeded in a manner worthy of respect up to

our time, since "in spite of overlooking certain aspects, and be-
lying others, his work continues to be the most comprehensive
explanation, in English, of the Brazilian colonial era." [23]

The reception of his work in the contemporary intellectual
world of Brazil does not seem to have been warm.[24] The extreme
nationalism of the first days of independence did not look
favorably upon a foreigner—and moreover a Protestant—who
busied himself with our history. This same nationalism, on the
other hand, was much more willing to follow a line not far
from the fervor of Rocha Pita. This is principally what the
foundation of the Instituto Histórico e Geográfico Brasileiro
in 1839 reveals to us. The illustrative speech of its first permanent secretary, Januário da Cunha Barbosa, is spoiled by al-
lusions to the "joyous as well as prodigious discovery" of Brazil,
a land admired for the

riches of her mines and forests, the products of her plains and mountains,
the greatness of her rivers and bays, the variety and lushness of her vegetation, the abundance and value of her fruits, the astonishing novelty of
her animals, and finally, the constant benevolence of a climate that makes
the mills of our countrymen as productive as the blessed soil of the climate.

Consequently, continues the orator, "we will always find an
inexhaustible treasure in our honorable past of interesting ideas
which should be made known to the world in their true light." [25]
He has praises for the land, but also for the men: "In the
period of a little over three centuries, will not men renowned
for different qualities and who merit the care of the prudent
historian have appeared on this fertile continent to offer themselves to the new generations as models of great virtue?" Finally,
we come upon a clear demonstration of bad humor, in view
of which the following words sound as a truly sour note in a
hymn of praise of our national treasures:

And are we always to leave it to the enterprising talent of foreigners to
write our history without the discernment that a Brazilian writer could
better obtain? . . . Our history abounds in models of virtue, but a great
number of glorious deeds are dying or sleeping in obscurity, without benefiting subsequent generations. Brazil, placed in circumstances dissimilar to
those of France can, however, through its history, present to its children

a long series of men distinguished for their knowledge and brilliant qualities, to be studied and emulated. The only element lacking has been someone to present these men in a well-ordered sequence according to time
and place so that they may be better understood by those who yearn to
follow their steps on the paths of national honor and glory. . . .[26]

The expressed reference which is immediately made to the
name of Rocha Pita does not leave us any doubt whatsoever as
to the principal model which the orator preferred. The author
of *História da América Portuguêsa* adapted himself to the
nativistic tendencies of the time, and left aside any separatist
position, to accept the link of the colony to Portugal.[27]

In the second issue of the *Revista do Instituto Histórico,* the
same note is struck by its president, the Visconde de São Leopoldo, in the historical program proposed to the members of
the society. His ecstasy incites him to flagrant disrespect for
geography, which gives us the impression that he is outlining
an imaginary picture and accentuates his lack of contact with
certain realities. Note the following example:

Brazil, beneath a benign and pleasant sky . . . where everything either
laughs or frightens; a great variety of sights and sensations awaken and
interrupt the tedious monotony. With Brazil located on the most advantageous geographic point for world commerce, with the most beautiful
harbors on the ocean, with great lakes, or rather, landlocked seas; . . . in
short, everything foretells that Brazil is destined to be, not accidentally,
but of necessity, a center of enlightenment and of civilization and the
arbitrator of the New World's politics.[28]

An examination of the nationalistic views in the *Revista do
Instituto Histórico,* which was the news medium of our major
center of historical studies during almost a century, would take
us a long way—up to the establishment of the [first university]
faculty of philosophy in our country—toward understanding
our historiographical development. It is necessary to emphasize
several aspects of this most important tendency of the Brazilian
intellectual world, or better, of this element without which it is
practically impossible for us to delineate something that can
justly be called Brazilian thought. Above all, our attention is
directed, paradoxically, to the effort of kinship with Europe,

through France. The extraordinary affinity for this nation, already revealed in the eighteenth century by Santa Rita Durão,[29] would assume new proportions with the independence movement, which was fatally inclined to seek sources of inspiration in the liberal principles that emanated from the French Revolution. In the field of history, the foundation of the Instituto Histórico e Geográfico occurred precisely when the romantic historians were flourishing in France, absorbed in ideas of liberty, of exaltation and nationalism, whose recent origins they sought to reestablish in their works. Let us mention only the case of Augustin Thierry with his "Récits des temps mérovingiens," already published between 1833 and 1837 in the *Revue des Deux Mondes* and collected into a volume in 1840. In the preface, perhaps in his best-known passage, Thierry gives us an account of his rapture for the episodes of the wars of the French, through the pages of Chateaubriand,[30] bringing us face to face with the romantic enthusiasm for the barbarous, the crude, but also, the pure. In Brazil, anti-Lusitanism, understandably unleashed by independence, reverted to the exaltation of the Indian as the legitimate and true ancestor of Brazil's nationality.[31] The phenomenon was not new, since Gregório de Matos in the seventeenth century had been able to deride those who boasted of their aborigine ancestors.[32] So, the meeting of the Indianist current with the influence of French romanticism was easy, especially when history encouraged the mission of finding a clear definition of the national sentiment; in the collection of the *Revista do Instituto Histórico* we constantly come across essays relating to the Indians; the frequency alone constitutes a fact worthy of thoughtful examination.

A national preoccupation is evident also in the continual efforts to find in history models for the new generations. It is inevitable that we see the prestige that surrounded the authors of classical times, as the result of an education which emphasizes their great role. The memory of Plutarch is alive in the biographical series on Brazilians distinguished for their power, letters, honesty, etc., published regularly in the *Revista do Instituto*. Rocha Pita naturally finds his place there; his biography was written by J. M. Pereira da Silva. His *História da América Portuguêsa* is considered "a very valuable and necessary work for all Brazilians who wish to know the history of their country, not only in that period still poor in historical works, but also in our times, which possess a greater abundance of material on Brazil." However, among his defects, Pereira da Silva does not fail to point out, and very significantly, the little attention given to the indigenous tribes.[33] Remembering, therefore, the life and work of the patron par excellence of nativism, he continues to insist on the nativist note. The flattering pragmatism expressed in the praise of the great figures of the past as examples had a long life in the prevailing mentality among the members of the Instituto, as one gathers from the following passage, just written in the twentieth century:

A century has already elapsed since Brazil revealed the opulence of its culture to the metropolis [Portugal] and to Europe with a vigor that was already a prediction of its independence. The twentieth century opened a page of glory for our country, written by our fellow countryman Santos Dumont, who conquered the domain of air for science. Casting a retrospective eye over the past from this high point, let us see what our countrymen were like at the turn of the nineteenth century. From this study, so worthy of the majesty of our history, comes a useful lesson for the new generations and a stimulus to repeat in the future that which our greatest men so nobly achieved in the past.[34]

Besides their patriotic intentions, at least two other facets characterized the founding group of the Instituto Histórico: a preoccupation with a new way of presenting history, and a consciousness of the necessity of finding documents—in other words, of careful research. The first of these facets is most clearly expressed in the oft-repeated reference to so-called philosophic history, beginning with the address of Cunha Barbosa himself.[35] I believe that a new reflection of contact with French culture can be discerned here, since "philosophic history" probably was found in works of Chateaubriand and meant the exclusion of the role of Providence in events for which natural and human causes should be sought.[36] Strict impartiality is emphatically required in order that such a history may be truly practiced: "The prudent genius of the historian, seating himself upon the tomb of Man, who ends his labors there at the grave, spurns biased arguments and flattering advice by conducting himself, in wisdom, as the severe priest of truth." There will be no prejudice of patriotism and pragmatism once "the love of national glory will lead us to cleanse our history of inaccuracies. . . . And will not a truthful history of our country offer these lessons which can so profitably be used by Brazilian citizens in the performance of their important duties?" [37] As for documents, they constitute the principal objective of the Instituto, as we gathered from the founding proposal signed by Raimundo José da Cunha Matos and Cônego Januário da Cunha Barbosa:

1. . . . members of the administrative council of the Associação Auxiliário de Indústria Nacional, recognize the lack of a historical and geographical institute in this court, which would concern itself principally with gathering innumerable valuable documents that are now scattered throughout the provinces and that could be used in the compilation of the history and geography of the empire, [a task] made difficult by the lack of a reference, or index, of which our writers could take advantage; . . . 3. The goal of this Instituto will be, besides those which may be designated by its regulations, to compile and organize the historical and geographical documents of interest to the history of Brazil.

Item 9 constitutes a proof, not only of the sentiment of a certain affinity with France,[38] but also of the consciousness of the importance of foreign institutions for achieving the desired objective:

The Instituto will open correspondence with the historical institute of Paris, to which it will remit all the documents of its constitution, and will do likewise with other [institutes] of the same nature in foreign nations; and it will seek to expand into the provinces of the empire in order to better gather the documents necessary for the history and geography of Brazil.

Nationalism, then, was not involved with the hatred of foreigners. The address of Cunha Barbosa naturally insists on the indispensable task of research and the organization of a deposit for documents, saying that the Instituto should "condense documents . . . purifying the errors and inaccuracies that obscure so much printed matter, both domestic and foreign." [39] He also wrote "A Lembrança do Que Devem Procurar nas Províncias os Sócios do Instituto Histórico e Geográfico Brasileiro" [memorandum on what the members of the Instituto . . . should search for in the provinces], to the end that the members might submit the following to the central office in Rio de Janeiro: 1) biographical notes, published or in manuscript, on Brazilians distinguished for their letters, virtues, exploits, services rendered, or any other notable quality; 2) authentic copies of the most interesting documents and extracts of reports in the secretariats, archives, and registers, both civil and ecclesiastical; 3) notes on the customs of the Indians, their religious practices and civilization; 4) descriptions of the internal and external commerce of the particular province, its industry, literature, and other general facts, even population and class divisions; and 5) notes on unusual facts.[40] Concerning the execution of plans for the existing material abroad, he required that the imperial government appoint a legation attaché to copy documents in Portugal and Spain; furthermore, his report of November 3, 1839, tells of "several of the most distinguished writers of the Old World, who, taking an interest in Brazil, have dedicated several strokes of their illustrious pens to us, making the riches of this our land better known in Europe." [41]

The entire task of organizing collections of source documents was along the line of historical research such as it was being practiced in Europe, especially in Germany. And it was precisely a German who sent us a famous essay on how to write the history of Brazil, in reply to the Instituto's request for the best method of compiling a general history of Brazil.[42] He was Karl Friedrich Philipp von Martius (1794–1868), the naturalist who, together with [Johann B.] von Spix, undertook a trip through Brazil from 1818 to 1820. For Martius, the first fact to really merit attention from the historian was the formation of the people:

Anyone who undertakes to write the history of Brazil, a country which promises so much, should never lose sight of the elements which contributed to the development of man there. These diverse elements come from the three races, namely: the copper-colored, or American; the white, or Caucasian; and the black, or Ethiopian. Because of the reciprocal and changing relations of the three races, the present population consists of a novel mixture, whose history therefore has a very particular stamp.

Each one of these races, then, is considered individually, and the direction of research is indicated in order to establish the degree of participation of each race in the unfolding of Brazilian history. In the case of the indigenous race the study of language would be required, from which pertinent conclusions could be drawn, "leading to ethnographical investigations and an understanding of a large part of the New World." As for the Portuguese, emphasis on the militia system would be worthwhile, since it encouraged and maintained the spirit of adventure that reverberated throughout the Lusitanian domain, and because it favored "the development of self-governing municipal institutions and helped to nurture a bold citizenry that took up arms to oppose the governing authorities and powerful religious orders." Moreover,

This period of the discovery and early colonization of Brazil can be understood only in relation to the Portuguese maritime, commercial, and military achievements. This period never can be considered as an isolated event in the history of the active Portuguese people. Brazil's importance to and relations with Europe are the same as those of the Portuguese expansion.

Also indispensable is the study of fifteenth-century customs, as well as the legislation and social conditions in Portugal at that time, the clergy in general, and the religious orders in particular, with the added complication that the latter take us beyond the Iberian Peninsula, because of the French and German Jesuit missions in Brazil. Europe, in its totality, is invoked in one of the most interesting passages in the entire dissertation of Martius:

An interesting task for the pragmatic historian would be to study the establishment and development of the arts and sciences in Brazil as a reflection of European life. The historian should bring us into the colonists' homes, show us how they lived in the city and the country in various periods and developed their relationships with their neighbors, servants, slaves, and customers. He should depict church, school, and government for us and take us into the fields, the plantations, and the sugar mills. We should learn something of the rural economy, the agriculture, and the colonial commerce of Brazil. . . . The Brazilian historian should analyze the progress of poetry, rhetoric, and the other sciences in Portugal; compare them with the rest of Europe; and show their influence on the scientific, moral, and social life of the Brazilians. . . . The historian will be drawn to the variety of the narrations about the many expeditions and forays into the hinterland from the coast. These *entradas* were undertaken to procure gold and precious stones or to capture Indians and make slaves of them.

The Negro, to whom Martius assigns considerably less observation than to the other races, should be studied from his origin, in his role vis-à-vis the Lusitanian colonization of Africa, as a slave influencing the "civil, moral, and political development" of the population. Finally, as to the form that a history of Brazil should have, though recognizing the inestimable value of the works previously published on the provinces,[43] he pointed out: "The vast extent of Brazilian territory presents the historian with a difficult problem, for he is surrounded by an immensely varied natural setting and by a population composed of very different elements with different customs and practices." Martius recommends, with an eye to avoiding the danger of compiling special histories of each province—and not a history of Brazil—that

those parts of Brazil that are similar in physical conditions and belong with each other can be treated together. Thus, the history of São Paulo, Minas, Goiás, and Mato Grosso converge into one; Maranhão and Pará can be treated as one; Ceará, Rio Grande do Norte, and Paraíba form a natural group influenced by Pernambuco; and finally, the history of Sergipe, Alagoas, and Pôrto Seguro will be the same as Bahia's.

The work of the German naturalist was considered to be on a level above the possibilities of the time in Brazil, something which should be taken as a start by future historians.[44] Such was the admiration dedicated to his memory that in the end he aroused the most violent criticisms of Sílvio Romero.[45] For him, there was practically nothing original in the ideas of Martius, since "a foreigner who visited us hastily, preoccupied with botanical matters and who, moreover, was almost completely ignorant of us," could have woven only a coarse cloth of commonplace facts about our history. A discussion of the matter does not belong here. But to deny the value of Martius's dissertation seems to us to be an unjustifiably extreme attitude when we take into consideration the dominant ideas in Brazil in 1843; it is sufficient to evaluate the difference in quality by comparing the work of the scientist [Martius] with that of Júlio de Wallenstein,[46] who was also competing for the prize offered by the Instituto for the best proposal on the matter which preoccupied it at the time.

In this way, between 1810 and 1843, we had Robert Southey, the first model for Brazilian history, worthy of note even today; the foundation of a sponsoring organization for documentary research; and a guide for the historians of the future. Given the importance assumed by research, the object of constant concern in the field of history, let us see how it [research] developed among us in the nineteenth century, up to Capistrano de Abreu.[47]

The Instituto Histórico pursued its activities incessantly, leaving us in its journal an excellent and varied repository of data for the study of the Brazilian past, above all the history of nineteenth-century ideas. In stimulating the search for documents by all the means open to it, the Instituto at the same time proposed topics to be developed and discussed by its members, such as "a determination of the true periods of Brazilian history and if this history should be divided into ancient and modern periods, or what its divisions should be,"[48] what was the influence on the country's civilization of various deceased members of the Instituto who, for their example, were revered by the public,[49] etc. Following the example set in the capital of the empire, institutes were also formed in the provinces, but not always with the ability to complete the undertakings stipulated in their programs. The Instituto Histórico e Geográfico de Ceará and the Instituto Arqueológico e Geográfico de Pernambuco are outstanding. In the journal of the latter institute,

Raposo de Almeida proposed to follow, for his state, the policies advanced in Rio de Janeiro by Cunha Barbosa. Private research was also carried out in connection with the Instituto Histórico, and names like Meneses Vasconcelos de Drummond and Francisco Adolfo de Varnhagen distinguished themselves. The first, in his capacity as a diplomat, was able to glean great numbers of documents, published or in manuscript, from several European countries.[50] These were donated to the Instituto Histórico or given to his disciple, Melo Moraes, himself known as a researcher, especially in the Arquivo Nacional and the archives of the secretary of the empire. Varnhagen, for his part, had already attracted the attention of Vasconcelos de Drummond, who recognized his talent and unusual capacity for work. In 1840 Varnhagen had donated to the Instituto manuscripts copied in Portugal; he then immediately dedicated himself to research in São Paulo, where he asserted he found in the Jesuit letters the best documents on the first period of Brazilian history.[51] His appointment as first-class attaché in Lisbon (1842) gave him the opportunity of collecting, organizing, and analyzing documents, in the capacity of a government official, a position which he was to hold until 1846. A letter of his, sent to the secretary of the Instituto Histórico in 1843, gives us an idea of the results of his work:

Though my inquiries may today relate to more remote times, I do not neglect to exert my best efforts to obtain copies of what is important to more modern times. So I am gathering and collecting the information which, by order of the court, was given in writing at the beginning of the last century by our frontiersmen who discovered Minas Gerais, Cuiabá and Mato Grosso.[52]

Transferred to Spain in 1847, he pursued his activities, searching through the major archives of that country, particularly those of Simancas. In this way he sought material referring to boundary problems with the old Spanish colonies. Until 1851, when he returned to Brazil, he was given, in addition, the opportunity of research in Dutch archives,[53] increasing the number of sources destined to be used in his *História Geral do Brasil*. A second stay in Europe, from 1851 to 1858, as always in the diplomatic service, was followed by a transfer to Paraguay, which afforded him new opportunities as a researcher, this time in the field of Spanish America. Upon returning to Europe in 1868, it was in the center of the continent, Vienna, that new archives were opened to Varnhagen. Until 1876 trips motivated by his desire for research were many, even though Portugal always detained him, since the preferred center of his studies and publications was in Lisbon.[54]

In Brazil, the Instituto sponsored a series of researches, with the names of Machado de Oliveira and Pereira Pinto being outstanding in São Paulo. The provinces of the North were explored by Gonçalves Dias,[55] by virtue of a mission conferred directly upon him by the imperial government. The result of his work could not have been encouraging, to judge from the words of José Honório Rodrigues:

From this investigation . . . was verified the state of abandon in which those records were found, the disdain for historical papers, the slow destruction of those records, many times consciously; and also that our poet was perhaps not the person really suited for a task of this nature. A total incomprehension about the exact nature of the probe and examination of the state archives influenced the shipment of material to the Arquivo Nacional, to the detriment of local studies, which remained without the indispensable firsthand sources.[56]

Furthermore, the visit of the poet [Dias] to Europe to find documents, until his replacement by João Francisco Lisboa, was not totally satisfactory. The latter immediately took care to put himself in contact with Varnhagen, from whom he hoped to find advantageous and wise guidance; this was what led him to dedicate himself to a search in the Arquivo do Conselho Ultramarino [in Lisbon].[57] Still in Europe, especially France and Holland, Joaquim Caetano da Silva,[58] to whom is owed a very rich collection of documents for the study of the Dutch in Brazil, and J. Franklin Massena, who concentrated on the archives of the Jesuit Society in Rome, gave outstanding performances. The desire of the imperial government to investigate the European archives motivated a second mission by Gonçalves Dias, in 1863–1864, and a mission by Ramiz Galvão in 1873, the latter resulting in the reform of the Biblioteca Nacional, the discovery of new sources, and the publication "of the best research, bibliographical, and cataloguing tools." [59] Under the sponsorship of the Instituto Arqueológico e Geográfico de Pernambuco, José H. Duarte Pereira undertook an important study in Holland (1885–1886) and in the British Museum, and F. A. Pereira da Costa examined the public archives of Olinda (1892). With this we arrive at the end of the nineteenth century, a period in which the name of Capistrano de Abreu was already beginning to have deep repercussions on the panorama of Brazilian historiography.

The most important historian of the time was Francisco Adolfo de Varnhagen, author of *História Geral do Brasil, antes de Sua Separação e Independência de Portugal*. The son of a German father, raised in the atmosphere of European culture and, on the other hand, tied to Brazil, he was in a privileged position to mark an epoch in our historiography.[60] History became his vocation, and he displayed exceptional gifts as a researcher. In his work (the first edition dating from 1854–1857) we truly come face to face with important signs of thinking along lines very diverse from those which marked the mentality of the Instituto Histórico and which furthermore continued to be widely accepted in the intellectual circles of the country. There is a notable restriction of the nationalist tendencies. The author hoped that his readers would discover in his work "by the display of a civilizing tolerance, the feelings of high and noble patriotism, not of another lamentable patriotism summed up only in the absurd display of vile and rancorous hate of everything that is foreign!" [61] Varnhagen did not exalt the Indian, the true passion of the nationalists. Rather he viewed the native as troublesome; this he mentions at the end of his preface to the first edition of the *História Geral*.[62] His awareness of pricking sensitivities by viewing the Indian in an unflattering manner can be recognized in the following passage:

With respect to what we said about the colonizers and the African settlers, we believe that in general there will be only a conflict of opinions. This does not hold, however, with respect to the Indians, who are little studied philosophically and profoundly. The Indians do not lack advocates dedicated to their glorification, for motives which are not always sound and which we do not acknowledge—we who as historians sacrifice everything to the convictions of our conscience. We are convinced that if for the symbolic idea of Brazilianism we would wish to exalt these motives unduly, we would end up by being unjust to these motives, to the colonizers, to humanity in general (since all constitute only one race) and, therefore, unjust to the present Brazilian nation, which we boast of belonging to.[63]

Correctly understood, this is far from meaning that he valued any less the participation of the Indian in Brazilian history, as one can gather from his prologue to the second edition of the *História Geral:*

Among these and many other unpublished facts selected exclusively by historical criteria, most noteworthy are those facts relative to the ethnography and anthropology of the Tupi, the study of whose languages we seek to popularize among us by completing the costly republication of the grammar and other valuable dictionaries of Padre Montoya. That was the best reply that we could give to those who thoughtlessly accused us of prejudice against the ancient inhabitants of this region . . . forgetting, in such accusations, that in 1840 we maintained the necessity of the study and teaching of the languages of this land to which we had already devoted ourselves; that in 1849 we proposed that certain information about the Indians be requested from the provinces; that we suggested the creation in the Instituto Histórico of the ethnographic section which now exists; and finally, that it has been in this field of studies that we have had the fortune of presenting the most important investigations on our history.[64]

Hearing the condemnation of the "fierce assassins of our first bishop, the barbarous 'quilombo' runaway slaves, the fierce Mascates," we do not feel far from Southey. Possibly Varnhagen could have avoided the issue, but he chose not to. He wrote,

If I had wanted to follow comfortably in the footsteps of some who, instead of studying and submitting the most difficult and ticklish point for public discussion, sought to avoid giving their opinion, it would have been very easy for me to write in such a way that, if it would not please everyone, at least it would not displease anyone, just as certain politicians do at times today.[65]

The influence of Martius seems clear, for example, from the persistence in his talk of "the comparative evaluation of the degree of civilization of the colonizers, of the barbarity of the slaves brought mercilessly from Africa, and of the savageness of the Indians, recent nomadic invaders who occupied the territory which we today call Brazil." The relation between the two authors is evident and led Capistrano de Abreu to the pure and simple affirmation that "with the plan of Martius, Varnhagen plunged wholeheartedly into his study." [66]

The influx of historical criticism, then in full vogue in Europe, is evident in the *História Geral do Brasil*. Varnhagen does not hesitate to counter expressly everything that would recall the tendency of Rocha Pita, whose work was considered "lacking in essential facts, destitute of criteria, and foreign to the high intentions of forming or improving the general national spirit." [67] The influence of geography on the development of Brazilian history—here it is possible to discern the ideas of Karl Ritter—is more clearly recognized than it had been up to that time. The land was hostile, its penetration difficult;[68] hard was the struggle of the colonist with the peoples in virgin, hostile jungles "before which man grieves, feeling his heart constrict, as if in the middle of the seas, surrounded by the immensity of the ocean." [69] Heroism was also not a thing to be put in prominence:

It behooves us to repeat here . . . that the love for truth will oblige us more than once to combat certain beliefs or illusions which we have already been accustomed to respect. To those who lament seeing some of these illusions of proclaimed heroism dispelled, we beg that they believe that we will have preceded them in their protests, and we ask that they resign themselves before the truth of the facts. . . .[70]

The policy was to seek the truth—that is, the facts such as they really happened—according to the policy of [Leopold von] Ranke, of whom it is impossible here to refrain from thinking.

The number of works left by Varnhagen was enormous.[71] Outstanding among the strictly historical ones are *A História das Lutas contra os Holandêses* (1871) and *A História da Independência do Brasil*, unfinished and only published in the *Revista do Instituto Histórico* in 1917.[72] Critics have been unanimous in considering him the greatest exponent of Brazilian historiography in the nineteenth century. Sílvio Romero praises his erudition, his direct study of documents in the archives and libraries, as well as his capacity to overcome his phase of small monographs by throwing himself into the broad works which brought him fame.[73] Capistrano de Abreu, in the obituary published in the *Jornal do Comércio,* thinks it "difficult to exaggerate the services rendered by the Visconde de Pôrto Seguro [Varnhagen] to national history, and his efforts to raise its standards." [74] However, he had several reservations concerning Varnhagen, applicable to all who open new roads in any field. In this respect, it is useful to remember that "Varnhagen was the first person to write the history of the eighteenth century. And it was he himself who said that his work left much to be desired," [75] and that "each century demands special qualities of him who studies it." [76] Whatever may be the defects of his work, "it is necessary to recognize the master in him." [77] With Varnhagen, a change is noticed in the historiography of the country; particularly worthy of mention was the support given him by the Instituto Histórico and by the emperor in spite of his position, which was contrary to the many principles made public by the nationalism of the period.

Varnhagen's figure assumes even greater proportions when we compare him with the only other contemporary historian to lay claim to a place in our considerations of national history: J. M. Pereira da Silva. Characterized by prolificacy, he [Pereira da Silva] classified his own works as historical, literary, political, and imaginative.[78] Outstanding among his historical works are *A História da Fundação do Império Brasileiro* (1864–1868), *Varões Ilustres do Brasil durante os Tempos Coloniais* (1858), *Segundo Período do Reinado de D. Pedro I* (1871), *História do Brasil de 1831 a 1840* (1879), and *Memórias do Meu Tempo* (1895–1896). Sílvio Romero himself, although repressing the disapproval with which he had confronted da Silva's work, did

not venture to seek out and indicate the qualities which by
chance were contained in it, and restricted himself to copying
the opinion of Joaquim Nabuco—for whom Pereira da Silva,
in the last analysis, was a superficial improviser[79]—and to
recommending caution with da Silva's exaggerations. We have
already referred to the manner in which Pereira da Silva considered the work of Rocha Pita, an example likely to give us
an idea of his view of history. The same biography presents another interesting aspect when the author seeks to outline his
ideal as a historian, which

once the truth of events is examined and known; once the voice of the
past centuries is heard; it still remains to recount and describe, and along
with the narration and description, to judge and to analyze. History is a
noble and high mission which perfects the intelligence, purifies the spirit,
clears the conscience, and embellishes the heart. Description and moral-
ization, painting and judgment, narration and reasoning, are indispensable
elements in sketching the great picture of human events, questioning their
causes, discovering their consequences, linking the life of the individual
to the life of the society, connecting man to the species, and forming in
this way the great lesson for which history was instituted.[80]

He does not shirk from giving us a summary of the historical
schools, concluding that "the only true historical school is that
of Tacitus and Thucydides, of Gibbon and Niebuhr, of Machi-
avelli and Müller, of Plutarch and Thierry, of Polybius and
Lingard," a considerably heterogenous mixture in which all
these authors—assuming that Pereira da Silva really read them
—are connected without one's knowing how or why. Also
significant is his repulsion for the "school created by Mignet,
developed by Thiers and Armand Carrel" and born from the
theories of the 1789 French Revolution, since it "corrupts life,
demoralizes the conscience and perturbs the spirit." [81] His tendency toward flattery is readily discernible just from the simple
title, *Varões Ilustres do Brasil*. For example, among the illustrious men, Alvarenga Peixoto recalls Petrarch and Metastasio by
presenting in his poetry "the colors of Raphael of Urbino, the
sentimentalism of Correggio, and something candid and pure
like the compositions of Murillo, or happy and sweet like the

Psyche of Canova." [82] In fact, this brings us closer to a Rocha Pita combined with a Théophile Gautier in his moments of bad taste than to the critical spirit of Varnhagen or the characteristic preoccupations of the European historiographical movement in the mid-nineteenth century.

Alongside national history, local history developed, the study of which—so it seems to us—could be fascinating, because of the conclusions to which it leads concerning the formation of the Brazilian nationality. Truly, the intellectuality of the provinces could offer something much closer to what there then was of a legitimately Brazilian mentality, than a center like Rio de Janeiro could. This city, favored by special benefits, constituted an environment unfit to serve as a base for us to evaluate the prevailing atmosphere in the northeast, in the center, or in the extreme south of the country.[83]

João Francisco Lisboa, whom we have already seen playing an important role in the research for documents, is one of the greatest proponents of this category of work. His *Apontamentos para a História do Maranhão* qualifies him to be a historian "in whose pages are felt some of the agitations of the soul of the masses, some of the pulsations of the heart of Brazilian nationality," since "here and there he refers more specifically to the State of Maranhão and Grão Pará, but what he says can be applied to Brazil as a whole." [84]

Another celebrated author is Joaquim Felício dos Santos, to whom *As Memórias do Distrito Diamantino* is credited and which was originally published in the weekly *O Jequitinhonha* in 1862.[85] Upon announcing his work, he addressed his readers as follows:

The colonial history of the unfortunate people who inhabited this diamond area, subject to the authorities of absolute power and governed by special laws, virtually forming a private colony isolated in the immense territory of Brazil, cannot fail to be interesting to every Brazilian. It was this population, precisely because of its existence on a rich soil, that most endured the vexations and exactions of the insatiable government in Lisbon, which sought only to extract every benefit from our country, the prosperity of which little mattered except to enrich the royal treasury. What we can guarantee our readers is the truthfulness of the facts that we are going to publish; proof will be found in documents existing in the secretariat of the Diamantina District, and when we have recourse to traditions, we will seek the accounts of trustworthy persons.[86]

Therefore, what is presented is the result of scrupulous research. But we can infer much more from these words: first, a sharp liberalism, confirmed by the political views of the author, who was decidedly Republican; second, the nationalism so character- istic of his time, reflected in his charges against Portugal; and we glimpse, perhaps, a notion of his breadth in the historical arena, with his declaration of the interest in a local matter for the entire country. What we have here is most pleasant reading. The reader will never forget the incidents and sufferings of the contraband *garimpeiros* [diamond miners]; the social life in Tijuco; the judicial career of João Fernandes de Oliveira; or the personality of the councilman, Manuel da Câmara Bitten- court. Special mention is due him for his care in relating the rejection by Portuguese authorities of the ideas of the French Enlightenment; these ideas penetrated the region with facility, not only as a result of the normal commercial relations with Lis- bon, but also by means of the contraband trade practiced un- interruptedly with European countries—England and Holland in particular. It was in this way that "our small society in this corner of the world also immediately awoke to the same philo- sophical spirit of the encyclopedists; their books were avidly sought after, and their ideas of freedom accepted with as much predilection as we had the necessity of seeing them attained." [87]

Both J. F. Lisboa and Felício dos Santos linked their names with Varnhagen's, something which does not fail to be useful for our sketch concerning their relations. The former was one of those who refuted the ideas of the Visconde de Pôrto Seguro about the indigenous peoples,[88] which only leads us to the con- firmation of the prestige of Indianism. The latter clarified one of the defects of the *História Geral do Brasil,* which consisted of sometimes molding events according to the vanity of the author;

so it was that in order to give his father the glory of having the first iron foundry in Brazil, Varnhagen underrated the Pilar Foundry, which made iron bars as early as 1815.[89]

The prolific Joaquim Norberto de Sousa Silva (1820–1891) also deserves special consideration for his work on the Inconfidência Mineira,[90] which was presented to the Instituto Histórico at the end of 1860. Southey had been the first to publish some details on the matter, and the introduction to his chapter in the *Revista do Instituto Histórico e Geográfico* testifies to the interest aroused by this initiative;[91] however, he had concentrated essentially on the court's judgment. It was left for Joaquim Norberto to utilize the legal proceedings of the investigation of the Inconfidência, thus completely revising the picture of the Mineiro movement.

The number of local studies was great, as one can verify, not only in the provincial periodicals, but also in the *Revista do Instituto Histórico* itself. These studies always constitute a significant source, when not directly for the matters they treat, then certainly for research on the prevailing mentality of the days when they were conducted. In short, the same thing occurs in any other literary branch, in any period of the country's history. For example, it is well known how much one can find on the history of customs or ideas, besides information for various other fields, in the works of the romantic poets: José de Alencar or Joaquim M. de Macedo.[92] At times, they are sources as important as documents for conscientious historians; they assume aspects of spontaneous and accurate testimony. Newspapers are another area to consider since "the freedom of the press maintained in practically the entire country made this source of information one of the most abundant contributions to the history of the empire." [93]

Brazilian historiography continued to be augmented abroad during the nineteenth century. In France, names such as Fernand Denis[94] and d'Avezac[95] were associated with that of Varnhagen; in England, John Armitage continued the work of Southey by extending it to independence and the reign of Dom Pedro I;[96] the German, Louis Schneider, was the author of a

famous *Guerra da Triplice Alianca contra o Governo da República do Paraguai* (Berlin, 1872–1875), published in its Brazilian
edition with notes by the Barão de Rio-Branco.[97] Heinrich
Handelmann, of the University of Kiel, published a *História do
Brasil* worthy of note for already being completely linked to the
development of German immigration: "The salvation of Brazil," one reads, "rests upon the uniquely spontaneous immigration of free European farmers." [98] However, the Brazilian atmosphere did not seem too encouraging to the eyes of
Handelmann, as we see by the final considerations in his
História:

However, in summary, repeating what has been said up to now: A more
frank reception on the part of the Brazilians, more tolerant in the political, religious, and nationalistic sense, would be welcome and necessary;
what still remains to be desired in the interest of immigration is no less
in the interest of the Brazilian people themselves.[99]

A new mark on our historiography was made by Capistrano
de Abreu; furthermore, he led us to turn our eyes to the surroundings that conditioned his early education—that is, a
regional setting enlivened by a series of new ideas appearing
from all sides of the horizon.[100] In 1870–1871 the conclusion of
the Franco-Prussian War considerably rocked the prestige of
French culture, at the same time that the end of the Paraguayan
War laid bare an immensity of weak points in the Brazilian
monarchy. Restlessness seized control of men who yearned for
new foundations, for a vision of the world capable of adjusting
to completely new conditions.[101] And in the Northeast, especially in Recife, there flourished a movement influenced by
German culture. Within that movement, Tobias Barreto was
particularly outstanding. English authors also came to be more
known, precisely because some of the most famous German intellectuals—such as Haeckel—drew their inspiration from Dar-
win. Sílvio Romero inveighed against the patrician atmosphere, charging that it was lamentable, empty, and predomi-
nated by banalities; he aspired to make contact with the true
Brazil, not with the false country imitating the stale common-
places of French origin.[102] Romero said of Capistrano:

He understood the weakness and inevitable death of romanticism and launched the beginning of another literary formula for poetry and for art in general. He appropriately appraised the necessity to examine all the old base for Brazilian sentiments and he introduced the true ethnographic principle into Brazilian criticism and history, until then falsified by the mania of Indianism. He wanted to be the man of his time and also the man of his country, and he always applied the new European ideas to national matters.103

German prestige grew, Spencer won new admirers, and all this demanded another way of viewing the past. Even Sílvio Romero, giving a speech as deputy of the province of Alagoas, turned against the "backward and nonscientific" methods of Brazilian historians, concluding later in the following manner: After Mommsen and Buckle, only immeasurable talent would justify adherence to the thinking of Michelet and Quinet.

In response to these demands, João Capistrano de Abreu arose. Born in Maranguapé, Ceará, in 1852, he went to Recife in 1869 to study law. In Recife he studied French and English, sought to familiarize himself with the philosophical ideas then in vogue among the local intellectuals, resolved to dedicate himself to history, and abandoned his law studies. After some time, we find him in Fortaleza, where, as in Recife, the young intellectuals were in a state of excitement.104 The Positivist Raimundo Antônio da Rocha Lima was in the center of one group whose participants called themselves the "French Academy." Rocha Lima himself, before adhering to Comte's thought, had pursued several paths, but by preference he always studied philosophy and history, mainly religious history in which he had recourse to Burnouf, Maury, Quinet, Reuss;105 Vacherot, author of *Science et Conscience,* had been one of his mentors, later displaced by Taine, who directed him toward recognizing the urgency for a complete transformation in his ideas.

This conviction came to be confirmed by a study of the writings of Buckle. Many ideas of the English thinker disgusted him profoundly, such as those which refer to the theory of moral laws; however, his exposition on mesological influence, his discussion of the introspective method, his conception of scientific history—much more defined than by Taine, a thousand fertile suggestions that swarm in the entire work, found a receptive mind and had a lasting, fruitful effect upon his thinking.[106]

In 1875 the group dispersed, with Rocha Lima a complete Positivist. Going to Rio in 1877 he already had begun to lean toward Spencer.

He thought that the hierarchical classification of the sciences was admirable; however, the classification of Spencer, without seeming to be less perfect, appeared perhaps to be less automorphic. It disgusted him to admit the Law of the Three States because, besides being an empirical generalization, it applied neither to all societies nor to all the phenomena in one society. He conjectured that the British thinker, coming after the revolution effected in biology by Darwinism and in psychology by the theory of association, could praise a more worthy monument than the Positivist philosophy. Finally, what fascinated him above all was the synthetic conception of the universe that reduced all realities to parts of an immense function—evolution—parts which are distinguished only by their greater or lesser degree of heterogeneity, by the greater or lesser proportion in which they are definite or indefinite.[107]

If we lingered on Rocha Lima, it is because we judge him suitable to give us an idea of the laborious studies of Capistrano himself, who gave Rocha Lima unlimited admiration to the point of confessing to consider him as his model.[108] Taine, Buckle, Comte, and Spencer were also influential in his [Capistrano's] education,[109] besides other German authors then known through French translations.[110] In Rio in 1883, his studies already had helped him to win the professorship of Brazilian history in the Colégio Pedro II, thanks to a thesis on the discovery and development of the region in the sixteenth century;[111] other works revealed him as a true innovator in the field of national historiography. From then on he remained in Rio dedicating himself exclusively to intellectual activities. His letters, so opportunely edited by José Honório Rodrigues,[112] fully show his constant preoccupation with historical research and the effort to keep himself up to date with important publications in Europe. Names of European authors appear frequently, and one notes particular attention to his German bibliography. His preference was toward specialists in political

economics, with Schmoller[113] deserving special note alongside
Buecher, whose principles—according to Capistrano—became
routine in his interpretation of historical facts in general, with
the exception of those facts concerning ancient history.[114] He
strove to know comprehensively all the works relating to the
history of America and Portugal,[115] but his curiosity extended
to the entire history of the Western world, since all of it, in the
last analysis, should be considered for the study and compre-
hension of the history of Brazil.[116] Psychology, through the
works of Wundt, was considered by him as an indispensable
element for the historian; and geography occupied a very notable place in his thinking. He translated into Portugese (sometimes with the collaboration of Vale Cabral) the small *Geographie* by [Johann Eduard] Wappäus, the *Allgemeine Geographie
Brasiliens* by [Alfred W.] Sellin, and a work by [Alfred] Kirchhoff on anthropogeography. He was attentive to the principles
formulated by Ratzel, taking them as the basis for an article on
the history of Ceará.[117] As is to be expected, it has been asked
in which way Capistrano allowed himself to be influenced by
the Germans. For José Honório Rodrigues, his relations with
German culture showed itself in his methods of work and in his
conception of history:

> The German methodology guided him in the rigorous study of documents;
> his geographical and economic knowledge focused his attention on the true
> structure of historical events; Wundt's psychology, the beginning of ex-
> perimental psychology, made him abandon a vague psychological orien-
> tation and prevented him from relying on fatalism for understanding the
> lives of people. These influences cause an about-face in his mind, toward
> more realism. His new conception is historical realism, adopted from the
> German experts, and his task is to recount what really happened.[118]

Castro Rebelo has another opinion, in which "it does not
seem possible to point out in any work of Capistrano any
sign of a change in his conception of history after the
direct knowledge he came to have of German historians when
he could read them in their original German." [119] We believe that it would be more appropriate here to indicate the
difficulties in determining the different influences to which

Capistrano was submitted. Above all, it is necessary to keep in mind that tendencies such as the strict verification of sources or research on the relations of man with his environment, although originating in Germany, by the end of the nineteenth century already belonged to the common domain of specialists in the West. Capistrano had an early knowledge of French and English works that could act as intermediaries for the research methods present in Germany; and such methods would have reached him even before he learned the German language. Furthermore, his works do not lend themselves to an evaluation of the degree of influences upon him; the majority were not published in book form during his lifetime but were scattered as articles, critiques, introductions to works of other authors, etc. This means that there was no preface to his books, which, collected after his death, appeared devoid of an explanation concerning the guidelines of the author in composing his work. The *Capítulos de História Colonial* itself, whose edition was directed by Capistrano, does not offer a preface. With these conditions, only his letters remain for us as sources for research on the guiding elements of his activities as a historian. They truly are extremely valuable material for the study of the life and ideas of Capistrano as much as for the history of Brazil in his time, since he never failed to recount and criticize the major contemporary events and personalities. The letters extend from 1880 until 1927, the year of his death. Those letters lead us to conclude that in fact there did not exist any cultural preference for, or any exclusive influence of, one author or country during any moment of his life. In that which touches on intellectual activity, he never sinned by one-sidedness. What was decisive for him can be easily inferred from words such as the following: "The soul is an organism; different capabilities coexist in interdependence. In order that culture be complete, it is necessary that all capabilities be cultivated at the same time." [120] Anyone who expresses himself in this way could not prefer German authors over all others, since he would tend to indulge himself in all works worthy of consideration, be they German or not. Similar to what is true of the soul, people also "coexist in interdependence," chiefly in that which refers to culture. Indisputably, however, it was by recognizing the respect given in the whole world to the profundity and value of German culture that Capistrano ventured to study the language and to derive every benefit from this; it is he himself, furthermore, who tells us: "I am not boastful nor am I ashamed of having studied the language. I did it because certain German books satisfied several curiosities in my mind, and to wait until they are translated would amount, in the best of estimates, to a delay of years." [121] This was the pure behavior of an honest intellectual, never a bias in favor of German culture.[122] Not only did the books referred to spring from all corners of the Western world; the same happened with magazines. At a time when no public library in Rio de Janeiro possessed collections of foreign periodicals specializing in history,[123] he sought by every means to bring himself up to date with the *Revue historique,* the *English Historical Review,* the *American Historical Review,* the *Revue de synthèses historiques,* and others. And his correspondence again attests that a predilection for the Germans is unnecessary in an application of the research methods initiated in their country; in fact, in writing to Guilherme Studart, Capistrano expresses himself as follows: "For what motive, therefore, do you revolt against an obligation to which all historians are subject, especially since the physiognomy of history has been renewed by the study of archives, the creation of historical criticism, and the criticism of references begun by Leopold von Ranke in Germany?" [124] All historians, therefore, independent of their nationality, already were proceeding according to certain principles begun in Germany. The position of Capistrano, in truth, is that of a true Westerner, for whom European culture appears as a whole which cannot be broken up by the limitations of political orders. This is the trait that best characterizes Capistrano, to our mind, and without taking it into account, one cannot possibly understand the new manner in which Capistrano faced the problems of Brazilian history, since this manner was conditioned, above all, by the mind and by the cultural education of the man.

Giving Varnhagen his due respect does not silence the deficiencies—really the defects—of his work, beginning with the lack of an over-all view of history, from which resulted a failure to establish relations between facts that are apparently remote from one another.

Varnhagen was not noteworthy for that understanding and engaging mind which, by imbuing the historian with the sentiments and situations that he comes across, makes him a contemporary and confidant of men and events. The major defect of the Visconde de Pôrto Seguro was the lack of a flexible and engaging mind. The history of Brazil did not seem to him to be a solid and coherent entity. He could dig up documents, show their authenticity, solve enigmas, unveil mysteries, not leave anything for his successors in the realm of facts. However, to understand such facts in their original context—their connection with the wider and more fundamental facts from which they spring, to generalize their actions and formulate a theory, to show them as consequences and demonstrations of two or three basic laws, all this he did not achieve, nor could he achieve.[125]

From these words, so full of implications about the ideas of Capistrano himself, is further inferred that the treatment of references left much to be desired in Varnhagen; really, how can one know what to look for, or what to choose, without the indispensable qualities to do this? Here it is the researcher who places himself under restrictions, according to the letters of Capistrano when he took it upon himself to prepare a new edition of the *História Geral do Brasil*. One can read the following, for example:

I tell you the pleasing news that I hope to put out the first volume of Varnhagen by the end of the year. It has given me some trouble; he is much more careless and inaccurate than I thought at first; it is enough to see the helter-skelter that he made of Francisco Caldeira and Alexandre de Moura. The entire military expedition to Maranhão must be rewritten. I had thought of asking you for an unedited document that Varnhagen possessed about this expedition, but now it is late." [126]

Care in documentation, then, is of first importance to Capistrano,[127] bestowing upon him an exceptional place as a researcher into Brazilian history. Once more we reiterate the wealth of data given in his correspondence. His letters to Lino de Asunção, João Lúcio de Azevedo, the Barão de Rio-Branco, and Guilherme Studart reveal an infinite preoccupation with the search for documentation, a task in which, furthermore, his collaborator, Vale Cabral, distinguishes himself.[128] Initially thinking of editing a large collection of unedited documents[129] touching on the sixteenth century,[130] he dedicated himself to the investigations that resulted in the publication of the *Tratados da Terra e Gente do Brasil,* the *Informações e Fragmentos Históricos do Padre José de Anchieta,* the *Diálogo das Grandezas do Brasil,* the *Primeira Visitação do Santo Ofício às Partes do Brasil,* and the *História do Brasil de Frei Vicente do Salvador.* The latter invites our attention by its importance, since it had already been consulted by Varnhagen and João F. Lisboa in Portugal, but remained unedited until Capistrano and Vale Cabral, in 1886, undertook its publication.[131] Frei Vicente (Vicente Rodrigues Palha) had finished his work in 1627, showing love for his native land and a certainty of its future, perceiving its possibilities as the center and refuge of the Portuguese government.

He was a master of the culture of his time, versed in sacred and popular Latin literature and in Portuguese literature, a reader of histories, voyages, and poetry; he knew Spanish and perhaps Italian. We may imagine that if the *História* by Frei Vicente, instead of remaining buried and lost for so many years, had come immediately to light, its consequences would have been considerable as a model. The archives were complete, and would have been consulted within the limitations imposed by time. The forays of the *sertanejos* would have attracted attention, and knowledge of them would not remain as the names of scouts, without biographical information, or supplementary geographical information—mere "subjects without verbs." [132]

Such words, from Capistrano himself, give an idea of the work's importance.

Among his [Capistrano's] original works, two demand special consideration: the *Capítulos de História Colonial* and *Caminhos Antigos e o Povoamento do Brasil.* His position in Brazilian historiography was put into focus by José Honório Rodrigues in words that seem excellent to us and which for this reason we repeat:

Capítulos de História Colonial is the most perfect synthesis ever achieved in Brazilian historiography. . . . The book was born out of the desire to publicize and modernize the understanding of our history in a simple, nonpedantic form. He wanted it to be more an economic and social history than a political history, as free as possible from the listing of names and dates and from the mere chronology of the viceroys and governors. . . . Nobody can read the *Capítulos* without immediately seeing that Capistrano was concerned about "the people, castrated and bled, and bled and castrated for three centuries." The work is a well-executed social and economic synthesis. . . . *Os Caminhos Antigos e o Povoamento* defined the major themes of the colonial period, explained the meaning of the various captaincies, and indicated a new direction for Brazilian historiography. Until the end of the century nobody, except Capistrano, attributed such importance to the conquest and settlement of the *sertão*. . . . *Os Caminhos Antigos e o Povoamento* is for Brazilian historiography what Frederick Jackson Turner's *The Frontier in American History* is for American historiography. . . . He [Capistrano] saw the *sertão* and the inland trails as the process of incorporation and expansion of the western frontier. It was a new approach and presented an original interpretation of the colonial development of Brazil. The *sertão* and the roads were vital factors in the creation of Brazilian life. . . . The *sertão* and the trails into it contributed to the development of a distinctive Brazilian history. . . . In the transformation of the *sertão*, the colonists were at first barbarous, but they changed as the *sertão* changed. This transformation created a new, distinctly Brazilian personality. . . . The role of the *sertão* and the roads profoundly changed the writing and methodology of history in Brazil. The history of colonial Brazil was not only the colonization of the Atlantic coast, but also the expansion into the interior, either occupied by or free of barbarians.[133]

Both works fall within the guidelines outlined by Martius, which helps to assert the importance of this naturalist.[134] And we are further reminded of him in considering another category of Capistrano's activities: the study of indigenous languages.

The recommendation for such study is included in the directives of Martius, and Capistrano earnestly dedicated himself to it. References to this study run throughout his correspondence; and the Indians will see for themselves that by sharing their life with him, they acted as the purest source for linguistic studies. Bacairi and Caxinauá were the languages to which he was most dedicated, writing the volume *Ra-txa-hu-ni-ku-i* on the latter. The role of the Indian in the formation of Brazil was very great. "My thesis is the following," he said, "what difference there may be between the Brazilian and the European, I attribute in the major part to the climate and the Indians." [135] We have here a phrase whose analysis can reveal much about Capistrano's position in Brazilian historiography. First, we note his serious tone, free of any illusions, dealing with a matter that had been so delicate during the nineteenth century. Is this not a sign of balance, resulting from a realization of national consciousness? In the second place, we note his certainty that the Brazilian is simply a European submitted to a process of differentiation whose force is far from sufficient to justify historical isolation. Do we not have here the trace of an integration on a higher level, in which America and Europe may always be linked? Finally, we note his recognition of the Indian's function as a factor of uniqueness only, without praise, without lyricism, without the worry of opposing an idealization of the Indian to the foreign image of an indifferent Europe. It is now the legitimate conscience of the Brazilian, feeling himself to be a participant in an uninterrupted and intricate chain of relationships, to which is given the name of history.[136]

In this way is explained Capistrano's profound effect, not only upon historiography, but upon the entire renaissance movement in Brazilian intellectualism. As was natural, he was not alone in the enrichment of our history; his personality alone would facilitate the awakening of vocations and stimulate the work of his contemporaries, who are remembered by Capistrano himself in 1882, on a page which we feel would be useful to reproduce here.

Brazilian historical studies are progressing. . . . Baptista Caetano's work places linguistic studies in the field of science. Barbosa Rodrigues, José

Veríssimo, and [Joaquim] Serra have tried to penetrate the native's soul and extract the secret of his organization. Before his death, [Charles F.] Hartt laid the foundation for Brazilian archaeology. Rodrigues Peixoto, aided by Lacerda, initiated the study of anthropology. [Antônio Joaquim de] Macedo Soares and Sílvio Romero extract from contemporary society the unknown origin of many traits. [Alencar] Araripe, Jr., is investigating the origins of our literature. Silva Paranhos tries to clarify the intricate labyrinth of the Rio da Prata. Augusto da Costa and Pereira da Costa are delving deeply into the history of Pernambuco. Franklin Távora tries to recreate the history of the Revolution of 1817. Assis Brasil and Ramiro Barcelos discuss the *rio-grandense* revolution. Alcides Lima reveals the history of Rio Grande do Sul. Henrique Leal jealously digs into the glories of Maranhão. Teixeira de Melo attempts to answer the international questions. Vale Cabral is establishing Brazilian bibliography and uncovering unpublished annals. Alencar Araripe is preparing the history of Ceará and of the revolutions of the regency. Severiano da Fonseca studies Mato Grosso. Moreira de Azevedo fences with the Sabinada. Paulino Fonseca is investigating the *Chrónica das Alogoas*. Ladislau Neto is preparing the catalogue of the anthropological exposition. Félix Ferreira, João Brigido, Pôrto Alegre, and many others bring their stones to the monument.[137]

This report of Capistrano is, above all, worthwhile as testimony to the existence of a fermentation, a feverish curiosity, running throughout the country. Several of the names are of interest only for strictly local history; and besides, the list refers to the year 1882. This is why we single out only one name of those mentioned among the contemporaries of Capistrano: [José Mária da] Silva Paranhos, Barão de Rio-Branco. Otherwise, it would be necessary to recall personages not included on the list: Joaquim Nabuco, Oliveira Lima, Pandiá Calógeras, and João Ribeiro. Nabuco and Rio-Branco, as diplomats solving border questions, undertook a documental research that by itself would guarantee them a place in Brazilian historiography.[138] Other works, however, assure them of such a place. In the biography of his father, José Tomás Nabuco de Araújo, Nabuco organized a work that is indispensable to the study of the Second Empire;[139] while in his autobiographical work, *Minha Formação*, he left a reference concerning the life of a patrician Brazilian family in the nineteenth century. Rio-Branco, for his part, directed himself to military history, as his notes to the translation of Schneider's work[140] and the "Esbôço Biográfico do General José de Abreu, Barão do Serro Largo" show us.[141] As for his *Efemérides Brasileiras,* let it be enough for us to refer to the opinion of Capistrano: "I have read his *Efemérides* in the *Jornal do Brasil* and duly enjoyed it. For the first time in this field, there appears a serious work based on references."[142] Oliveira Lima distinguished himself by his research on documents in England, and his activities as a historian were also facilitated by his diplomatic functions.[143] Among his works, the most important, regarded as a broad source of information on the reign of Brazil over the Portuguese Empire, is *Dom João VI no Brasil* (1808).[144] Pandiá Calógeras, in close connection with Capistrano,[145] wrote his *Formação Histórica do Brasil* partially in the spirit of the *Capítulos de História Colonial.* Of his labors, there is further left to us, the *Política Exterior do Império* and a number of studies to which fall the merit of revealing "the ample prospects offered by the exploration of that almost virgin domain: our economic history."[146] João Ribeiro is noted for his small *História do Brasil,* of a didactic nature, also organized under the influence of the ideas of Martius;[147] it continues to be worthy of new editions in our day.[148] Outstanding among compilations of documents are the *Atas da Câmara de Santo André* and *de São Paulo* (both begun in 1914), the *Registro Geral,* the *Inventários e Testamentos,* and the *Registro Geral das Sesmarias.*[149]

We could certainly lengthen the list of works for inclusion in our outline. For example, we could dwell on Guilherme Studart, researcher into the history of Ceará; on Euclydes da Cunha with *Os Sertões, Contrastes e Confrontos,* and *À Margem da História;* on Tobias Monteiro with his studies of independence and the empire; on Rodolfo Garcia, collaborator and continuer of Capistrano's work;[150] on the mass of facts accumulated by Rocha Pombo in his *História do Brasil;* or we could select several among numerous works worthy of being considered as references for the history of customs, for social history, and for other areas. Let us limit ourselves, however, to recalling what we have said before: that, in general, everything that is published—or that is written—is worthy of attention from those interested in history, and many times the most surprising results arise from unexpected sources. All the major authors just mentioned shared at least one common characteristic: All of them, in one form or another, had their minds open to European culture, all of them wrote history with a mind imbued with Europe. In the diplomacy of Rio-Branco, Nabuco, and Oliveira Lima, in the enthusiasm of João Ribeiro for the German culture, in the high posts occupied by Calógeras, the opportunities to expand a point of view dominated by nationalism were always present. The circles in which they moved, it is true, limited the depth of their views a little in a legitimately Brazilian sense. This is why we must return to Capistrano de Abreu, in order to arrive at the new stage of studies on Brazil's history, the new attempt at final emergence from isolation in historical studies, at attaining that which—with the restrictions demanded by such an expression—corresponds more closely to a Brazilian historical reality, at opening the possibility for research to the broadest strata of the population. This is what leads us to the elimination of the works of Rocha Pita and to the modernist movement and to the foundation of the university.

We once more turn to the correspondence of Capistrano. His letters reveal his zeal to understand Brazil such as it is and not as one would wish that it were. And the result is not all flattery for the country, in which Capistrano seeks reasons for great enthusiasm in vain. Let it be noted that this has nothing to do with his love for his country; in his letters are found unmistakable expressions such as, "I love and admire Brazil, and I hope for her. The bad Brazilians pass, and Brazil remains." [151] And exactly because of this, he wanted to face the truth as much as possible; he was far from letting himself be lulled by praises that had already become commonplace. The land, considered alone, did not appear to him as something marvelous: "The most fertile land in the world. . . . Where? Not in Amazonas, where, once a layer of earth is scraped away by the backwoodsman, sterility is struck. In the other states it is almost invariably the same." [152] The people did not seem so intelligent to him as many claim,[153] and political life was a source of constant deception.[154] From him comes that melancholy phrase with which he meant to sum up Brazil: The *jaburú* is "the bird that for me symbolizes our land. He has a stout stature, thick legs, robust wings, and spends his days with one leg crossed over the other; sad, so sad, that austere, dead, and vile sadness." [155] It was not by chance that Paulo Prado took this passage as the epigraph for his *Retrato do Brasil,* the book that takes self-criticism to extremes, and therefore places itself under the sponsorship of Capistrano. For this reason, it has already been said that the *Retrato do Brasil* is a work of Capistrano although written by his friend.[156] Curiously, we note that another characteristic concept of the intellectual world in the nineteenth century, Indianism, in spite of all the importance given to it as an idea as well as to the more practical studies of the Indians and their languages, was held as outmoded, according to what one gathers from a letter to Mário de Alencar dated 1914: "Why bother with the Indians? It is a useless waste. I do not know very well what you intend to seek, but I assure you right now that you will end up disillusioned." [157] Linking this opinion to other passages in Capistrano's work we could conclude that his only objective in such a study was to understand its significance in the formation of the nineteenth-century mentality, or perhaps to appreciate the contributions the Indians had made in the past. The new Brazil, bubbling from the ambition which São Paulo and the southern states were manifesting, was benefiting from the immigration movement and was breaking the arrangement of the three races extolled by Martius. To those who lamented the transformations occurring from then on, replies were put forth in this manner:

São Paulo was, continues to be, and will always be intimately Brazilian. This does not hinder a hundred races from confronting each other on its ethnological chessboard; it is precisely these immigrating groups, peaceful and hard working, who, nationalized by the birthplace of their children, became . . . São Paulo, one of the most beautiful and prosperous states in the country.[158]

And certainly, Capistrano understood this fact.

Capistrano, the historian, who could attain the level characteristic of his work only through the greatest possible identification with Brazilian reality, whose view of the past was based on live, conscious, and uninterrupted contact with his contemporary world, was better able than anyone else to illustrate the passing to a new stage in whose atmosphere historical studies would undergo a total renovation. We are referring to that which, lacking a more appropriate expression, has been designated by the name of *modernismo,* a name not in any sense restricted to art or literature but interpreted broadly, as Ronald de Carvalho clarifies: "The new man in Brazil wants to live the reality of the moment. To be modern is not to be futurist, nor to forget the past. No one can forget the past. However, to repeat the past would artificially break up reality, which is continuous and indivisible." [159]

Paulo Prado, one of the sponsors of the Modern Art Week of 1922 who had faith in the movement and valued the importance of "the brave and very beautiful work of the Week of Modern Art," which aspired to a transformation in Brazilian cultural mediums and was also favorable to a political change,[160] was also a friend of Capistrano and turned to history. His *Retrato do Brasil* is the opposite of Rocha Pita's work, since it reads:

We give to the world the spectacle of a people inhabiting a land that legend, more than the truth, considers an immense area of unequaled riches; and not knowing how to exploit and profit from its share . . . Brazil . . . sleeps in her colonial dream . . . In spite of civilization, we live isolated, blind, and immovable within our own mediocrity, in which the rulers and the ruled please each other.[161]

Such words, which seem mild in view of the deep bitterness of the entire volume, are the result of a reexamination of the past, in a seizure of conscience in the present.[162] The yearning to reach the heart of Brazil—such as in Capistrano—catches our eye, and also as in Capistrano, the preoccupation with Europe is permanent, combating provincial nationalism and seeking to find the right place and the values representative of Western culture, where Brazil should have a place.

In the field of historiography, the results of the new tendencies were immediately felt. Documents, the publication of which had been uninterrupted, were used to accelerate the new trends; *Os Inventários e Testamentos* aided Alcântara Machado in his *Vida e Morte do Bandeirante*. Along with several others, such as Washington Luís, Basílio de Magalhães, and Alfredo Ellis, Jr., Paulo Prado dedicated himself to rewriting and revising Paulista history. Although a stranger to *modernismo,* Afonso de Taunay, also a correspondent of Capistrano, who gave him considerable advice for his *História Geral das Bandeiras Paulistas* (1924–1951), stands out because of the breadth of his research.[163] The fermentation characteristic of teaching in the 1920s expressed itself in the yearning for renovation, including the campaign for the founding of universities in the country. The fundamental step toward the realization of this goal was taken with the establishment of the faculties of philosophy, letters, and sciences in São Paulo and in Rio de Janeiro in 1934 and 1935, respectively. And, according to Fernando de Azevedo, who makes the point very well, there was more than ever a desperate need among us for personalities really worthy of exercising the responsibilities of university teaching duties in the various areas of intellectual and scientific specialization.[164] In the particular case of history of civilization, we were faced with an almost absolute vacuum. In truth, a factor which made understanding of and historical research about Brazil quite difficult was the complete lack of a base in general history.[165] The perfunctory manner in which the subject was taught in secondary schools did not allow its use for clarification of innumerable aspects of Brazilian history, resulting in the almost total divorce between national and world currents of historical development. From primary school on, Brazil was seen as something more or less isolated from the rest of the world. In view of this, we can appreciate the growth of the *ufanistas* [braggart] dogmas against which Capistrano and his followers reacted. There were, it is true, those who made contact with general historical works superior to the texts in the secondary schools. What were these works? First, the *História Universal* by César Cantú, written between 1837 and 1848 and considered in Europe a popular work of an inferior quaity;[166] and then, the great *História Universal,* published in Germany under the direction of [Wilhelm] Oncken and translated into Portuguese. In reality, it was a collection of historical works of very uneven value, but which boasted among its collaborators respected names such as Edward Meyer. The simple consideration of such a work as the last word on the matter immediately reveals to us the manner in which the material was approached. The necessity of a continuous contact with the European historical publications was not felt; or better, the great majority, so large that we could call it a totality, hardly knew of the existence of these new works. It is interesting to note that, in spite of the great attraction in the realm of history for France, so important for the development of pro-French enthusiasm, the works that enjoyed the greatest fame here were written by an Italian and by a group of German professors.[167]

With the recently founded faculties of philosophy, those who felt attracted by the study of history, for the first time in this country had the opportunity to attend courses in which the subject was treated according to European standards; in this way, the fundamentals were put forth, upon which it was hoped that a modern Brazilian historiography could grow. French professors whose names will never be forgotten came to São Paulo and Rio de Janeiro to treat the cultural history of our country: Emile Coornaert, Fernand Braudel, Henri Hauser, Eugène Albertini, Jean Gage. Under the direction of the latter, the departments of history in São Paulo began to award their first degrees. As imperfect as were the theses presented, one cannot deny that they represented great progress (in view of the prevailing conditions). For the first time in Brazil, under the direction of a European master, work was done methodically and critically. Such innovations encouraged the Brazilian elite to view their country as a part of the world, or at least of the West. It was then understood how sterile the previous atmosphere had been, in which one had the impression of living isolated from the rest of humanity. Naturally, this was only the beginning—and a very modest beginning. There were, and still are, many for whom the preoccupation with studies relative to ancient times, the Middle Ages, or any other area not specifically Brazilian, was a real lack of wisdom or loss of time. According to this point of view this activity was useless, since we did not find ourselves in a position to undertake original research on matters of this nature; in compensation all support should be given to research efforts in Brazilian history or, in the final analysis, to research in Portuguese or Iberian history, according to the situation. We believe that such a way of confronting the problem is open to argument. In the first place, we think that a history of Brazil outside general history is not possible; or, it is not possible to give Brazilian history its full meaning without considering general history. In fact we consider Brazil's integration with the Western world indispensable at least to correct the tendency toward isolation and historical uniqueness. Even more, the familiarization with problems of general history has as a result, particularly for the specialist in Brazilian history, the opening of new horizons, of new possibilities in method. And in this case, even a work on distant and foreign regions could have favorable repercussions, including local research into national history. A sound background of general history is indispensable for the development of a legitimate Western conscience, so much more so for the Brazilians, a people of colonial origin whose roots are in Europe. Several centuries are not enough to destroy the force of language, religion, social forms, and an enormous mass of traditions by means of which we are forever linked to Europe.

Several negative aspects deserve emphasis if we dedicate ourselves to a calm examination of what the historical studies have been in the universities. São Paulo serves as an example. Let us turn, however, only to what the university gave us in the positive sense. Above all, the establishment of the *Revista de História* attracts our attention. Conceived and realized by E. Simões de Paula, it appeared in 1950, constituting the first Brazilian periodical devoted to history in general and possessing the permanent collaboration of foreign specialists.[168] Founded in 1942 and reorganized in 1950, the Sociedade de Estudos Históricos continued to function and was associated with the same group as the *Revista*. Also the task of organizing a specialized library was not neglected, a rather thankless task which was handicapped by numerous obstacles. Everything had to begin from practically nothing: the acquisition of periodicals, basic works in European historiography, collections of published documents, descriptive material. All this demanded and continues to demand considerable financing and good will, which are not always found.[169] At last, works that revealed an effective renovation in the manner of confronting history were published. With her eyes on Brazil, Alice P. Canabrava completed two works on the history of the Americas which were warmly received by the critics:[170] *O Comércio Português no Rio da Prata (1580–1640)* and *A Indústria do Açúcar nas Ilhas Francêsas e Inglêsas do Mar das Antilhas (1697–1735)*. The novelty of her contributions is shown in the introduction to the first volume:

The history of the Luso-Brazilian contribution to the evolution of the Platine countries has been seen principally under the aspect of military campaigns, while other aspects perhaps more interesting, such as the deep influence exercised by Brazil in the social and economic formation of these countries, have been passed by unnoticed. Our work, seeking to show the Luso-Brazilian commercial expansion in the Spanish territory of the viceroyalty of Peru in the unified period of the Spanish and Portuguese crowns, represents an effort in this sense.

Still in the scheme of American history, Olga Pantaleão published *A Penetração Comercial da Inglaterra na América Espanhola (1713–1783)*. Certain aspects of the work are applicable to Brazilian situations. Concerning Brazilian history in a strict sense, the research for documents relative to colonial Brazil found a dedicated and honest student in Myriam Ellis, while

Nícia V. Luz explored such a little-known subject as Brazilian economic nationalism.[171]

In the history of ideas, let us remember João Cruz Costa, with *O Desenvolvimento da Filosofia no Brasil no Século XIX e a Evolução Histórica Nacional,* which highlights themes of great relevance, as one discovers in the following passage from his introduction to the book:

Thought is always the product of the activity of a people; and so it is to our history in its relation with world history that we should dedicate ourselves to understand our own significance, the feeling of our spirit, in order that we may better comprehend the transformation of ideas that came to influence our environment. Many ideas changed, and many theories born on the other side of the Atlantic took on expressions here that do not appear perfectly in keeping with their original premises. There is a style peculiar to different environments, a style conditioned by the historic traits of the people, which determines or influences the transformation of systems developed by the intelligence to explain life.

Others with contributions worthy of attention are Laerte Ramos, with his *A Formação Filosófica de Farias Brita* and research concerning the educational reforms of the Marquis of Pombal, and Roque S. Maciel de Barros, who studied Luís Pereira Barreto and the movement of ideas during the Second Empire.

Lourival Gomes Machado, turned toward political studies and tread a path of enviable beauty by relating political studies to the history of Brazilian art. Despotism and the baroque in this way constitute a single, wide horizon on which his live intellectual curiosity is exercised.

Under the direction of the tested master Fernando de Azevedo, and with the collaboration of Roger Bastide, sociological studies advanced enough to open new roads into historical research itself. It was in this area that Florestan Fernandes and Egon Schaden completed works about the Indian, a field in which the Department of Ethnography and Tupi Language headed by Plínio Airosa distinguished itself. In the field of geography numerous volumes appeared, mainly under the direction of Aroldo de Azevedo, of importance, above all, to the history of São Paulo.

The intellectual fermentation existing in the Faculty of Philosophy at the University of São Paulo is undeniable, in spite of all the handicaps inherent in the circumstances of a country destitute of a university tradition, and a world war which erupted at such a delicate moment for our cultural development. However, the growth of our historiography in the last decades was not limited to the University of São Paulo. Other institutions have the merit of sponsoring and stimulating research and publication of documents. The systematic cataloguing and protection of the state, local, ecclesiastic, and private archives, whose contents may well be of interest for the history of Brazil, fell to the Serviço do Patrimônio Histórico e Artístico Nacional [National Service of Historical and Artistic Heritage].[172] The Biblioteca Nacional in 1928 initiated the collection of the *Documentos Históricos* and in 1935–1938 made public the valuable *Autos da Devassa da Inconfidência Mineira;* the Ministério de Educação, immediately after being established, began the publication of references; and the same path is being followed by other institutes.[173] The Arquivo Nacional and the Academia Brasileira de Letras published considerable material of value. Individuals made their own private contributions. Such was the case of J. C. Macedo Soares with his *Fontes da História de Igreja Católica no Brasil.* Bibliographic indexes worthy of attention were, among others, *O Manual Bibliográfico de Estudos Brasileiros* and *A Bibliografia Brasileira* by Rubens Borba de Morais.[174]

The *História da Companhia de Jesús no Brasil* (ten volumes, 1938–1950) by Padre Serafim Leite, or the fourteen volumes of *A História do Café no Brasil* by Afonso de Taunay were publications of great importance. Outstanding names in the study of economic history are Roberto Simonsen and Caio Prado Junior, also author of *A Formação do Brasil Contemporâneo,* including at the present, the colonial period.[175] The phase of discoveries in which the Portuguese delved so much aroused the interest of a researcher with polemic tendencies who has already produced international repercussions: T. O. Marcondes de Souza.

History through the biographical prism has its greatest representative in Octávio Tarquínio de Souza with his ten-volume *A História dos Fundadores do Império do Brasil;* it is outstanding in

the part dedicated to examining the contributions of the main personalities who appeared at the historic moment of the emancipation of Brazil and who acted to establish its political institutions. In this collection of biographies, the men appear indissolubly linked to events, historic men and not mere spirits, concrete and not abstract men, associating nature and culture, nature and history—"anges et bêtes," at the same time, to draw on the thought of Kierkegaard. When it was within the possibilities of the author, his biographic work was in good part inspired by the lessons of Dilthey; and based on the best documentary sources, he strove to discover the effective tie between his historical characters and the environment in which they lived and reacted.[176]

Alberto Rangel, Castro Rebelo, Alvaro Lins, Wanderley Pinho and others also are outstanding.

The work of Pedro Calmon is vast, from work on the Bahian expansion, to research in Portuguese archives,[177] to a large *História do Brasil* and a *História Social do Brasil,* a field in which Nelson Werneck Sodré also distinguished himself with his *Formação da Sociedade Brasileira.*

Afonso Arinos de Melo Franco, J. F. de Almeida Prado, José Maria dos Santos, José Maria Belo, Hélio Viana, and numerous others in regional—or even local[178]—history could be mentioned if it were our intention to give a long list of names. In place of this, it will suffice to refer to the work of José Honório Rodrigues, *Teoria da História do Brasil,* where, besides an attempt at systematization, bibliographic information is found to satisfy anyone who may want to delve into the matter.[179]

In the area of sociology, at least three names have deep repercussions on historiography: Oliveira Viana, Gilberto Freyre, and Fernando de Azevedo—the first, with *As Populações Meridionais do Brasil* and a series of essays inspired by the history of the empire; the second, with *The Masters and the Slaves,* one of the books with the greatest repercussions in modern Brazil;[180] and the third, with *Brazilian Culture,* in which the author, "familiarized with procedures of social investigation, especially those which derived from Durkheimian theories, applies them to the examination of our social, cultural, and political evolution." [181]

Not only did a movement worthy of "discovery by Europe" occur in Brazil; also in several European centers a new phase, initiated around 1920, brought about a "discovery of Brazil." [182] This is what explains the interest given to Brazilian history by men such as C. R. Boxer, E[mile] Coornaert, Henri Hauser, [Allan K.] Manchester and [Lawrence] Hill; by specialized periodicals, as in the case of *Annales* and the *Hispanic American Historical Review;*[183] or by G[ermain] Bazin and R[obert] C. Smith in art history.

Finally, in the work of Sérgio Buarque de Holanda, the fruits of Brazilian intellectual restlessness are discerned. He attributes to Brazil a most agreeable place in the history of the aspirations of the entire Western world, perhaps of humanity. The fact that he started with an examination of the *Raizes do Brasil* in 1936 and arrived at the *Visão do Paraíso* in 1959 is highly symbolic. In fact only through diligence in searching for the Brazilian reality is our historic integration in the Western design admissible, and only by eradicating the vice of considering the history of Brazil as an impenetrable and isolated compartment will we attain the realization of a truly human ideal, one that is universally human.

CAIO PRADO JUNIOR

A Guide for the Historiography
of the Second Empire

CAIO PRADO JUNIOR, one of the most important contemporary economic historians of his country, emphasizes
in this essay the significance of the Second Empire (1840–
1889) as the transition period from colonial to modern
Brazil. Independence in 1822 brought few, if any, fundamental changes. Emperor Pedro I ruled surrounded by
Portuguese advisers and engrossed in Portuguese affairs.
After his abdication in 1831, he returned to Lisbon to
govern Portugal in the name of his young daughter. The
Regency Period, the nine hectic years (1831–1840) while
the Brazilians waited for the child-emperor Pedro II to
come of age, was too chaotic to permit any activity except a desperate effort to maintain unity. The accession
of Pedro II to the throne in 1840 brought much-needed
tranquillity to the realm. His long, peaceful, and fruitful
reign gave an impetus to progress and prosperity, which
in turn wrought some fundamental changes in the mori-
bund colonial institutions. Caio Prado discusses here
those changes, the salient themes during that vital half-
century, and some of the important works written on
those themes.

For those interested in understanding modern Brazil, the
Second Empire is perhaps the most interesting period of Brazilian historical evolution. Coming after the pacification of the

This essay is translated from the Portuguese "Roteiro para a Historiografia do
Segundo Reinado (1840–1889)," in Caio Prado Junior, *Evolução Política do
Brasil,* 3d ed. (São Paulo: Editôra Brasiliense, 1961), pp. 199–208.

post-independence social and political struggles, the Second Empire represents the transitional phase between the colonial past and contemporary Brazil. The Empire's historical significance can be measured by the extent of its transformation of the colonial structure to the modern one. Much of the colonial structure remains even today; other parts of it were only partially affected; but a group of institutions (economic, social, and political institutions, in the full sense of the word) underwent a radical change. The history of the Second Empire— when the country underwent the process of fundamental, though incomplete, change—helps to explain the complexities of modern Brazil, where we find a modern civilization side by side with the vestiges of the colonial past.

Because of the difficulty of the subject, there are no comprehensive studies of the Second Empire. All the historian can expect to find are partial works and abundant documentary sources. The researcher needs a guide through this large mass of scattered data. Such a model guide would be related to what was said above: The Empire is a transition between the colonial past and present-day, modern Brazil. The historian should investigate the extent to which the colonial institutions have been transformed.

Naturally the first topic of his research is the subject of labor. The colony of Brazil was a regime of universal slave labor; little or nothing of importance (except the positions of management) mattered, other than the slave. It fell on the Empire to transform slave labor to free labor. The bibliographical material on this is quite abundant, but it is usually unscientific. With today's perspective, the critical historian will be able to orient himself with some effort and understand the slow and difficult process of this evolution. The basic work is by Agostinho Marquês Perdigão Malheiro, *A Escravidão no Brasil: Ensaio Histórico-Jurídico-Social* (Rio de Janeiro, 1867), an old but as yet unequaled book with a careful analysis of the social and legal situation of the Brazilian slave, African as well as Indian. From the many other works, we will select only Evaristo de Morais's *Campanha da Abolição, 1879–1888* (Rio de Janeiro,

1924), which studies the parliamentary debates on the slave question; as well as Sud Mennucci's book, *O Precursor do Abolicionismo no Brasil* (São Paulo, 1938), which covers the popular campaign for the abolition of slavery. There is a lack of any comprehensive analysis of the slaves' own struggle through revolts and especially mass escapes from the fazendas where they worked. These mass flights became increasingly numerous on the eve of abolition and contributed decisively to the final suppression of slavery in Brazil.

The documentary sources on slavery are relatively scarce in Brazil. The first republican government destroyed all the documents on slavery in the public archives, for sentimental motives and to avoid any damage claims from the former slaveowners. Much material still unused will be found in the published parliamentary debates. Furthermore, English archives possess many documents related to this subject, for English foreign policy was very much concerned with slavery in Brazil, especially during the period of the eradication of the African slave trade, which was effectively suppressed only in 1850. This English documentation has not been sufficiently exploited.

The topic of European immigration runs parallel to the slave question, for it was stimulated especially to replace African slave labor. Its consequences are of great importance. To convince us of this we need only compare the regions where the European immigrants flocked (especially the south and central south of Brazil) with those regions where they did not go for one reason or another. There are profound economic, social, political, and ethnic differences between the regions; perhaps the major cause is the unequal settlement of the European immigrants. The best summary of this material is found in Eduardo Prado's short work included in the collection *Le Brésil en 1889* (Paris, 1889), edited by Santana Néri.

The organization of free labor, based on the abolition of slavery and on European immigration, is of great interest because, contrary to what would be assumed, the law of May 13, 1888, that liberated the slave did not entirely resolve the matter. Even today in many regions of Brazil, there has been a continued strengthening of certain labor practices that a modern capitalistic economist would hardly classify as a pure form of salaried labor. In many cases after the suppression of the slave system, there was a quite successful adaptation of former slave labor to a state of labor legally free yet still keeping the same conditions. This system of neo–slave labor constituted a basic element in the economic, political, and social evolution of contemporary Brazil. The historian of the Empire ought to seriously consider this fact: The process of abolition did not entirely resolve the slave question, and it left many complex problems for the future.

After the topic of labor, the investigator will next focus his attention on the great material transformation of the Second Empire. Brazil came out of the colonial period in a precarious economic condition. Everything about Brazilian technology and productive processes was deplorable. Colonial industry was nothing more than inferior craftmanship without any artistic qualities; the land was exploited by rudimentary and devastating methods; the mining of gold and diamonds—an important aspect of the colonial economy—was not in any better shape; transportation and communication were the most primitive possible, without one carriage road in the whole country at the beginning of the last century (only in the great plains of the extreme south did nature furnish these gratuitously), and there was hardly a vehicle of any kind. One factor summarizes all these statements: As a form of energy there existed only humans and animals—and even the latter was insufficient because of the inferior quality of the cattle used. The use of the energy of wind or water was rare and practically worthless. These indices are enough to give a general idea of the low material level inherited from the colonial period. It would remain for the Empire to raise it, and this was one of its great accomplishments. The development of science and modern technology came from Europe, but Brazil had to have the competency, at least in part, to know how to employ these conquests of knowledge. Steam navigation was first introduced in Brazil in 1819, but the real progress in steamboat navigation belongs to the second half of the century. Soon after 1850, the first railroads were built by the initiative and resources of Brazilian financiers. The great manufacturing industries (large in comparison to primitive colonial craftmanship rather than in absolute terms) had their beginnings under the Second Empire. During this period, the country's material progress was considerable in many other sectors.

We find here also that the specialized bibliography is imperfect. To study and keep up with bibliographic progress, it will be indispensable to consult the official reports published annually by the ministries of agriculture and public works and of the treasury, as well as by the different provincial governments. The large collection of works published by the *Sociedade Auxiliadora da Indústria Nacional,* and the *Almanaques* of the various national and international expositions in which Brazil took part (Rio de Janeiro, 1861; Vienna, 1873; Rio de Janeiro, 1875; Philadelphia, 1876; and Paris, 1889) are especially important. The historian should not forget [the Visconde de] Mauá, the first great Brazilian businessman, who spread his industrial and commercial enterprises throughout Brazil, and abroad as well. Uruguay owes its first bank to him. Of the various biographies published about Mauá, there are two outstanding works: One is a eulogy by Alberto de Faria, *Mauá: Ireneu Evangelista de Sousa, 1813–1889* (Rio de Janeiro, 1926); and the other is a critical reply by Castro Rebelo, *Mauá: Restaurado à Verdade* (Rio de Janeiro, 1932). Finally we should remember the *Autobiografia de Mauá,* with preface and annotations by Cláudio Ganns (Rio de Janeiro, 1942).

The production of coffee made an important contribution to the economic development during the Empire. Although coffee had long been produced in Brazil, its production rapidly expanded only in the last half of the last century because of the opening of the large consumer markets of Europe and the United States. Until then production was centered in the basin of the Paraíba River (in the provinces—today states—of Rio de Janeiro, Minas Gerais, and São Paulo); later it expanded further into the Paulista territory. Besides its economic importance, coffee has another significance for the historian. While the Empire based its economic vitality on coffee production, it did not succeed in detaching Brazil from its colonial habits, and it failed to create a really national economy. It repeated the same problem with coffee that had already been illustrated by the major colonial economic activities: brazilwood, sugar, gold, diamonds, and cotton. Brazil continued to be a producer of primary materials for the foreign markets, as it always had been; it would not overcome this fundamentally colonial economic status. There is a voluminous work on the history of coffee in Brazil by Afonso de Taunay, *História do Café no Brasil,* a twelve-volume edition by the Departamento Nacional do Café (Rio de Janeiro, 1939–1943); although devoid of either a critical spirit or organization, it is the only large repository of data on the evolution of our coffee production. A very interesting study was commissioned by the Dutch government toward the end of the last century, and published by its author, Van Delden Laërne, *Rapport sur la culture du café en Amérique, Asie, et Afrique* (The Hague-Paris, 1885).

After analyzing these economic transformations, the historian should concern himself next with the evolution of the Second Empire's political and administrative institutions. In colonial times, Brazil lived under the absolute rule of the Portuguese kings who were represented in Brazil by viceroys, captains general, and governors. Practically speaking, the law was the will of the monarch and his representatives, who exercised a despotic and unrestrained power. The colony had some representative institutions, the *câmaras* [i.e. the municipal governments], whose members were elected to office by the most important citizens of the city or town. In the early colonial period, the *câmaras* had some autonomy and importance, but toward the end of the colonial period they lost all their power and became merely the executors of the governors' orders. With independence, the sovereign's absolute power disappeared. Brazil became an empire. Yet it enjoyed a parliamentary regime with its chambers of deputies and lifetime senators representing the Brazilian landed classes. The emperor Dom Pedro II, the second and last emperor and the one we are interested in here, allowed the parliament to function freely and relinquished his power over the administration and political control of the country. He was accused of using personal power and improper intervention in a constitutional regime; this accusation is exaggerated, if not baseless. Although very upright, Dom Pedro II was a rather mediocre man with little foresight. The emperor attentively supervised public affairs, preoccupying himself with the selection of individuals of unquestionable personal honesty for public offices, from the ministries to the lowest administrative post. He sought to appease partisan passions by avoiding violent and extreme conflicts. He allowed the politicians who surrounded him, selected as they were by popular suffrage or elevated to governmental posts by public opinion (at least of the dominant social and economic classes), to manage governmental affairs freely. The press always enjoyed the most unrestricted freedom; and parliament as a rule functioned normally.

From parliament came the ministers who wielded the executive and administrative powers of the country. For our public men of the Empire it was a question of honor to imitate faithfully the parliamentary models of the European countries, especially England. Naturally Brazil lacked the political maturity, even in its upper classes, to copy the British model exactly; consequently, the imperial chambers functioned very artificially and with an exotic air. The historian will note the imitative abilities of the chaotic and unstable society inherited from the colonial period. Until independence, only the ruler's personal power was known in politics and administration. Some adaptations were successful experiments, but others were failures. Most students of the Empire have analyzed this subject well. Doubtless the most important contribution is Joaquim Nabuco's book, *Um Estadista do Império, Nabuco de Araújo: Sua Vida, Suas Opiniões, Sua Época,* 2 vols. (Rio de Janeiro, 1936). The more meticulous historian will be able to follow the functioning of the imperial parliament in the *Anais da Câmara dos Deputados e do Senado.*

On a par with the political institutions, and ultimately linked to them, are the administrative and juridical institutions. During the Empire there was a great transformation in those institutions. In the colonial period almost all the administration had been concentrated in the person of the governor, under whose direct orders the small bureaucracy functioned. When the Portuguese king Dom João VI, actually only regent when he arrived, transferred his court to Brazil in 1808, he brought all Lisbon's administrative organs with him. At the time, it was jokingly said that in Rio de Janeiro the king confined himself to copying the *Almanaque de Lisboa,* an official publication that annually listed all the Portuguese public administrative departments. Our country had to support a highly expensive, complex apparatus that was unadaptable to Brazilian conditions and therefore detrimental and inefficient. The Empire's considerable task was to transform these defective institutions, which could not function well in Brazil, into an administration capable of managing public affairs. The problem was even more difficult. For besides these institutions, Dom João and his court also brought a staff, almost all of whom remained after the king's departure and Brazil's independence. For a long time they perpetuated themselves in power through their ties of family and friendship. Thus this Portuguese staff's routine and spirit were transmitted to and continued by their successors in the Second Empire. This was one of the main reasons why the Brazilian administration always functioned so badly. These great obstacles, inherited from past traditions, hindered the development of efficient adaptations, and retarded administrative progress. Today we still suffer from this old affliction.

The Empire's legislation was its most brilliant achievement. We entered the Second Empire with completely revised criminal and penal procedure codes. The Second Empire gave us a magnificent code of civil procedures, which has lasted until just recently. The essential outline of the commercial code, promulgated in 1850, is found in force today. The civil legislation had a slower development; only the republic succeeded in codifying it. During the Empire the old *Ordenações do Reino de Portugal,* dating from the beginning of the seventeenth century, were kept in effect. Nevertheless there was considerable legislative and juridical work, for it can be said that the Empire developed a new civil law, although it was not codified until after the end of the Empire. The republic had to gather it into a code.

As we have seen in the other elements of the Second Empire's evolution, Brazilian legislation was not always successful in escaping the past and inaugurating new institutions more compatible with contemporary civilization. For Brazilian jurists were very attached to the past and referred too often to the past without understanding the present necessities. They relied excessively on models from Europe, where they preferred to seek their learning, without properly considering the different Brazilian conditions. We have many instances of an artificial and inapplicable law; and many unique Brazilian situations were omitted in the making of our juridical precepts. Perhaps the most flagrant case of this is land tenure, so important in an agricultural country which is still largely uninhabited; in spite of this, it was never properly treated in Brazilian law. As we have found previously, the Brazilian laws were copied from European legislation, which was formulated for a completely different situation. The sole experiment regulating Brazilian land tenure, the land law of 1850, was never executed effectively; therefore, we still suffer from a great deal of confusion about land tenure, even today. Even if we consider only the occupied land, only a small fraction of the Brazilian territory is properly registered; to verify this one needs merely to consult the long list of litigation on land questions. This is only one of many examples of the failure of the Empire's juridical development. During the Empire the breaking away from the old metropolitan Portuguese law was partially effected, but the transformation of Brazilian law failed in innumerable important instances. It will be very interesting for the historian to weigh the achievements with the failures. There is no single comprehensive work on the subject, but he can use the copious contemporary legal works; the outstanding of these are by Teixeira de Freitas and Nabuco de Araújo. The parliamentary annals will furnish some important documentation. Another recommended work is the *Livro do Centenário dos Cursos Jurídicos* (Rio de Janeiro, 1928), which includes a volume on the historical evolution of Brazilian law. Although it was written without any sociological criteria, it is a useful summary and a first attempt at the topic.

While many institutions were being transformed, Brazilian thought underwent a revolution during the course of the Second Empire. Portugal bequeathed to us a scholastic mentality. The rationalistic and scientific concepts that transformed European philosophy in the beginning of the seventeenth century did not penetrate the Iberian peninsula, especially not Portugal. The Jesuits directed Portuguese higher education at the University of Coimbra. Pombal's great educational reforms came too late. When Brazil liberated itself from Portugal, the earlier intellectual mold had not been transformed. At the time of independence, the encyclopedists' philosophy was very influential in Brazil in breaching the medieval conscience of the country. Accompanying the other political, social, and economic reforms of the second half of the last century, Brazilian thought took a really new direction, though still feeling the handicap of the scholastic heritage. This awakening to modern thought was emphatically agnostic. Our religious skepticism did not scorn the Catholic tradition but concentrated on the essentials of faith and worship. It was an expression of the intellectual awareness of the country under the Second Empire. The emperor, himself a great patron of letters and a scholar, participated in this spirit, which prepared the way for the separation of Church and State, realized soon after the proclamation of the republic, and for the dominant irreligiosity of the first part of the republican period.

The principal political repercussion of this new thought was Positivism. Auguste Comte's doctrine received a welcome in Brazil that it never had in his own country. Although the number of orthodox Positivists was always quite small, their influence was considerable. Positivism was the only coherent body of ideas in Brazil during the second half of the last century. It assumed a political role after it had penetrated the armed forces

through the teaching of Benjamin Constant Botelho de Magalhães, an enthusiastic Positivist who spread his ideas throughout
the Escola Militar, where he served as a professor of mathe-
matics. It was under the aegis of Positivism that the republic
was declared, and this action was successful thanks mainly to
the participation of army officers in the events. The evolution
of Positivism should not escape the attention of the historian
of the Second Empire. There is a voluminous bibliography on
Positivism. The annual *Circulares* of the *Apostolado Positivista*,
the organization of the Brazilian Positivists, are the most important publications of their active propaganda campaign. The
two most outstanding names in this propaganda are those of
the *Apostolado's* two great masters, Miguel Lemos and Teixeira
Mendes.

During the Second Empire, profound social changes in class
relations, psychology, and habits of life coincided with transformations of the political and economic structure and its ideological character. Brazilian society acquired a new tone, entirely
different from that of the colonial period. In the short space of
barely half a century, society was completely revolutionized
by a rising standard of living, or at least that is true among the
upper and middle groups; the fruits of economic progress; intellectual developments; a rhythm of life more in harmony with
the outside world; increased contacts with foreigners, something unknown in the colonial period; and the large immigration of Europeans of the lower, middle, and even upper classes,
likewise unknown in the colonial period. The interrelationship
of all these factors completely revolutionized Brazilian society
in the short space of half a century. Beside this favorable progressive revolution, there were the adjustment crises of a poorly
assimilated new order. These conflicts of the whole economic,
social, political, and psychological order were kept relatively
quiet by the paternalistic government of Emperor Pedro II
and the conservative nature of his reign. Violent conflicts
erupted under the republic, making its stabilization very difficult, and often endangering its normal development. A good
synthesis of the whole social evolution of the Second Empire

is the very well-written little book by Oliveira Lima, *O Império Brasileiro* (São Paulo, n.d.). Wanderley Pinho's *Salões e Damas do Segundo Reinado* (São Paulo, 1945), a more recent work, uncritically analyzes the social life of the Empire's upper classes. The other necessary data on the profound social transformation accomplished under the Second Empire can be found in the works already cited.

JOSÉ HONÓRIO RODRIGUES

Problems in Brazilian History and Historiography

THE BIBLIOGRAPHY of José Honório Rodrigues (1913—) is extensive, and its quality matches its quantity. His most outstanding books are *Civilização Holandêsa no Brasil* (São Paulo, 1940), *Historiografia e Bibliografia do Domínio Holandês no Brasil* (Rio de Janeiro, 1949), *Notícia de Vária História* (Rio de Janeiro, 1951), *A Pesquisa Histórica no Brasil* (Rio de Janeiro, 1952), *Brasil, Período Colonial* (Mexico City, 1953), *Teoria da História do Brasil* (São Paulo, 1957), *Historiografia del Brasil, Siglo XVI* (Mexico City, 1957), *Aspirações Nacionais* (São Paulo, 1962), and *Historiografia del Brasil, Siglo XVII* (Mexico City, 1963). This brief but representative list of some of his works indicates his preoccupation with historiography. He has written more than any other Brazilian—indeed, possibly more than all the other Brazilians together—on that topic. He is the author of three of the nine essays in this book, and it was a constant temptation to include more of his studies. The three chosen, however, will be more than enough to demonstrate the depth and importance of his contribution to the study of Brazilian historiography.

In the following essay Professor Rodrigues discusses some of the major obstacles in writing a history of his country. He points out that Brazilian historians during the national period have given most of their attention to an examination of the colonial past. One might add that that general trend is noticeable throughout Latin Ameri-

This essay is translated from part of Chapter I, "Os Problemas da História e da Historiografia Brasileira," of José Honório Rodrigues's *Teoria da História do Brasil*. (São Paulo: Companhia Editôra Nacional, 1957), I, 9–28.

can historiography as well. Several reasons account for it. As anyone who has done research in Latin America can testify, material on the colonial period is both more readily available and better organized. Also, history generally has been written by patricians, who have tended to look back to the "good old days" when life was peaceful, social classes well defined, and their class firmly in control. These patricians have shown a fondness for the period when Latin America formed but an extension of Europe. Historians in general have also shown a reluctance to get involved adversely in contemporary politics. In a society where relatively few participate actively in the national political life, there are in positions of power too many sons, grandsons, and great-grandsons of the historical figures of yesterday, and so historians tread lightly and tend to avoid recent history. These as well as other reasons combine to keep historical output concentrated on the colonial period. José Honório Rodrigues laments the contemporary emphasis on and preoccupation with the colonial past and makes a convincing plea for a more intensive study of the national period.

Brazilian historiography is a mirror of Brazilian history. Like the other branches of human endeavor, historiography is an integral part of society. There is an intimate connection between the historiography of a period and the preferences and characteristics of its society. The connection is economic and ideological. Scholarship is not a luxury; it depends on society's support.

Until recently, and even today to some extent, Brazilian historiography has represented mainly the traditional Brazilian society to which Pierre Denis and Jacques Lambert referred.[1] It has been overwhelmingly devoted to colonial history, an expression of the society's fondness for the old Luso-Brazilian culture and traditions, which form the philosophic basis of Brazil's social character and personality. Archaic Brazil is rural Brazil. Sixty-nine percent of Brazil's total population is rural, the opposite of the new, highly developed, more stable society of São Paulo and the extreme south of Brazil.

Between 1850 and 1950, about 4,800,000 immigrants came to Brazil, and approximately 3,400,000 remained. The majority were Portuguese, and their personality seems to have been the dominant influence on Brazilian character. Until 1930, there was a continuity of population, personality, and culture, and the rural class dominated. Although this basically rural Luso-Brazilian character was dominant, it did not cause all the cultural changes, but it did furnish the direction and define the manner of the adaptations. Thus, we have two fundamental elements for understanding Brazilian history and the directions of its historiography: the basic Portuguese character and the rural society. Furthermore, a rapidly growing society with a high demographic potential, molds a certain type of social character that Riesman called traditional,[2] meaning that the individual learns to adjust to life rather than to change it. In the relatively stable society of feudal Brazil with its persistent customs, the social character is traditional; that is, it assures the traditional patterns of conformity to certain elements of productivity, politics, leisure, and culture. Its rituals, routine, and etiquette orient everything. Little energy is devoted to discovering new solutions for old problems.

As an expression of that Brazil, Brazilian historiography is devoted mainly to the colonial period. A good proof of this is that more than 60 percent of the contributions in the *Revista do Instituto Histórico e Geográfico Brasileiro* during its first hundred years were on the colonial period; the same is true for its special issues.[3] Most of the important topics undertaken and resolved by historical research are on colonial history. The general histories either do not go beyond the colonial period or overemphasize it. The colonial period undeniably dominates the fields of diplomatic, religious, economic, and political history. The great majority of the historical documents found in the great source collections are colonial.[4]

During the first thirty years of this century, colonial history was still the first choice of Brazilian historians and editors of historical documents. Brazil was hardly a vital link in the Portuguese overseas empire during the colonial period; later when it assumed a more significant part in the world drama, Brazil came under British influence. This excessive fondness for the Portuguese and European past is an expression of the traditional society and of an immaturity that provoked certain emotional maladjustments resulting in *mazombismo,* which led us either to disparage Brazil and love Europe or to engage in flagrant self-glorification, or even in a certain critical flagellation, to which Vianna Moog referred.[5]

It is not only this psychological consequence that reveals the domination of Brazilian history by the outmoded social life. A characteristic Luso-Brazilian trait is an emphasis on friendly, personal relationships, rather than on impersonal ones.[6] This personalism, which has had disastrous political consequences, has led to biographical history, to the study of personalities and heroes as the leaders and creators of history.

The politics of the empire or [first] republic—a partial liberation from the colonial spirit—were synonymous, in those times, with imperial or republican biography, a personalistic form bound to the social character of traditional and feudal Brazil. The studies on the Indians and the Negroes, as well as on art, are devoted mainly to the colonial period. The Indian and especially the Negro are the only groups which have made important contributions to the development of the Brazilian people from the beginning of colonization but are without a historical study of their cultural influence on modern society and contemporary Brazil.

The historiography of the new Brazil gradually began to appear, especially in economic and social history. In the period from 1890 to 1914, social history occupied 44 percent of the material published in the pages of the *Revista do Instituto Histórico e Geográfico Brasileiro;* in the period from 1915 to 1938, 55 percent; and in the special issues between 1889 and 1914, 95 percent.[7]

As an expression of the new Brazil, the new historiography was initiated by Capistrano de Abreu. In *Caminhos Antigos e o*

Povoamento do Brasil (1889), he rejected the emphasis on European origins and relations in colonial history. While he wrote about the colonial period, his topic was entirely national. He invited Brazilian historians to concentrate not on the coastal communities, strongholds of traditional Brazil, but on the interior, the autonomous origin of the new Brazil, with its trails, expeditions, and mines. His rejection of the traditional approaches to the past is made explicit by these very selections of colonial themes. From 1875 on, Capistrano considered Brazilian independence as an emotional change from a sense of inferiority to Portugal to an awareness of our superiority to Portugal, but not as a change in our inferiority complex toward Europe.[8]

Capistrano's orientation toward the new historiography interests us here. Thanks to his background, he enriched historiography with new concepts: He substituted the concept of culture for that of race; his contemporary studies of the Brazilian Indians renovated our ethnography; the importance of social history and customs appeared for the first time in his *Capitulos;* and in 1910 he was the first to notice the importance of the peculiar system of the *casa grande* and *senzala* in the Northeast. Capistrano suggested to his friends and followers new and unresolved problems and theses, such as the history of land tenure, the history of legislation, parliament, and political parties, and the making of a Brazilian historical dictionary and atlas.

As Sérgio Buarque de Holanda said so well, "The historiography of the 1930s contains largely interpretive writings which simultaneously clarify and distort the facts by characterizing them in a particularly nationalistic manner." [9] This master historian of São Paulo recognized the importance of those works, stimulated by an epoch of crisis and transformation, which helped to indicate a new direction for historical studies.

Since the 1920s, because of rapid economic transformations and the pressure of cultural and technological changes, the historian has manifested a desire to expand his studies beyond the colonial past. He wants to get closer to the present, the national period. He has become interested in employing the "utilizable past" and, thereby, inclined to give less attention to the colonial period and more to the national. It is evident that action and interest are not always the same thing.

One of the examples of the historiography of the 1930s that Sérgio Buarque de Holanda cited was the *Retrato do Brasil* (1928) by Paulo Prado, author of *Paulística* (1934), and a Paulista historian intimately linked with the school of Capistrano de Abreu. Supported by copious historical evidence, Prado proposed to show that the country was sleeping in "its colonial dream." Two years before the movement of 1930 [the revolution of the Aliança Liberal, which brought Getúlio Vargas to power], he stated the necessity of "making a *tabula rasa* before thinking of total renovation." As Capistrano's disciple, he desired to liberate Brazil from the pressure of the past—which merely weighed Brazil down—by understanding the illness from which we were suffering.

It does not seem that José Maria dos Santos's *Política Geral do Brasil* (1930), which, without any undue praise, is the most intelligent critical analysis of the Second Empire and the First Republic, adopts an attitude opposite to that of Sérgio Buarque de Holanda. Santos's work should not be characterized as an appeal to the remedies of the recent past for the evils of the present. But, as Henri Hauser said,

With a really definite rupture with the colonial past, history should push aside all the pious legends and patriotic fictions to disclose the naked truth. Analyzing the excesses of the Comtian ideology, thinking about the parliamentary corruption, the military insurrections, and the replacement of the monarchy not by a regime of free speech but by a presidentialism whose absolutism was moderated by almost periodic revolutions, Santos had the quiet audacity—and, as Michelet would say, the lack of respect that is the first obligation of a historian—to call part of his book "the republican deformation that led to that which we call the Second Republic." [10]

If fondness for the colonial past is a sign of immaturity, so is a total rejection of it. Both books [*Retrato* and *Política Geral do Brasil*] are dominated by the excesses of the first attempt at analysis. In both, there is a rejection of the past, and the remorse that must emerge as a natural consequence of this immature solution. A true catharsis consists of a liberation from and an assimilation of the past—ambivalent attitudes toward the whole historical experience.

One can agree with the lucid idea of Sérgio Buarque de Holanda that

one finds numerous formative studies published in the 1930s. There is a persistent appeal to what an American essayist called the 'utilizable past' for some exciting formulas to be used as the perfect cure for all our ailments. These imagined reconstructions are hardly concerned with historical investigation, and in their extreme form they lead to manifestations of totalitarianism, especially to the Integralista doctrines.

The thought of Capistrano de Abreu, Paulo Prado, and José Maria dos Santos reflects the historical process of Brazilian life. Now it is not only a matter of understanding the present from the past, to employ the language of Marc Bloch, but also of understanding the past from the present. A lively imagination is an essential quality of a historian. In order to understand the fundamental characteristics of certain problems, it is necessary to observe and analyze the present landscape, because only it will give the complete perspective that we must have to begin a historical study. The strong ties between the past and the present require an eternal quest and an understanding of change, for history is the science of change.

The most recent problematic orientations of Gilberto Freyre and Sérgio Buarque de Holanda reflect the new historiography of the new Brazil in all its vitality and acuteness of interpretative vision. Clearly a vital historiography is not one which deals only with current themes. This would be incomprehensible, for the historian should not formulate his questions with answers already in mind. Often questions are made according to present circumstances, but the answers depend on research. If it were done in any other way, the historian would be biased and unscientific.

When the interest in the national period surpasses the interest in the colonial period, we will have entered successfully into a new phase of our historiography. Without rejecting the colonial heritage or trying to assimilate it into a dialectic contradiction or into an analytic catharsis, we will add to the formation of a new Brazil a new historiography.

If Brazil grew from 18 million inhabitants in 1900 to 60 million in 1956, at a demographic growth rate of 2.5 percent per year and a 5 percent growth rate in national income, the highest proportional rates that can change an underdeveloped country to a developed country, the task and problems of Brazilian historiography must be presented in a new way because of their complexity, variety, and magnitude and because of the new fields of activity and thought that this growth offers Brazilian historians. Unfortunately these rates of growth in population and national income have not been accompanied by educational development. We continue to have 50 percent illiteracy, whereas we had 80 percent in 1880; but we now have 37 faculties of philosophy, with 1,693 history students.[11]

. . . .

The study of contemporary history is one of the principal duties of Brazilian historiography. We cannot continue to ignore and avoid modern Brazilian history and have it dealt with only in the annual meetings of American historians or by Soviet historians in international congresses, as recently happened. It is necessary to pay attention to the "living zones," to use Fidelino de Figueiredo's term, as well as to the extinct ones.[12] A nation in transition to its complete economic development cannot continue to dissipate its historical intelligence in colonial recollections. It must deal with topics that will aid it in confronting present problems. J. R. M. Butler has pointed out that there are powerful objections to contemporary history as well as obvious advantages.[13] The world would be immeasurably poorer if contemporary history had never been written. One does not have to recall the examples of Thucydides, Polybius, and Tacitus to realize that the secrets of the past cannot be uncovered in books and documents but are found in the hearts of men, the majority of whom want to preserve the reasons for their actions.

.   .   .   .

Every day history conquers new fields and concerns itself with new problems. Of all the new ramifications of historical studies the most important at the present moment is without doubt economic history and its varied subfields, such as the history of business.

Social history is not a novelty. Since 1920, it has found many adherents and has produced a really valuable bibliography. The Institute of Social History of Amsterdam,[14] the new Institute of Social History of Paris, and the Hoover Library on War, Revolution, and Peace, of Stanford University, are especially devoted to the history of social movements, which was the topic of a speech by Professor Carlos Rama of Montevideo at the Tenth International Congress of Historical Sciences.

In the most advanced countries, demographic, immigratory, urban, and rural history have developed, but in Brazil they have received little or no attention. Brazilian intellectual history has been limited to literature and has given very little attention to ideas. Our history continues to be very narrative, chronological, and biographical. Because the Brazilian people are essentially sentimental and because personalistic solutions prevail in Brazil, it is not surprising that the great majority of our historical works are biographies.

Brazilian historians still have not been attracted to study the development of the rural and bourgeois consciences. The latter appeared before the advent of an urban class. The rural population has always been the largest in all of Brazilian history, and at present it constitutes 69 percent of our population. There has been no study made either of the role of the urban middle class or of the role of the rural classes in the frontier regions, which have been so important in Brazilian historical evolution in these last thirty years.

Bernard Groethuysen wrote a magnificent essay on the formation of the bourgeois conscience in France during the eighteenth century, based mainly on sermons.[15] Such literary sources, so indispensable for his impressions of the spiritual environment, have not yet been used in Brazil.

There have been no studies of the voting public's opinion, nor of the character of political activity. Our historians have been interested neither in the history of international relations nor in studies of national character, which are investigated in the centers of highly developed historical research. These are very important for understanding present attitudes and tensions.

Toynbee noted that during the establishment of peace from 1919 to 1921 medium-size states were reintroduced into the political scene by the reconstruction of Poland and by Brazil's aspiration to overcome its status as a small power, even if it could not be considered as having attained the dimensions of a great power. Europe was growing and would soon see itself surrounded by a dozen giant powers, when Canada, Argentina, and Australia had populated their vast spaces and when Russia, India, China, and Brazil had become industrialized. What have we, the Brazilian historians, done to clarify the reasons for our national direction and search for international power and respect? What have we done about recognizing special climates of opinion, characteristics of certain epochs and places, the character of our culture, the basic personality of our people and their special national traits? [16]

What have we done to explain the principal aspects of contemporary Brazilian life? Jacques Lambert said that Brazil is like a metropolis with its own colonies, the North and the Northeast. They exhibit such an economic disequilibrium that they threaten or can threaten national unity. The economists of the Mixed Brazil–United States Commission emphasized the enormous disparities in rates of growth and in the regional distribution of income between the economic center of Brazil and the north and northeast regions, which have 40 percent of the national population. What has been done to explain the reasons for this different behavior, which would be logical in a country with such an extremely varied localism and provincialism, and especially the reason for this profound economic and cultural disequilibrium that threatens national unity?

These economic problems affect historiography, and it is to be hoped that the growing economy will stimulate a broad historiographic development as it did in the United States. There will be different opinions about the direction of reform and what specific solutions should be undertaken to promote it, but national integration will be a great political achievement. Its enormous historical effects will decide the new areas of historiography, which will be more national than state or local.

The fundamental problems of modern Brazilian historiography are not only thematic. Of what importance is it to know all about the expansion of the fields of research if we do not consider some fundamental problems of historical thought and method? The philosophic controversy has had little effect on historical research and writing. It has neither created new methods nor greatly modified past usages. As Henry Hauser already noted in his previously cited study, two of our shortcomings are the lack of methodological preparation and the consequent reliance on self-instruction. It is important to constantly repeat the litany that we cannot expand our historiography if we do not introduce the disciplines of methodology and historiography into our departments of history.

These are the capital sins of Brazilian historiography. The venial sins, which Professor Charles Boxer recently considered as the mortal sins of Portuguese historiography,[17] are responsible for some of the deficiencies of our historiography. Among them are verbosity, attraction to speeches and lectures, lack of consultation of foreign works, and lack of good indexes. There is a curious coincidence of those observations of Professor Boxer on the defects of Portuguese historiography with those of Professor Hauser on Brazilian historiography. The similarities were the rhetorical methods, the routine and inertia of certain institutions, the excess of biographies, and the academic elogies, the commemorations and homages for our dead heroes.

There are other strengths and weaknesses of Brazilian historiography. Recent activities and successes lead us to believe that we will be able to overcome some of the deficiencies that hinder its free development. The growth and improvement of Brazilian historiography can be advanced by freeing the academic curriculum—so antiquated, with its five traditional professorial chairs and without any choice of disciplines; balancing the excessive emphasis given to certain periods of history, and the lack of study of the most important modern areas, such as the United States, Russia, and the Orient; and establishing professional standards, professional recognition, and state aid.

Jacob Burckhardt once said that he did not want to build for today or tomorrow but for always. In his closing speech to the Tenth International Congress of History, the great German master Professor Ritter said that he can understand only the historian who works also with his heart. He who really knows history will be protected from sensationalism but will not be able to face historical problems without a profound emotion, at least when he deals with the future of his own land and people.

JOSÉ HONÓRIO RODRIGUES

The Periodization of Brazilian History

TO BETTER understand history, to make it meaningful and to make it manageable, it is advisable to divide it into coherent periods. For certain areas and for certain times, there has been a concurrence of opinion concerning the establishment of and adherence to specific historical periods. José Honório Rodrigues indicates in this essay that there has been no such concurrence about the periodization of the Brazilian past. It is a topic very much open to discussion and suggestions. As this essay reveals, many suggestions have been made. However, few of them have been as thought-provoking or as convincing as those put forth by João Capistrano de Abreu. Professor Rodrigues discusses those suggestions here within the historical and intellectual context in which they were made.

The intricate task of dividing our history into periods originated with our first historical books. At that time it was purely a necessity, either didactical or logical, of classifying the material. There was not any concern for the ideological, philosophical, or theoretical character of the material. Only much later with the development of Brazilian historiography were there contributions of a philosophical or sociological character. The understanding of the importance of periodization and the

This essay is a translation of Chapter V, "A Periodização na História do Brasil," of José Honório Rodrigues's *Teoria da História do Brasil* (São Paulo: Companhia Editôra Nacional, 1957), I, 152–81.

necessity of having a standard emerged in Brazil with the foundation of the Instituto Histórico e Geográfico Brasileiro, which was the principal stimulus for historical studies.

At the very first meeting of the Instituto, on December 1, 1838, Januário da Cunha Barbosa proposed the following problem for discussion by the various members: "To decide on the true periods of the history of Brazil, and if that history should be divided into ancient and modern [periods] or what should be its divisions." [1]

This problem was going to be the principal business at various sessions of the Instituto.[2] In the second session, Brigadier General Cunha Matos, Lino de Moura, and Silvestre Rebêlo read their papers and participated in the discussion. In the third session, on January 19, 1839, Silvestre Rebêlo and Cunha Matos continued to read their works. Cunha Matos's work was later published, slightly modified, in the *Revista do Instituto* with the title "Dissertações acêrca do Sistema de Escrever a História Antiga e Moderna do Brasil." [3] After an account of the various sources of Brazilian history, Cunha Matos proposed three periods: the first, relating to the aboriginal peoples; the second, including the era of discovery by the Portuguese, and the colonial administration; and the third, including all the national events since independence. He stated that there were some disagreements about the beginning of the first and third periods, each person having good reasons for setting different dates. After a series of considerations on each of the three periods, he responded to the general claim that a philosophic history of Brazil should be written. He proposed that because of the general ignorance about many provinces, it would be better first to write a history of each province and only later to write a general chronological history. He also made a philosophic classification of the periods and said that many historians first described the traditional accounts of the fabled past, then the heroic times, and finally the ancient and modern periods. These classifications of Cunha Matos suggest, in a certain way, the three cycles of universal history proposed by [Giovanni Battista]

Vico. Cunha Matos also divided the history of Brazil before its discovery into three periods. Thus he made the first theoretical exposition of the different periods of Brazilian history.

The problem was not resolved nor were the discussions ended. The Instituto Histórico, in an effort to establish historical methods and prepare philosophical questions, continued to discuss the problems of periodization in later sessions. In the fourth session, in 1839, Januário da Cunha Barbosa, who originated the concern with Brazilian periodization, proposed this question: "What are the best methods to periodize the establishment of the captaincies general in Brazil, the foundation of Brazilian bishoprics, and their interrelationships?" Only in the sixth session, on March 2, 1839, was a committee on Brazilian periodization formed; it approved of the division of Brazilian history into three periods.[4] It is evident that the committee was influenced by the previously mentioned work of Cunha Matos. After the approval of this division, the Instituto continued to discuss questions related to periodization.

General José Inácio de Abreu e Lima, in his *Compêndio da História do Brasil,*[5] was the first to claim to carry out the idea discussed in the Instituto Histórico. In a letter to the Instituto, presenting his book to the learned association, Abreu e Lima wrote:

There is one consequence of my compendium that suffices to give it some value. Everything written about Brazil was without method and historical plan, and was a heap of facts haphazardly thrown together *without any discernible periods.* It was so bad that recently the Instituto became concerned with this matter, trying to survey the terrain, which needs a clever cartographer to sketch the map of our history.[6]

Because the Institute had not decided definitely on this important question, he said that he had decided to do it in his compendium, adopting eight periods or chapters to divide up the history of the fatherland until the coronation of Dom Pedro II. He added,

Here is the manner in which I divided the periods: 1) Discovery. The first explorations. Physical state of the country. 2) Colonization. 3) Transition to foreign domination. 4) Return to Portuguese rule. Dutch War. 5) State of the colony. Improvements. Internal administration. 6) Establishment of the Court in Brazil. 7) Independence. Administration of the First Empire. 8) Minority of the emperor. Administration of the Regency. Elevation of the emperor to the throne.

He declared that the fifth period, embracing a century and a half, could be divided into two periods, with the first part from 1654 to 1763 and the second [from 1763] to 1807. Abreu e Lima said,

This fifth period is so sterile of important events that I do not see any characteristic that would differentiate it clearly into two parts. The two most well-known events are Duguay Trouin's invasion of Rio de Janeiro and the Spanish occupation of Santa Catarina. Both were transitory events that left no other vestiges in the country except to confirm the inherent dissolution of all short-lived conquests.

He added that this whole space of time should form only one period because any other way it would overemphasize these two "unfortunate episodes of our history." Likewise, any change would greatly affect the body of the compendium, which he had carefully calculated and described, if it were to maintain a proper proportion with the whole. He ended his letter by saying that in "the division of the periods he always sought a characteristic that would distinguish them, but that this characteristic ought to be such as to be obvious at first glance. In order to be well understood each period must have its particular stamp; that is, a change, a variation, from the preceding period." In his letter, Abreu e Lima boasted that he had attained one of the first goals of the Instituto with his division of periods.[7]

When the compendium was offered to the Instituto, Francisco Adolfo de Varnhagen was commissioned to give his opinion of the work. One of the most violent polemics of Brazilian historiography arose from the judgment that Varnhagen wrote and the Instituto approved.[8] Abreu e Lima immediately entered the field with his rebuttal, published in Pernambuco in the same year, 1844.[9] It should be emphasized that Varnhagen's criticism of Abreu e Lima did not cover the issue of periodization. His main point was that the work was based almost entirely on Alphonse Beauchamp's *História do Brasil,* which everybody knew was a plagiarism of Robert Southey's book. According to Varnhagen, the compendium was full of serious errors, caused by the model that was copied. Beauchamp, although plagiarizing Southey, made occasional digressions of his own into the domain of Brazilian history, which gave rise to unpardonable errors.

Varnhagen was unable to discuss the problem of periodization because he did not have a theoretical background in the subject, as we will see later in discussing his *História Geral.* In reply Abreu e Lima once again took advantage of the opportunity to state that without the perfect division of these periods it would be impossible to write a history according to the rules of chronology. He added that he found his first period perfectly in accordance with Aires de Casal and the others, including Rocha Pita, Brito Freire, Simão de Vasconcelos, Frei Rafael de Jesus, Berredo, Frei Gaspar da Madre de Deus, Monsenhor Pizarro, and Armitage; and that what he wanted to do was to use the important events as landmarks to fix the boundaries of the periods.[10]

Abreu e Lima's reply was written in such violent language that Januário da Cunha Barbosa, saying that it exceeded the limits of decency, proposed that the Instituto Histórico insert a note in the newspapers declaring that it would not reply.[11] On the other hand, Varnhagen, in his *Réplica Apologética de um Escritor Caluniado e Juízo Final de um Plagiário Difamador que se Intitula General,*[12] limited himself, in order to terminate the discussion, to publishing corroborative evidence that his nationality was Brazilian, rather than German as asserted by Abreu e Lima.

Abreu e Lima's criteria for his periodization are very susceptible to criticism. In the first place, he was too concerned with purely administrative aspects, in spite of declaring that he always sought a characteristic that would immediately distinguish the period and give each period its particular stamp.

He lacked the important ability of penetrating into the historical facts, which would have enabled him to make a more definite division of his periods. Of course, he cannot be criticized for the lack of social and economic factors in his periodization, because social and economic history are very recent developments and were not available in his time.

The most serious criticism that can be made of Abreu e Lima's periodization is that which he himself stated in his reply to Varnhagen's *Juízo*. Abreu e Lima stated that he did not begin his theoretical periodization with an insight into and knowledge of the raw material of Brazilian history. He said that he based his ideas about preparing a compendium, upon a general understanding of the different periods of our history. All he had to do was to fill in each period with the secondary facts in their chronological order, accompanied by an adequate narration.[13] Thus, Abreu e Lima arrived at a classification first and at the facts second, when the proper thing would be to do the opposite.

Abreu e Lima's *Compêndio da História do Brasil* in one way was the initial attempt to gather the facts into periods. But the Instituto Histórico was so unfair in its criticism of Abreu e Lima that the Instituto considered Henrique Luís de Niemeyer Bellegarde's work, an elementary textbook then used in the schools, superior to the General's.[14]

Bellegarde adopted six superficially different periods in his *Resumo*.[15] Like the old chroniclers, he was more concerned with the distribution of materials in equal groups than with the limits of the periods. Unlike Abreu e Lima, the author had no interest in periodization. His work preceded the concern of the Instituto Histórico with the problem by four years. His six periods were: 1) Brazil before the conquest; 2) Brazil conquered by the Portuguese; 3) Brazil under Spanish rule; 4) Brazil free of the Spanish yoke; 5) Brazil as the seat of the Portuguese monarchy; and 6) the constitutional and independent Brazilian Empire. Although both men made compilations of facts—or, better stated, used and abused glue and scissors—and committed some of the same mistakes, Abreu e Lima's work is clearly superior, not only because he interpreted and tried to weave the facts together but because he wrote a better narrative.[16]

Therefore the Instituto Histórico, which had been concerned with the problem of periodization since its first session, was even more unfair when it decided a few years later to ignore Abreu e Lima's contribution to Brazilian periodization. It confined itself to a bare criticism of the factual materials included in each period, and for its model cited Bellegarde's work, which was merely an elementary textbook making no attempt at periodization, and which was very inferior to Abreu e Lima's work, especially in the part on the Kingdom of Brazil.

At that time, it was easy to confuse real periods with ephemeral intervals. Antônio Ladislau Monteiro Baena's work *Compêndio das Eras da Província do Pará*[17] and the anonymous "Compêndio das Épocas da Capitania de Minas Gerais desde o ano 1694 até 1780"[18] organized their material as a chronology in the first case and an almanac in the second.

Thus we have seen that Januário da Cunha Barbosa introduced the problem of periodization, Brigadier General Cunha Matos initiated theoretical discussion of it, and Abreu e Lima made the first real effort to implement periodization in the writing of history. Bellegarde's work was didactic, and Baena's book was a chronology. Finally, the Visconde de Cairu, José da Silva Lisboa, in his *História dos Principais Sucessos Políticos*,[19] restricted himself to a colorless organization of his collected material. He was commissioned by Pedro I "to perpetuate the memory of national events since the day of independence." He divided Brazilian history into ten periods: discovery, division, conquest, restoration, invasion, mining, viceroyalties, kingdom, states, and constitution of Brazil. This, then, obviously had an excessively politico-administrative character. Furthermore, the author was especially concerned that the heroic deeds be honorably transmitted by history to posterity.

The most important impetus and best contribution to the periodization of the history of Brazil to appear in this whole era was the work of the German naturalist Karl Friedrich

Philipp von Martius (1794–1868), "How the History of Brazil Should Be Written," dated January 10, 1843.[20] In the 51st session of the Instituto Histórico, on November 14, 1840, Januário da Cunha Barbosa, whose name is indissolubly linked to this subject because he participated in all the initiatives on periodization, offered a one-hundred milreis prize for a plan to write an ancient and modern history of Brazil, organized so as to include political, civil, ecclesiastical, and cultural material. The Instituto considered it an excellent idea and added one hundred milreis more to the prize when it was announced. There were two candidates, Martius and Wallenstein. Martius won the prize.

Martius's plan was not an attempt at or a guide to periodization. Rather, it contained many general ideas on the problems of Brazilian history; it was going to be the point of departure for various later works, which were inspired by Martius's method. The power of Martius's insight, as well as his acute observations on Brazilian history, were going to help those who were guided by his more precise delimitations of the types and divisions of our history.

Martius was the first to draw attention to the important contribution of the three races to Brazilian history. He was the first to say that it would be an error, in view of the principles of historiography, to neglect the influences of the Indians and the imported Negroes, who, along with the Europeans, contributed to the physical, moral, and civil development of the whole population. He suggested the necessity of studying the Indians, their customs, usages, and language. While studying the role of the Portuguese, he suggested that it be remembered that the period of the discovery and early colonization of Brazil can be understood only in relation to the Portuguese maritime, commercial, and military achievements and that this period can never be considered as an isolated fact in history. The Brazilian historian should never forget that in the history of the colonization and the civil and legislative development of the country the influences of world commerce were extensively incorporated into our history.

Martius indicated the necessity of studying the history of the legislation and the social conditions of the Portuguese nation in order to follow the gradual development of the very liberal municipal institutions that were transplanted to Brazil and of investigating the causes for their perfection in this country. He emphasized the role of the Jesuits and indicated the necessity of studying the development of ecclesiastical and monastic relations. He suggested that a very interesting task for the historian would be to study the reflection of European life in the development of Brazilian arts and science.

Not forgetting the smallest detail, Martius added that the historian should show how the colonists lived, bringing the reader into their homes, in the city as well as in the country, whether they be citizens or slaves. To avoid the duplication of special histories for each province, which was a popular idea of the age, he thought that it would be better to treat jointly those portions of the country that belonged together geographically. This could be done through histories of large regional groups. Thus he proposed, for example, the unity of the histories of São Paulo, Minas Gerais, Goiás, and Mato Grosso; of Maranhão and Pará; of Pernambuco, Ceará, Rio Grande do Norte, and Paraíba; and the writing of the history of Sergipe, Alagoas, and Espírito Santo together with that of Bahia. He made the first proposals for regional histories in our country.

It goes without saying that even if Martius did not propose any classification of periods, his ideas improved the critical criteria for relating facts, grouping them, and organizing them. The opinion of the Instituto, which was delivered on the two plans competing for the prize and of which Freire Alemão was the author, said that Martius's work was ably conceived. It also said that his plan was too good and could not be put into practice at that moment but would serve as a model for the future. It added that the plan's utility at once indicated the direction that historical investigation in Brazil ought to take.[21]

Wallenstein presented the other proposal to the Instituto Histórico.[22] His was much longer than Martius's work. He considered it most prudent to follow Livy, João de Barros, and

Diogo de Couto, to explore history by dividing it into decades, and to narrate the events within certain periods. He maintained that this was the only way to connect all the events together. The text ought to emphasize political history, which he considered the most important. Civil, ecclesiastical, and literary history ought to be treated separately, at the end of each decade, as an observation on the text.

In 1854–1857, Francisco Adolfo de Varnhagen, Visconde de Pôrto Seguro, published his *História Geral do Brasil*, which, even today, undeniably contains the greatest number of facts. Although the author considered himself powerfully inspired by Martius's proposals, the plan of his work did not produce any new material on periodization. The main lines of his classification are almost the same as in Southey, or even in the older historians, who confined themselves to following the classics, dividing history in decades. If it is true that he did not limit himself to a pure recital of the political facts or a biographical history of the dominant figures and that he tried to concern himself principally with the facts more in relation to the real development of Brazilian civilization—as he wrote in his prologue —it is also true that he was incapable of understanding the facts or of connecting, grouping, and relating them in characteristic periods.

Varnhagen's method of work was almost exclusively to carry out the investigation of the facts that Martius had indicated were important and significant, but he had no capacity to generalize, a capacity which would have allowed him to create an original scheme of classification of these facts. Martius stated the necessity of studying the Brazilian Indians, their language, usages, customs, and social organization. Varnhagen investigated the facts related to these topics, but he did not have enough imagination to realize that he was dealing with a coherent body of facts and to put them into a single chapter that would deepen our understanding of the indigenous people of Brazil. Martius indicated the necessity of studying the colonial laws and social legislation, and Varnhagen put the colonial laws in the same chapter with the laws of the donees. However, the laws established in the first *Regimentos,* in the *Códigos Manuelinos,* and especially in the *Códigos Filipinos* were not laws characteristic of any one period. They lasted beyond the colonial period. Only the laws of the donees gradually disappeared as their captaincies were absorbed by the crown.[23]

Varnhagen really was not the least concerned with periodization. This is exactly what he said in his prologue:

We could well gather these topics into definite periods, taking great care to make smooth transitions. We suppose that we can dispense with adopting these pedantic and academic divisions into large periods, and be content with a simple division into sections as in the previous edition.[24]

As Capistrano de Abreu said, Varnhagen knew how to excavate documents, demonstrate their authenticity, solve enigmas, unravel mysteries, and reveal a multitude of facts. However, he never succeeded in understanding the origins of these facts and their connection with the deeper roots from which they came, nor did he succeed in generalizing and organizing them into a theory.[25] Varnhagen's incapacity to theorize made it impossible for him to make a well-planned division of periods for the most complete history contributed to Brazilian historiography. Varnhagen employed the generally accepted chronological approach in his compilations, but he disregarded periodization.

Justiniano José da Rocha proposed a purely chronological division, based on political actions and reactions:

From 1822 to 1831, period of inexperience, and struggle between the monarchist and democratic elements; 1831–1836, undisputed democratic triumph; 1836–1840, reaction of the monarchist party, and the campaign to declare the majority of Pedro II; 1840–1852, domination of the monarchical principle, a reaction against the social achievements of the democratic element, which did not know how to defend itself except by violence, and so was smashed; 1852 to present [1855], cooling off of passions, the present quietness, the anxiety for the future, and a period of transition.[26]

This was a very contemporary view of political life, but also a very valuable suggestion for the study of our history.

When the exposition of Brazilian history was held in 1881 at the Biblioteca Nacional, Ramiz Galvão made a purely chronological classification based on bibliographical material. He adopted eight periods: 1500–1548; 1549–1639; 1640–1762; 1763–1807; 1808–1821; 1822–1831; 1831–1840; and 1841–1881.[27]

It is not by chance that the best Brazilian historian, not because of his material contribution but because of his acute critical capacity, made the best periodization of our history. Capistrano de Abreu felt the spiritual necessity to seek, with critical research methods, the roots of our true, distinct, unique, and singular periods. His periodization was not only objective, based empirically on source materials and facts, but sociological as well. It was free of any scheme or arbitrary distribution of material. He was the first to emphasize the basic socio-economic patterns and motives of each period, and he left open the relations between these fundamental patterns and the ideal superstructure. Capistrano de Abreu was the first to analyze political and socio-economic components in order to study the various cultural relationships. His periodization grew out of his understanding of the economic motivations—influenced by natural geographic circumstances—and their transformations and continuity in each period.

Like the other historians of his period, Capistrano was quite influenced by geographic determinism, the theory of evolution, and Comtian Positivism. This explains why his work appears to be based more on geographic characteristics than on socio-economic factors. It would be a mistake, however, to let this label obscure the essential elements of his periodization. Furthermore, the geographic, natural, and anthropological characteristics, which appear to be his main preoccupation, also are the foundation for the socio-economic factors. He forgot neither to analyze the complicated socio-economic factors nor to relate them to the different elements of the spiritual and psychological superstructure.[28]

The first conscientious probing of the problem of periodization appeared in the article that Capistrano de Abreu wrote

about the Visconde de Pôrto Seguro, Francisco Adolfo de Varnhagen.[29] This was the most profound page ever written on the
periodization of Brazilian history.

The history of Brazil from 1500 to 1614 has its own character. The period
deals mainly with the occupation of the coast, the colonists being forced
to face the sea, not only because the Indians prohibited their movement
into the interior but because they had to ward off continual French attacks. During the period from 1614 to 1700, the coast was completely populated, with the exception of a portion of the south and the lands north
of the Amazon. Then began the movement into the interior along the
rivers.

The phase of the conquest of the *sertão* was characterized by
the expeditions on the Amazon and its tributaries; Paulista
bandeiras followed the Tietê down to the Paraná and Uruguay
in order to expel the Jesuits, moved along the banks of the
Paraíba, climbed the Serra da Mantiqueira, explored Minas
Gerais, and, following the Mogi Guaçú, crossed over the Rio
Grande and reached Goiás. "On the San Francisco River, descending Paulistas met ascending *baianos* and *sergipanos*. Its
banks were rapidly populated and cattle herding assumed enormous proportions." A cattle herder discovered Piauí, and Gomes
Freire de Andrade ordered the opening of a road between
Maranhão and Bahia.

Mining dominated the half-century from 1700 to 1750. Minas
Gerais, Goiás, Cuiabá, and Mato Grosso were explored and
populated, and agriculture abandoned. Rivalries broke out, and
anarchy assumed fearful proportions. The process of expansion
into the interior continued with the populating of Santa Catarina and Rio Grande do Sul and the discovery of the route to
Mato Grosso via the Madeira River, descending the Tocantins
and Parnaíba and ascending the Itapicurú.

"During the period from 1750 to 1808, the colonial system
was consolidated." The local governments were abolished; industry, prohibited; the captaincies, taken back from the donees;
the mines declined; the Jesuits were expelled; and the capital
was transferred to Rio de Janeiro. "The Brazilian-born colo-

nists and the Portuguese-born rulers experienced jealousies and rivalries that resulted in the idea of independence. The following period, which began in 1808, saw the decomposition of the colonial system." Dom João VI initiated it and Dom Pedro continued it. The Regency concluded with its legal codes, and Dom Pedro II subdued the separatist attempts. "Since 1850 a new period has begun which will be called either 'centralist,' 'imperialist,' or 'industrial'." The steamboat put Brazil in rapid communication with Europe and the provinces; the slave trade ended, and slavery declined, while industry was established. "These six periods exhibit sharply separate characteristics, as well as similar aspects." Capistrano de Abreu added that the basic defect of Varnhagen's *História Geral do Brasil* was the author's inability to distinguish these characteristics and others perhaps more important, although less known.

A new examination of periodization appeared later in his introduction to *Informações e Fragmentos Históricos de Padre José de Anchieta*.[30] He wrote that the most important characteristic for the definition of the first period was scorn for the land and scorn for the natives. Beginning with Cabral's discovery of Brazil and ending with the conquest of Maranhão, this period can be called the "transoceanic" period. The primitive colonists found the land to be sad, and they were in constant dread because of their privations, the internal risks in the form of wild animals and Indians, and the external dangers from foreign interlopers. The Portuguese settlers' sons born in Brazil were treated with scorn because of their "lack of ability" and fondness for Indian customs.

The transoceanic period was followed, in 1614, by the period of the exploration of the interior—with the exception of São Paulo, whose inhabitants had begun to explore much earlier because the narrow coast that separates the ocean from the Cordilheira Oriental forced them immediately to climb that range. The *bandeiras* spread out, and the conquistadors extended the limits of civilization. Cattle herding was extended, and in 1697 a land route was discovered between Bahia and

Maranhão, via Piauí. This land connection encouraged unity
and helped to diminish the disdain held for the territory and
people.

The third period began in the first years of the seventeenth
century with the discovery of the mines, and the consequent
psychological revolution. The differences that separate this
period from the transoceanic period were shown by the disputes, the war against the *emboabas* in Minas Gerais, and the
war of the *mascates* in Pernambuco. Now those disdained were
no longer the *mazombos* and the *caboclos*.

It would not be an exaggeration to say that Capistrano de
Abreu, with these few pages, rose to a height still not attained
by any other Brazilian historian. In these pages, he commented
on Varnhagen's fundamental shortcoming—his lack of philosophic perception—and then went on to show incisively the
particular philosophic element of the history of Brazil. He
demonstrated his penetrating ability to theorize, an ability that
separates him from the pedants and bookworms of history and
raises him to the level of a true historian. Large, well-defined
periods clearly reveal themselves. He not only sought the historical category of a period in the socio-economic structures
and the natural and anthropological foundations, he also sought
the boundaries of his periods in the goals, way of life, sentiments, and ideas of the inhabitants. Therein lies all the grandeur of his periodization. The profoundness of Capistrano de
Abreu's revelations are shown in the close relationship he attributed to economic and psychological motivations. The essential trait of a period is at times defined, not by subordination
and hierarchy, but by the psychological fact of *scorn* that characterizes the period or by the substitution of a feeling of superiority for a feeling of inferiority.

Capistrano de Abreu published his *Capítulos de História
Colonial* a few years later.[31] Although it covers only the colonial phase, as the title indicates, it deals more with the distribution of historical material than with periodization. Nevertheless
the division of the book into eleven chapters very well characterizes the periods, each of which constitutes a well-delimited

and outlined unit clearly separated from that which precedes or follows it. The titles are "Indian Antecedents"; "Exotic Factors"; "First Discoveries"; "First Conflicts"; "Hereditary Captaincies"; "Crown Captaincies"; "The French and the English"; "The Dutch War"; *"Sertão";* "The Development of Boundaries"; and "Three Centuries Later."

This division of chapters certainly did not follow any periodic design, but it would not have been difficult for Capistrano de Abreu to follow in this book his previous divisions into six perfectly delineated periods. Capistrano noticed the vagueness of the second and the last chapter titles, as well as the lack of uniformity of the basic dividing lines. In characterizing his six periods, he always linked the economic bases with the superstructural elements; he knew that the fifth and sixth chapters followed almost completely politico-administrative criteria; the first chapter, a more geographic judgment; and the others, historic ones, except the last chapter, which was held together only by the title. But Bauer observed that all classification of periods ought to be based on the same criteria, either closely following historical transformations or based on facts of politics, administration, etc.[32]

Contrary to Bauer's opinion, it is almost impossible for Brazilian history to follow always uniform criteria for its periodization. There are large gaps in our knowledge of the historical development of Brazil. This is clearly demonstrated in our colonial history, where our contemporary historians with an understanding of the facts—periodization ought to be based always on facts, from which theory develops, and not the reverse as in Abreu e Lima—have been able to use social and economic criteria of classification, which have not been used for the history of the empire or of a half-century of the republic.

Finally, two observations should be made about Capistrano's division in this work. The first refers to the criticism d'Avezac made of Varnhagen's periodization, censuring him for having begun with Europe and not with Brazil. He should have begun with a description of the country and its indigenous inhabitants and only then gone to the era of the Europeans' arrival.[33] Varnhagen replied that his work began with the arrival of Cabral to Pôrto Seguro, the first chapter being merely an introduction which he intended to link with the history of humanity.[34] It appears that Capistrano considered d'Avezac's observation just, and thus began his narrative with the Indian antecedents. Furthermore, Capistrano purposely overlooked certain formative intellectual movements of the national conscience, such as the eighteenth-century revolutionary movements—the Inconfidência Mineira, for example. This particular movement could be overlooked, but not the national intellectual environment, which he so well pointed out as one of the fundamental characteristics of the fourth period.

A very important stage in the development of Brazilian historical periodization is represented by Joaquim Nabuco's *Um Estadista do Império*. Some of his proposals for the political divisions of Brazilian history expand Capistrano's contribution. At first he adopted Justiniano José da Rocha's classification,[35] and considered the Paraguayan War as "the divisor of contemporary history," [36] for although it marked the apogee of the empire, the principal causes of the decadence and fall of the dynasty arose from this war. When he tried to divide the history of the empire, he perceived, with all the lucidity of his historical vision, certain decisive moments of complete reversal.

The reign of Dom Pedro II (1840–1889) can be divided into six distinct periods: 1840–1850, consolidation of internal order, end of the revolutions, perfecting of parliamentary government, fight against the slave trade; 1850–1863, foreign policy, Platine equilibrium, political conciliation, industrial undertakings, bank issues, opening of the country by railroads, growing centralization; 1864–1870, Paraguayan War; 1871–1878, gradual emancipation, diplomatic liquidation of the Triple Alliance, beginning of the democratization of the system (cheap printing and transportation— the street cars, which began in 1867, revolutionized the old habits of the population—republican ideas, and the emperor's democratic character, displayed in his imperial voyages and assumed thereafter); 1879–1887, direct election, abolitionist agitation, the major importance of the South because of São Paulo's rapid progress, disappearance of the old statesmen, appearance of new patterns, processes, and ambitions; 1887–1889, the illness of the emperor, his gradual withdrawal from public affairs, discontent of the army, sudden abolition, prevention of the Third Empire (by the large landowners, against Princess Isabel, and by the army, against the Conde d'Eu, the future emperor), abundant gold, stock-market fever, the final surprise of November 15, 1889.[37]

A better general picture could not be given; the periods and the transitions between them are intimately related. Nabuco saw the evolution of historical continuity and had a feeling for the appearance of new periods, which subsequent changes characterized as singular unities because of their individuality and peculiarity. In spite of being a mainly political periodization, Nabuco saw the unity of historical life with the same historical objectivity and philosophic conception as Capistrano de Abreu. He presented a guide for understanding the historical process, and this insight revealed the great distance separating him and his book from his contemporaries. Capistrano and Nabuco were the two major figures of our historiography at the end of the century.

The lessons of Capistrano de Abreu and Joaquim Nabuco were too recent to be used by João Ribeiro, Oliveira Lima, and Pandiá Calógeras. João Ribeiro's contribution was limited to a didactic *História do Brasil*. In spite of the considerable didactic influence that this book had—it would be better studied in a chapter specifically dedicated to didactic historiography[38]—he did not do any decisive research. There were a few outstanding, original interpretations in his superior compendium of the history of Brazil. The contemporary vogue for geographic determinism did not interfere with skillful periodization, which contributed to the better delimitation of the different historical periods of our evolution. There was a relation of the structure and the superstructure, of the natural bases and the political elements in his work. The chapter titles were mainly political, and a few were juridical. For example, from the early editions, there are Chapter IV, "Spanish Rule"; Chapter X, "Absolutism and Revolution"; Chapter XI, "The Empire, Progress of Democracy"; and Chapter XII, "The Republic." [39] His reliance on political-juridical periodization was proved conclusively in the title of "Absolutism and Revolution," for the designation "period of absolutism" comes from constitutional law, as Bauer indicates.[40]

João Ribeiro, influenced by Martius, observed a characteristic spirit in each of the country's regions: In Bahia it was religion and tradition; in Pernambuco, republican radicalism and extreme revolutions; in São Paulo (including Minas and Rio), moderate liberalism; in the Amazon, Indianism and perhaps separatism; in Rio Grande do Sul, overinvolvement in the Prata. Excluding the feelings of the last two regions—the first of which resented its abandonment and the second of which was extravagant—there were certain characteristic traits visible that can help clarify in the future the complicated research on the relations between structure and superstructure, an indispensable task for a more accurate periodization.

Oliveira Lima's work was one of the most profound collections of interpretations of Brazilian life, especially of the pre-independence and independence periods. Like João Ribeiro, he was not concerned with objective periodization in his more general works, such as *Formação Histórica da Nacionalidade Brasileira*[41] or *Aspectos da História e da Cultura do Brasil*.[42] There was in these works an excellent arrangement of the material, which was not confined only to political aspects, but included sociological, economic, and anthropological considerations. There were some helpful original ideas indicating profound relations between the intellectual and economic bases. Avoiding the gross error of dealing with literature as an appendix to each chapter, as secondary texts do, Oliveira Lima always interrelated economics and literature in an integrated expression of ideas. He tried to make an internally consistent link between these two elements in his *Formação da Nacionalidade,* which was a new and serious attempt to solve this problem and was a measure of the essential difference that separated him from João Ribeiro. *Dom João VI no Brasil,*[43] one of the best and most accurate Brazilian historical studies, interpreted the period's well-defined intellectual characteristics and decisively advanced the best periodization of the Brazilian kingdom. We have already noted that the research and knowledge of the colonial period is sufficiently advanced to allow us to make an objective periodization, which cannot be done so clearly for the period after the colonial system began to disintegrate. From *Dom João VI, O Reconhecimento do Império*,[44] and *Império do Brasil*,[45] an admirable work of synthesis, we begin to get a better understanding of the whole period of history that began to take form in 1808 and ended in 1889.

Pandiá Calógeras's position in Brazilian periodization was similar to that of Oliveira Lima. His contribution does not come from his major work, *Formação Histórica do Brasil*,[46] which had no design for periodization, but from his presentation of his profound understanding of selected aspects of our life. According to the author, the *Formação Histórica do Brasil* was inspired for the nineteenth and twentieth centuries by the example of Capistrano's unsurpassable *Capítulos de História Colonial*. Since Calógeras habitually separated social and economic aspects from the political and administrative, the book is not very helpful for periodization. For example, the chapter on "Discovery and Colonization" precedes one on economic organization and mineral wealth; the two together form the colonial part of the book. In the space concerning independence, he devoted three chapters to the politico-administrative and military facts and again had a separate chapter for the problems of economics, labor, and the slave trade. Consequently he not only disassociated the period's inseparable facts, but almost completely ignored the cultural aspects in order to devote excessive space to politics. Although this was a magnificent work of synthesis, perhaps superior in this respect to Oliveira Lima's *Formação Histórica da Nacionalidade Brasileira*, Calógeras made no valuable contribution to the periodization of Brazilian history in it.

Calógeras's important contributions came from his analytic works, such as *As Minas do Brasil e Sua Legislação, La politique monétaire du Brésil*, and *A Política Exterior do Império*.[47] The first work is a minute examination of the structural bases for certain definite periods of our history. Nobody has made a better detailed analysis and logical characterization of our history's third period, according to Capistrano's classification. Wilhelm

Dilthey has observed that the energy which determines the fundamental direction of an age can be found in its legislation. While studying the legislation and the economic bases of the period, Calógeras revealed the period's spiritual elements embodied in them. Thus he objectively analyzed the amalgamation of the whole culture of a period. In this book as in the one of Oliveira Lima, the regency of Dom João VI began a new period when "a series of provisions, some technical and others administrative, were made for the purpose of encouraging the revival of the mines." [48] According to Calógeras, the year 1819 was a characteristic one for Brazilian mining.[49] Extending the work to bring it up to the present day would help to clarify one or another point which, according to Capistrano de Abreu, might otherwise be more apparent than real.[50]

In his *Politique monétaire,* Pandiá Calógeras outlined a new study of the economic basis of our life, thus preparing for a logical characterization of periods. The great contributions of this historian and public figure, one of the best prepared we have had for public and academic service, were not made in his *Formação Histórica do Brasil,* but in his various detailed economic analyses, a task which demanded, as Capistrano de Abreu stressed, broad shoulders and a deep breath.

Finally we come to the contributions of Oliveira Viana, Gilberto Freyre, and Sérgio Buarque de Holanda. They brought new criteria for the research and interpretation of Brazilian history. As with Martius, they achieved a new acuteness in and arrangement of our historical facts.

The works of Oliveira Viana were more concerned with anthropology and sociology than with politics. They characterized the rural aristocracy as the most important human factor in the evolution of Brazilian society and indicated that it had the role of developing political institutions, not only in the colonial period but also during the empire. Perhaps his chapters on racial evolution are completely superseded today because of his racist views. However, his *A Evolução do Povo Brasileiro*[51] was a landmark for Brazilian historiography and represented a very important contribution to the periodization of our history.

Casa Grande e Senzala[52] deserves the happy honor of having begun a period of discovery that brought us to areas never previously explored. It is the most exhaustive study that we possess today of the formation of the Brazilian family under the system of the patriarchal economy. As Gilberto Freyre said, the *casa grande* complemented by the *senzala* represents a whole economic, social, and political system: production—monoculture latifundia; labor—slavery; transportation—the oxcart, the carried hammock, the buggy, and the horse; religion—Catholicism; the extended family—the chaplain subordinated to the paterfamilias and the cult of death, etc.; sex life and the family—patriarchal polygamy; hygiene of the body and the home—the river bath, the sitz bath, and foot washing; and politics—favoritism and patronage.

For the first time, the formation of an agrarian, slavocrat, and hybrid society was perfectly studied, with a broad base, and following the general characteristics of the Portuguese colonization of Brazil. It was the first realization of Martius's old plan to study the Indian, the Portuguese colonist, and the Negro slave in the development of the Brazilian family and society. If Varnhagen followed Martius's plan, it was only to collect the material. It was Gilberto Freyre, demonstrating his enormous interpretive ability, who gathered and related the facts into a general characterization of the Brazilian society and family.

The plan of *Casa Grande e Senzala* was developed for the next period in *Sobrados e Mucambos*,[53] which Gilberto Freyre completed with *Ordem e Progresso*.[54] Thus the old periodic trilogy according to Cunha Matos's plan, which was discussed and approved by the Instituto Histórico, again returns to dominate Brazilian periodization. The first period of the development of the Brazilian family within the patriarchal economy is followed by the transitional period, covering the decadence of the rural patriarchy in Brazil and the modification of Brazilian society during the eighteenth century and the first half of the nineteenth, and is concluded with the period of the substitution of free labor for slave labor with *Ordem e Progresso*. Thus the triangular study of Abreu e Lima is realized with very well-defined social and anthropological aspects in the complete works of Gilberto Freyre.

The titles are very suggestive for the characterization of the periods of Brazilian history: *Casa Grande e Senzala* (1934), *Sobrados e Mucambos* (1936), and *Ordem e Progresso* (1959). Naturally, not everybody accepts the periods as definitive. But in any form, the truth is that Gilberto Freyre's works made it possible for us to have a better understanding, a better orientation with respect to the tremendous number of causal connections, and a better division of the Brazilian historical events.

In *Raízes do Brasil*,[55] Sérgio Buarque de Holanda outlined a truly valuable suggestion for the periodization of Brazilian history. He pointed out that the most important moment in the evolution of Brazil was 1888, the date of the abolition of slavery, the dividing line between two epochs. Beginning with that moment, national life clearly shifted from one pole to the other, from a rural to an urban civilization. According to Sérgio Buarque de Holanda, there are two periods: one period of agrarian rule until the eve of the republic; and the other period beginning with abolition and the influence of the young university graduates, the cities, Romanticism, Positivism, and the transition from slave labor to free labor. The author himself recognized that he had slightly exaggerated the boundaries of the second period.

It seems that the truth is more with Gilberto Freyre. According to him, agrarianism waned and the social scene altered gradually during the second half of the nineteenth century. Oliveira Viana also put the limit of the "rural aristocracy" (or the "rural patriarchy," to use Freyre's expression) at the last decade of the nineteenth century. According to Freyre, the rural nobility kept some of their privileges, principally their decorative splendor, almost intact until the end of the nineteenth century. As with all ritual and liturgy, this decorative element had an extraordinary ability to prolong the grandeur, or at least the appearance of grandeur, of institutions already dead at their roots. The decadence of the rural patriarchy, which began with the arrival of the Prince Regent, the foundation of the cities and the first beginnings of an urban bourgeoisie, and the foundation in 1827 of the faculties of law and the consequent prestige of the urban, academic, university degree, had its final important phase between 1850 and 1875. An industrial era then began, with the enormous development of material civilization in Brazil.

Thus, between 1850 and 1888 there was only apparent rural control; or better yet, it was a period of transition from rural patriarchy to urban bourgeoisie. The year 1888 marked the end of that period because from then on neither the ritual nor the liturgy gave any brilliance to the grandeur of those rural institutions which still existed as slavery began to be replaced by free labor.

Another important theoretical contribution of Freyre was the concept that the transition from one period to another does not always happen the same way throughout the national territory. Taking from anthropology the concept of a cultural area and applying it to the particular case of periodization, Gilberto Freyre showed that the changes in one cultural area did not coincide with the changes in the others. In one cultural area the transition might be very rapid from the first to the second period; and in another cultural area the transition might be slower. Thus, the purely historical criterion of *time* is closely related to the criterion of *space,* which is not only physical but cultural. Freyre's boundaries for his periodization are based on his knowledge of anthropology and are not bound to the ideas of the old authors. The possibility of variations in the periods is much closer to the reality of historical events.

According to Troeltsch, the most outstanding historian is the one who periodizes best. In Brazil, Capistrano de Abreu and Joaquim Nabuco knew how to develop the most empirically exact classification by deducing from detail and fact the spirit of a period. Both made profound studies of the causal relationships between the structure—the specific period under consideration—and the superstructure—the broader sweep of history. This enabled us to gain a better understanding of the tremendous number of causal connections, and a better orientation for a periodization of the historical events of Brazil. The still continuing contributions of Gilberto Freyre and Sérgio Buarque de Holanda represent an interpretive advance toward the determination of periods. As the initiator, pioneer, master, and guide, Capistrano de Abreu has been the most effective contributor, both empirically and philosophically, to Brazilian historiography.

OILIAM JOSÉ

The Periodization of the History of Minas Gerais

THOSE undertaking to write regional or local histories
likewise face the problem of periodization, but their perspectives, of course, will be different. The periods for
local history need not, and often do not, coincide with
those for national history although they will certainly
be influenced by them. Oiliam José is one historian who
has sought to periodize state history. In his study of the
historiography of the state of Minas Gerais, he devoted a
short chapter to periodization. It is translated and included in this collection to show the solution he arrived
at as well as to serve for contrast and comparison with
the suggestions for national periodization discussed in
the previous essay.

Historical periods do not suddenly come to an end because
the events that produced them end. The period's temporal and
spatial influences endure, either actively or latently, sometimes
for decades, and subsequently create new events. Historical
periods change, but historical continuity assimilates all changes.

Paraphrasing Leibnitz's well-known aphorism *"natura non
facit saltum,"* it can be said that *historia non facit saltum.* This
same phenomenon is found in the vast field of literature. The
period of influence of a literary school or doctrine or a group
of poets or writers extends beyond the conventional limits of

This essay is translated from the chapter entitled "Períodos da História Mineira"
in Oiliam José's *Historiografia Mineira* (Belo Horizonte: Itatiaía, 1959), pp. 21–
24.

the period. Thus it is hard to defend the contention that Parnassianism or *modernismo* emerges in a definite period and disappears in another period. There are always Parnassian poets, and everybody is modern in his own time!

It is easy to see that what is true in the field of literature is also true in the field of historiography. There can be no really rigorous division of the periods of development of historical studies in any Brazilian region. As this is completely true in Minas Gerais, the historical researcher is obliged to speak in relative terms about the periods of the historiography of that state.

Only with these rigorous limitations for didactic purposes do we agree to the following periods for historical research, synthesis, and bibliography in our state of Minas Gerais: 1) the period of the first historians, from the sixteenth century to 1808; 2) the period of the traveler-historian, 1808 to 1870; 3) the period of the classical historians, 1870 to 1910; 4) the period of the contemporary historians, 1910 to the present.

We are aware that other periodizations could be made and perhaps adopted. Other divisions deserve similar consideration and possible utilization. Some prefer to analyze the history of Minas Gerais in terms of its economic cycles. Others would base their approach on such themes as administrative, political, religious, economic, military, educational, literary, artistic, racial, and municipal history, or the history of folklore, journalism, genealogy, and biography.

There are important reasons which lead me to prefer the proposed periodization. It is less complex, and closer to the actual status of our historical studies. If we still do not have a definitive history of Minas Gerais for the past four centuries, what can be assumed about the maturity of the scientific spirit of study and the quantity of information and critical material?

The first period fits within a well-defined political era, the colonial. (Some authors contend that nothing that happened in Brazil can be considered "colonial," but that whatever occurred must be thought of as an event in an "overseas state" of Portugal.) During the colonial period, the Portuguese predominance bestowed a characteristic tone on all that was planned and done in Minas Gerais, the field of history included. With the arrival of the royal family in Brazil in 1808, the situation was altered by the new circumstances, which began to shape events in Minas Gerais. Thanks to these [circumstances], cultural conditions developed which justify the existence of a new period in the intellectual development of Minas Gerais.

Beginning in 1808, a powerful eruption of culture occurred in this country as a result of the presence of scientific and artistic missions brought into Brazil by the Portuguese royal family. Foreign painters, sculptors, urban planners, geologists, botanists, zoologists, anthropologists, and geographers began to work here and to penetrate our mysterious interior. The result was the appearance of numerous studies and projects—mainly the formation of rich botanical, zoological, and mineral collections, which were soon sent to Europe—and the publication of works about Brazil and its inhabitants. This was a period of intensive studies, thanks to the travels of foreign scholars as well as to other notable contributors. They bequeathed to us precious material for our history.

Because the works considered fundamental to our historical studies were published by Diogo de Vasconcellos, Xavier da Veiga, and Don Silvério Gomes Pimenta, during the period between 1870 and 1910, we have designated it as the period of the classical historians.

The contemporary period began in 1910, when there was an unusual increase in the research and publication of studies about *mineiro* history. This was due especially to the then recently created Instituto Histórico e Geográfico de Minas Gerais and the interest shown by the *mineiro* government in publishing historical works. It was a definite beginning which reflected the humanistic culture imbibed by the majority of our public figures in the Seminário de Mariana and in the Colégio de Caraça, our two leading institutions of higher learning several generations ago.

JOÃO CAPISTRANO DE ABREU

A Critique of
Francisco Adolfo de Varnhagen

FRANCISCO ADOLFO DE VARNHAGEN (1816–1878) was the first outstanding historian in the national period, and one of the foremost Brazilian historians of all times. His early inclinations toward historical studies were encouraged by an appointment in the diplomatic service which permitted him to travel through Europe and South America. He took advantage of those travels by spending most of his time in foreign libraries and archives. The rewards were many. He uncovered manuscripts which shed new light on the colonial past. An indication of his production and contributions will be found in the *Bibliografia de Varnhagen* by Armando Ortega Fontes (Rio de Janeiro, 1945), which lists his writings in twenty-nine pages. Without doubt his greatest work was the *História Geral do Brasil*, in two volumes, the first published in 1854 and the second in 1857. The *História Geral* treats events from the discovery to the declaration of independence.

The essay which follows is a general critique of the *História Geral* and its author by Brazil's ablest historian. Trimming away the usual bombastic rhetoric and blind praise, Capistrano de Abreu gave a refreshingly impartial analysis. He saw both the accomplishments and the failures of Varnhagen. His purpose was not to belittle but to strike a balance. This essay and a companion piece,

This essay is translated from the Portuguese "Appenso sôbre o Visconde de Pôrto Seguro," in the third volume of the third edition of *História Geral do Brasil* by Francisco Adolfo de Varnhagen (São Paulo: Melhoramentos, n.d.), pp. 435–44.

also by Capistrano de Abreu, entitled "Necrológio de Francisco Adolfo de Varnhagen, Visconde de Pôrto Seguro" (*História Geral do Brasil,* 3d ed., I, 502–8) are the solidest historical criticisms that have been written of Varnhagen. Capistrano de Abreu assigns Varnhagen to his true place in Brazilian historiography, and an important place it is.

Francisco Adolfo de Varnhagen [the Visconde de Pôrto Seguro] once complained that we did not know enough about a certain governor of Brazil. After praising the governor, Varnhagen reproached him for not having made a will. Ever since, we have kept a sharp lookout for the will that our historian would make. We were right, too, for his will was a curious document. Varnhagen ordered his wife never to consider re- marriage and requested the erection of a monument to his memory.

The monument has been erected. The eminent historian can now rest satisfied in the tomb, with his last wish fulfilled. He can justly be satisfied, for he earned it honorably. In his child- hood he aspired to write a history of his homeland, and he ac- complished that. There is no greater happiness than that, as the poet of *Eloa* so well expressed: "What great achievement for a man to see realized the ideas of his youth." Now that the monument at São João do Ipanema is stirring up a little news about the Visconde de Pôrto Seguro, let me take this oppor- tunity to write a few lines about his *História Geral do Brasil.*

As d'Avezac has already observed, the Visconde de Pôrto Seguro adhered in writing the history of Brazil to the program masterfully outlined by the great naturalist Martius. That is a very accurate observation, which is obvious to anybody who knows the work of Varnhagen and Martius. What has not been noted is that in the second edition of the *História Geral* the author grafts onto the ideas of Martius the brilliant views of d'Avezac, whose principles he had at first protested against.

Varnhagen ventured boldly into his study with Martius's

plan. He was one of those men who are not deterred by difficulties. Any problem was a question of sheer endurance. Each manuscript had to be read. Every letter of every word was an enigma to be deciphered. He concentrated on them, and finally the mystery was unraveled.

He explored the hitherto uninvestigated Portuguese archives. Each day new documents appeared, and the discoveries multiplied. This series of fortunate discoveries was such that it would have been enough to animate even a person with little penchant for historical research. The discoveries of Varnhagen were considerable, especially for the first century of our history. He did not renovate the basic concepts about the period, but he discovered enough material for the person who can and wants to, to make a definitive study.

The discovery of Pero Lopes de Sousa's *Diário da Navegação*[1] and the *Livro da Não Bretôa*[2] clarified many obscure points. Another important task was to edit the account of Gabriel Soares de Sousa,[3] the geographer, historian, ethnologist, and living encyclopedia of our sixteenth century. The publication of Fernão Cardim's *Narrativa Epistolar*[4] made known information and clues which gave us a more adequate conception of contemporary society, as well as an engaging picture of the period that was so delicately depicted by José de Alencar in *Minas de Prata*. One of the best contemporary chronicles was *A Informação do Brasil em 1584*,[5] an anonymous work that Cândido Mendes [de Almeida] has demonstrated to belong to Padre José de Anchieta. The various letters of Duarte Coelho, Duarte de Lemos, Guillem Jeronymo de Albuquerque, and others have enlightened us and expanded the scope of our knowledge.

In short, it would be unjust to deny that Varnhagen did more to make the sixteenth century understood than anybody else who has written about the history of Brazil. The only Brazilian who can be remotely compared with him is the late Cândido Mendes. He also studied the sixteenth century, but only disjointedly. He took some obscure points and dug into them until he discovered a treasure. These researches illuminated their surroundings, but such limited monographs can be compared only remotely with a complete and continuous history.

Varnhagen also made some discoveries about the seventeenth century. As they were not overly important, the history of that century is not very indebted to him. His most complete work is the history of the Dutch War. Up to the time of Accioli and Fernandes Gama, everybody who dealt with these great events relied only on the Portuguese sources. [Robert] Southey was the first to consult the Dutch sources. [Priter Marinus] Netscher continued on the same path, or rather opened it again, for Southey had hardly begun. At the same time, a rich harvest was made in the Dutch archives by a Brazilian, Joaquim Caetano da Silva, who should always be respectfully remembered as Brazil's most erudite scholar. Afterward Varnhagen utilized the materials impartially gathered by Dr. Silva, Netscher's book, and both published and unpublished Portuguese documents, to give us the most complete history of these events. Another part of the seventeenth century that Varnhagen studied carefully was the history of the State of Maranhão.[6] There he made some important discoveries, such as Maurício de Heriarte's *A Descripção*.[7] Furthermore, he never let the great historian of the North, João Francisco Lisboa, distress or influence him as a result of their disagreements.

Varnhagen worked a great deal on the eighteenth century, but the task was much harder. In the sixteenth century settlement existed along the coast and extended into the interior for only ten leagues, according to the author of the *Diálogos das Grandezas*.[8] In the seventeenth century it began to move inward, but only at a few points along the banks of the Amazon, São Francisco, Paraíba, and Tietê rivers. In the eighteenth century, however, Brazil suddenly came alive and in a single move peopled Rio Grande do Sul, Santa Catarina, Minas Gerais, Goiás, Cuiabá, Mato Grosso, and Piauí.

This dispersion is not the only difficulty. It was the century of mining, the Spanish wars, boundary demarcations, the expulsion of the Jesuits, the attempts at independence, and so many other important events which are almost all scantily studied. The historical terrain is only partially explored. We are totally ignorant of the history of Sergipe, Pôrto Seguro, and Ilhéus. The history of the Jesuits in Maranhão is hardly known. The War of the Mascates[9] overshadows any other study of Pernambuco. The history of the mines lies in obscurity. How can this remaining work be done at one time?

Southey has already written a part of this history, but only a part. The most difficult and important work is untouched. Varnhagen was the first person to write a history of the eighteenth century, and his work leaves much to be desired. However, it is only fair to say that we do not have anything to compare with it.

The history of the nineteenth century owes not a little to Varnhagen, and it would have been very indebted to him if he had published the *História da Independência,* which he had finished on his last trip to Brazil. Where is this book? Will it come to light someday? According to him, it was a book full of revelations.[10] In Vienna he found the diplomatic correspondence between Metternich and the Baron de Mareschal.[11] It related Mareschal's private conversations with Pedro I, and many other things. Varnhagen gathered his information from this correspondence and from the contemporaries of the Seventh of September.[12]

Some years ago, after the publication of Varnhagen's *História Geral* and before their feud, João Francisco Lisboa wrote that the history of Brazil would not be written again soon. His words are being verified. The job is very large, and the facilities are small. Besides this, the men that can undertake it are disappearing. We look to our Instituto Histórico as the organization which is the focal point of our historical studies. There we find distinguished men who have added to our understanding of different questions; however, none of them would be able to write a history of Brazil. The reason is that certain special qualities are required for the study of each century. The sixteenth century requires aptitudes that are unnecessary for the seventeenth. The eighteenth century requires other skills.

In the Instituto Histórico all the researchers are principally interested in the study of contemporary history and are insensitive to our early history. Up till now, Cândido Mendes is the only exception. Varnhagen did not have all the necessary qualities to study the three centuries, but he possessed them in part.

Only two Brazilians could have written the history of our country better than he did. They were Joaquim Caetano da Silva, with his marvelous perspicacity, lucid spirit, relish of minutiae, algebraic style, and incredible knowledge; and João Francisco Lisboa with his opulent manner, acid irony, morbid poignancy, provident pessimism, and an intuition that seethed from his pages. They would have produced two beautiful books if they had written. They did not. We return to the Visconde de Pôrto Seguro.

One day an intelligent man said that history was not a chronicle. Canon Felipe approved of the idea, divided our history up into pieces, and distributed it to twenty-four of his colleagues.[13] Since that time, from each new historical work one hears, in a semibanal, semimalicious tone, these words: History is not a chronicle. It is easy to say, but harder to determine precisely where history begins and chronicle ends, or to point out a book which possesses one of these characteristics exclusively. For example, Varnhagen's work has many characteristics of a chronicle, but it is full of pages that reveal a great deal of perspicacity. It contains observations that would slip by an ordinary mind. Without doubt, it also has the character of a history.

Varnhagen's work has many ideas and thoughts that clarify facts that were previously poorly understood. After the facts pass through his hands, they are made to reveal new facets such as the first relations between the colonists and the Brazilian natives; an appreciation of the effects of the Dutch War; the causes that led people to explore the *sertão;* the influence of the contiguity of the Tocantins, Paraíba, and São Francisco river basins; and many other ideas which would take too long to enumerate. If this is not generally understood, it can be partly attributed to the fact that the *História Geral* has not been studied with the attention it deserves, and partly also to our historian's lack of artistic ability.

The *História Geral* is a difficult book to know. One can read it as many times as he wants, confront it, and meditate about it, but there is something that escapes, that resists, that cannot be found when one searches for it, yet which must be sought, in order to be found. There are details that are simultaneously excessive and deficient because they lack the accompanying facts necessary to show them in their true light.

The fault is not exclusively Varnhagen's. It rests partly in our contempt for patriotism, the general devastation of the archives, and the hastily prepared monographs. His was the tread of the *sertanista* on the barren land. Varnhagen found himself exactly in the position described by Alexandre Herculano: He had to do almost everything, alone. That was too much for one person to do.

Thus we agree with Lisboa, the history of Brazil will not be written again very soon. It ought not be written for some time. For the present there is a need for conscientious monographs. Among the youth who are studying today is there nobody who wants to know about some obscure point of the past? There are many such unknown aspects of the past, and each is very important. Nobody has yet written a history of the *sesmarias*. There is no history of the municipalities that were first discussed by Lisboa. The history of the *bandeirantes* is scattered in books and archives. Hardly anything is known about the history of the Jesuits, other than the period narrated by Simão de Vasconcelos, and that is almost nothing. Finally we need a history of the mining region.[14] If these monographs seem too complex, there are others that are equally important, but easier. Why has there not been a history written about the Casa da Torre, which began with Thomé de Sousa and continued through the colonial period? Why has no one written the history of roads yet? Why . . . ?

Even without these monographs, Varnhagen could have presented a better work if he had had some artistic skill, that is, if he had been able to synthesize, to give some design to his work, and to show the interrelation of the various elements of Brazilian history. He never emphasized the important events, but rather dwelt on lesser facts such as the dismissal of governors, treaties made in Europe, the death of kings, etc. Occasionally he was right, for Portugal's relations with her more powerful European neighbors had important consequences in Brazil during the eighteenth century. But this was not true for the whole country, since Rio Grande do Sul and Colônia do Sacramento did not constitute all of Brazil.

In Varnhagen's hands, the history of Brazil was standardized, its distinct features demolished, its characteristics mixed together, and its colors faded. It appeared to be a flat and level surface, which reminded one of the pages of a book that a heedless bookbinder had carelessly repeated. Even people who know infinitely less about Brazilian history than Varnhagen could see that his periods followed each other without reference to what preceded them and often without continuity. This monotony need not exist. I suggest the following periodization.

Brazilian history from 1500 to 1614 offers its own unique features. The settlement of the coast was the principal concern, not only because the Indians prevented internal movement, but also because the continuous French attacks required the colonists' presence near the ocean.

In the period from 1614 to 1700, the coast was settled, except for a portion of the south, and the lands north of the Amazon still disputed by the French.[15] The internal expansion began by using the rivers. The location of the city of Belém made it a natural center of this movement.[16] These little-studied explorations started from there and culminated in the marvelous expedition of Pedro Teixeira.[17] These expeditions were made principally on the Amazon, but its tributaries which were unobstructed by waterfalls were also used. São Paulo was at the headwaters of the Tietê, on the banks of the Paraíba, and at the side of the Mogi Guaçú. The Paulistas plunged down the cataracts of the Tietê and went along the Paraná and Uruguay rivers to expel the Jesuits. The Paulistas expanded along the banks of the Paraíba, climbed the Serra de Mantiqueira, explored Minas Gerais, followed the Mogi Guaçú, crossed the Rio Grande, and entered into Goiás. On the São Francisco River, the Paulistas descended and the *baianos* and *sergipanos* ascended. Its banks were rapidly populated, and cattle raising assumed enormous proportions. One of the cattlemen, following the Indians that devastated his property, casually discovered Piauí. Almost at the same time, Gomes Freire de Andrada ordered the exploration of a route between Maranhão and Bahia.

The mines dominated the period from 1700 to 1750. Minas Gerais, Goiás, Cuiabá, and Mato Grosso had already been traversed by slave hunters and then were invaded by gold hunters. All the interior was explored and populated. Agriculture was abandoned. Slaves were imported in great quantities. Anarchy assumed unprecedented proportions. Racial rivalries erupted and were never extinguished. Santa Catarina and Rio Grande do Sul were settled in this period. A route to Mato Grosso via the Madeira [River] was discovered. The Tocantins and Paraíba [rivers] were descended and the Itapicurú, ascended.

The period of consolidation of the colonial system was between 1750 and 1808. The municipalities had their powers reduced. Developing industry was violently uprooted. All the captaincies were redeemed from the donees. The mines declined. The Jesuits were dramatically expelled. The capital was transferred to Rio de Janeiro, and battles with the Spanish were endemic. Rio Negro was raised to a captaincy, as an advance guard. The Madeira [River] became preferred over the Rio da Prata as the means of communication with Mato Grosso. The rivalry between the *mazombos* and the *reinóis* was revealed, and resulted in the idea of independence.

Beginning in 1808, the next period marked the decomposition of the colonial system. The first blow was made by Dom João VI when he declared the Brazilian ports open to all nations of the world. Dom Pedro I continued the task by proclaiming independence. The period concluded during the regency, with its legal codes and other radical measures, the elevation of

Emperor Pedro II to the throne, and the final defeat of the separatist movements.

After 1850 a new period began; it can be described as centralizing, imperial, and industrial. It is the period which we are still passing through. The steamboat has put us in prompt communication with Europe and the provinces. Slave traffic has ended, and slavery is declining. Printing, represented by the newspaper, vainly tries to introduce books. Journalism and parliamentarianism have as their results more carefully conceived plans and virile resolutions. Next to institutions that do nothing, individuals work. Complementary to the supply of primary material, attempts are made to develop industry. There are many movements underway which will last a long time, but which only future historians can reveal.

These six periods present, besides similarities, characteristics that distinctly separate them. Varnhagen did not know how to distinguish these characteristics and other perhaps more important ones which are still unknown. This is the basic defect of his book. Now we will see others.

[Émile] Zola said that art is a corner of nature seen through a temperament. "Through an *artistic* temperament" ought to be added, because Varnhagen saw everything through a brash temperament and therefore left us nothing that even suggests art. It is necessary to define Varnhagen's temperament to understand his *História Geral* well. In one of the comedies of our dramatist [Martins] Penna, an authority who is tired of the observations made about him by others declares the constitution abolished. More than once Varnhagen also abolished history. Let me give some examples.

The question of Amerigo Vespucci had resisted the research of the most competent historians until Humboldt studied it and arrived at a generally satisfactory conclusion about him. When Varnhagen analyzed this conclusion, he committed what d'Avezac called a "historical solecism." One would suppose that Varnhagen would have recognized his error when he was admonished by the eminent French geographer. Far from this, he persisted, added new arguments, and so jumbled and complicated the question that it will take a great geographer to clarify it again. Varnhagen had a spirit that admitted contradiction with difficulty. Lisboa, in a note that I consider to be one of his best pages, made some just and severe observations about the way Varnhagen examined certain problems and evaluated certain individuals. This was putting fat in the fire, for Varnhagen strengthened the notes in his second edition and almost deleted Lisboa's name from his *História Geral*. He reached the point of not even mentioning the ludicrous expedition of Achuí only because the illustrious Lisboa brought it to his attention.

Varnhagen was frequently neither benevolent nor just with his fellow historians who had acquired some fame. There are certain things in his book that were personal affronts. He employs the mysterious abbreviation of *Br. H.* to cite Melo Moraes's *Brasil Histórico;* another time the citation "P. da S." deciphers to "Pereira da Silva"; he did still worse with Joaquim Norberto.

There was a book about the diamond district that combined the rigor of history and the appeal of a romance.[18] It would have had many editions among any other people. This book claimed that the first large iron foundry was established by Ferreira da Câmara, and with documents denied this to Federico de Varnhagen, the historian's father. Varnhagen pretended not to know the book, and he used the argument that the historical theme of diamond prospecting was trifling. This is one of the most curious arguments in our history, and worse than any freshman would try. Of course, it is possible that he did not know about this book, but that is very difficult to believe.

When some recent historian had dealt with a subject, Varnhagen sometimes omitted it and sometimes only touched on it, without even citing the author who had made the more extensive study. Thus Varnhagen did not even mention the name of the courageous explorer, Manuel Félix de Lima, whose journey from Mato Grosso to Pará was studied in detail by Robert Southey in his usual superior manner. With his predecessors

Varnhagen is rarely just. He considered Monsignor Pizarro's *Memórias do Rio de Janeiro*[19] "a confused, diffuse, and at times obtuse, work," while not remembering that he used many of Pizarro's facts himself.

He found Southey's book to "lack any focus and to be a tiresome repetition of boring descriptions, more a collection of various manuscripts and chronicles by many authors than a competent and unified history." These evaluations of Southey are flagrantly unjust. Doubtless Varnhagen had many more facts than Southey, who wrote before Baena, Accioli, Pizarro, Lisboa, São Leopoldo, Fernandes Gama, and other analysts who clarified and expanded previous concepts. Besides, Southey wrote his book in England, where he could not find the numerous materials that Varnhagen found in the Torre do Tombo,[20] the Évora Library, and other places. To compare the two books is impossible.

Southey wrote to his friend Townshend in an outburst of just pride that his book would be one of those which was destined not to die for centuries, and would be for the Brazilians what Herodotus' work was for Europe. Varnhagen's work will also be read for centuries, but only by professional historians, who will consult it as an archaic dictionary such as Santa Rosa de Viterbo's *Glossário*. People will know about it only by tradition. Forgive me for adding that he did not think so. For that reason, he constantly adopted certain attitudes with a view to posterity. At one point he reminds one of a statue; at another of a small chapel which ought to be Gothic, and later on of other things, as the reader will easily discover.

These aspects of his temperament as well as many others made him generally uncongenial. One must read him not once, but many times, for to read him only once is the same as never reading him. It is necessary to discover his qualities under his defects, to become familiar with his ideas, for to grasp them is to understand him. He must be read completely, not partially. One must compare him with his predecessors and successors in order to evaluate his contribution to our history. If we are to consider him fairly, we must stifle momentary displeasure and not be shocked with his rude manner, and we must recognize the great body of facts he added to our knowledge of history. Such recognition should give rise to a frank, dispassionate admiration of his deep roots.

To summarize, Varnhagen's *História Geral* is inferior to Southey's *History of Brazil* in form, conception, and intuition, but it is inferior only to that work. No Brazilian can actually be compared to Varnhagen. Pereira da Silva wrote only about one period;[21] besides, what good there was in his work was owed to João Francisco Lisboa. Moreover his work was a cicerone so careless and unreliable that it does not deserve much credence. Silva Paranhos,[22] who knows the Southern question like nobody else, accused him of having invented a battle that never took place, of even giving the number of wounded and dead. Abreu e Lima was an intelligent, honest compiler, but his work was outdated when it appeared, and even more so now after forty years of historical research.[23] [Alexandre José de] Melo Moraes is a collector. He has published many important things, however extraneous, in his five volumes of *Corografia,* four volumes of *Brasil Histórico, História do Brasil Reino e Império,* and *História da Independência.* What is actually his is so little that it is hard to find. Perhaps he has changed his system for his proposed *Crónica;* yet even if he radically changes it, he will be a very, very great distance from Varnhagen.

Varnhagen stands out from the midst of his contemporaries —with his statue erected, with his expression hardened, with his eyes reflecting his feeling of superiority—holding the ferule of the tutor. "Clap your hands! Clap your hands!" We must recognize the master.

Brazilian historical studies are progressing. The *Catálogo da Exposição de História* is an enormous contribution. Batista Caetano's work places linguistic studies in the field of science. Barbosa Rodrigues, José Veríssimo, and [Joaquim] Serra have tried to penetrate the native's soul and extract the secret of his organization. Before his death, [Charles F.] Hartt laid the foundation for Brazilian archaeology. Rodrigues Peixoto, aided by Lacerda, initiated the study of anthropology. [Antônio Joaquim de] Macedo Soares and Sílvio Romero extract from contemporary society the unknown origin of many traits. [Alencar] Araripe, Jr., is investigating the origins of our literature. Silva Paranhos tries to clarify the intricate labyrinth of the Rio da Prata. Augusto da Costa and Pereira da Costa are delving deeply into the history of Pernambuco. Franklin Távora tries to re-create the history of the Revolution of 1817. Assis Brasil and Ramiro Barcelos discuss the *rio-grandense* revolution. Alcides Lima reveals the history of Rio Grande do Sul. Henrique Leal jealously digs into the glories of Maranhão. Teixeira de Melo attempts to answer the international questions. Vale Cabral is establishing Brazilian bibliography and uncovering unpublished annals. Alencar Araripe is preparing the history of Ceará and the revolutions of the regency. Severiano da Fonseca studies Mato Grosso. Moreira de Azevedo fences with the Sabinada. Paulino Fonseca is investigating the *Chrónica das Alogoas*. Ladislau Neto is preparing the catalogue of the anthropological exposition. Félix Ferreira, João Brigido, Pôrto Alegre and many others bring their stones to the monument. When all these works are finished, when many others are collected, when a superior spirit breathes life into this mass of information, Varnhagen will descend from his pedestal. Until then he will remain the teacher and the guide.

JOSÉ HONÓRIO RODRIGUES

Capistrano de Abreu
and Brazilian Historiography

"CAPISTRANO DE ABREU became a legend in the field of historiography, where everybody pays homage to the master," asserts the author of this essay. It is a judgment with which few historians would quibble. His interpretive studies are far superior to the usual expository histories written by his compatriots. Capistrano de Abreu looked beyond the facts to find their meaning and significance. He was not a prolific historian but nearly everything he wrote was important. His complete works are listed by J. A. Pinto do Carmo in *Bibliografia de Capistrano de Abreu* (Rio de Janeiro, 1943). However, José Honório Rodrigues points out that his principal works number four: *Os Capítulos de História Colonial* (Rio de Janeiro, 1928), *Os Caminhos Antigos e o Povoamento do Brasil* (Rio de Janeiro, 1930), a critical edition of the *História do Brasil* by Frei Vicente do Salvador (Rio de Janeiro, 1889), and a critical edition of the *História Geral do Brasil* by Francisco Adolfo de Varnhagen (Rio de Janeiro, 1907).

Professor Rodrigues suggests in this essay many of the original ideas and innovations contributed to Brazilian historiography by this one scholar. For example, he initi-

This essay is translated from the Portuguese "Capistrano de Abreu e a historiografia brasileira," which has been widely reprinted. It first appeared in Portuguese in the *Revista do Instituto Histórico e Geográfico Brasileiro,* CCXXI (Oct.–Dec., 1953), 120–38; then it appeared as part of the introduction to *Correspondência de Capistrano de Abreu* (Rio de Janeiro, 1954), I, xxxvii–lvi; and most recently it forms a chapter in *História e Historiadores do Brasil* (São Paulo, 1965), pp. 34–53.

ated an important movement of historical revision by
calling attention to the importance of the Brazilian interior and its contributions to national formation. It is
curious to note that in 1889, four years before Frederick
Jackson Turner read his address on the American frontier, Capistrano de Abreu in his *Os Caminhos Antigos*
set forth the theory of the importance of the frontier in
the shaping of national character. A self-taught scholar
from the provinces, João Capistrano de Abreu continues
to be the most perceptive historian who has written about
Brazil's past.

On February 7, 1876, Counselor Tristão de Alencar Araripe,
a historian and member of the Instituto Histórico, gave a lecture
on how to write a history of the nation. This title is a good indication of the position of Brazilian historiography nearly a
year after the arrival of the young historian João Capistrano de
Abreu in Rio de Janeiro. Alencar Araripe believed that only
two historians since Rocha Pita knew how to discharge their
mission skillfully: Robert Southey and Counselor [João Manuel]
Pereira da Silva. He expressed a typically severe opinion of
Varnhagen, who by then had renovated Brazilian historiography
with his immense work and was preparing the second edition
of his *História Geral do Brasil*. Alencar stated, "Francisco
Adolfo de Varnhagen wrote uncritically and unstimulatingly,
wasting many pages with insignificant facts while he left events
worthy of more attention only vaguely outlined. Varnhagen
has done a great service for national history by investigating
ancient documents. If he has merit as an investigator of historical sources, his works, *História Geral do Brasil* and *Holandêses
no Brasil,* do not distinguish him as a historian."

An about-face in historical thought took place two years later.
It was brought about by a young man of twenty-five, just out of
the provinces, who had an up-to-date theoretical education, an
unusual knowledge of facts, a new ideal for Brazilian history,
and an incurable craving for knowledge. In an obituary of Varn-

hagen published in the *Jornal do Comércio* (December 16 and 20, 1878), João Capistrano de Abreu analyzed the work of the father of Brazilian historiography in this manner:

It is difficult to exaggerate the Visconde de Pôrto Seguro's service to our national history, or his efforts to improve its quality. He did not restrict himself to listing the kings, governors, captains general, generals, or battles, nor to making a chronicle of the minor issues and intrigues which beset the colonial period. Without doubt he considered these aspects because they were a useful means of relating events to each other, because they recalled dates that are flattering to national pride, or because they better clarified the motives that influenced different actions. However, he did more. In his work, an important place was given to the explorations into the interior, the bloody crusade against the Tupi, the population growth, the beginnings of industry, the discovery of the mines, literary works and associations, and relations with other nations.

This was the beginning of the rehabilitation of Varnhagen, now reputed one of the greatest Brazilian historians. It was strange that this quick and encompassing vision was that of a young man, who did not have the authority with which [Joaquim] Nabuco—addressing the Instituto Histórico in 1898, when he was forty-nine—assigned a provisional place in Brazilian historiography to Pereira da Silva because his work was uncritical and lacked definite standards. Indeed, it was Capistrano who began to question Pereira da Silva's reputation in an article on the *História da Fundação do Império Brasileiro* in 1877 (published in *O Globo* on March 10). He said that it was not unusual to find the author contradicting himself several times on just one page.

As of then no one had discussed with such clear, logical, and exact perception the real accomplishments and the future tasks of Brazilian historiography—its discoveries and its present state of development—as this young man did in his essays from 1878 to 1882. They are still the best ever written. In one of these essays Capistrano defined Varnhagen's contributions, pointed out his accomplishments, compared him with his predecessors and contemporaries, and concluded that no other

Brazilian equaled him in that period. He did not limit himself to indicating what the master, the guide and leader of his generation of the nineteenth century, had done. He examined the deficiencies, pointed out lacunae, reviewed the condition of Brazilian historiography, named its scholars, and enumerated the works that they were contributing to historical studies in Brazil since the passing of Varnhagen.

Whoever begins in that way, begins well; he knows what he is doing, what must be done, where the road ends, and where he should go from there. Capistrano's articles about Rocha Pita (March 23, 1880), Melo Moraes (October 30, 1880), Oliveira Martins (October 19 and 22, 1880), and Teixeira Mendes's *Efemérides* (April 8, 1881) demonstrate his knowledge of past Brazilian historiography.

In "Uma Grande Idéia" (1880), he discussed how to accomplish the writing of Brazilian history according to the plan outlined by Beaurepaire Rohan in *Organização da História Física e Política do Brasil*, published in 1877. He lacked no knowledge of the facts, theoretical development, or method. In this article he is implacable with historians like Pereira da Silva, Joaquim Manuel de Macedo, Moreira de Azevedo, César Marques; indulgent with others; and admiring of scholars like Capanema, Beaurepaire Rohan, Ramíriz Galvão, Vale Cabral, and Sílvio Romero.

His idea of a history of Brazil varied with time, his studies, and his researches. At twenty-one, in 1874, after reading Taine, Buckle, and Agassiz, he was planning a history that would show the permanent influences of nature on civilization. In this period he read much John Stuart Mill, Spencer, Buckle, and Taine. He knew French, English, and Latin well. "When I came from Ceará," he recounts, "I wrote English well and regularly as a result of having been on intimate terms with Shakespeare and Dickens for a year." Up to the period of his articles in the *Gazeta de Notícias* and *O Globo*, the two most important influences on him were Taine and Buckle. Still in Ceará in 1874, he searched, in the manner of Taine, for the primordial origin of Casimiro de Abreu, and compared Abreu's beginnings with his later successes in the same way that Taine established parallels between virtue and vice, sweet and sour.

On April 25, 1875, he arrived in Rio de Janeiro motivated by the best aspirations, full of ideas, and convinced that it was possible to attain an outstanding social and intellectual position in court with his studies. He was not yet contaminated with the pessimism that would reduce his aspirations in his last years to leaving this world as he had entered it—without personal scandal—and that would bring him to sign his letters to his friends as "John Nobody." He taught at the Colégio Aquino between 1876 and 1879, and made his debut in *O Globo* in 1875, publishing the lectures he gave at the Escola Popular do Ceará. Soon after, in 1876, he wrote two articles on "O Caráter Nacional e as Origens do Povo Brasileiro," as a critique of Sílvio Romero. His private teaching and historical and literary criticism, based on the doctrines of Positivism and Darwinism, comprised his activities.

In 1879 he began to frequent the Biblioteca Nacional, where he had the chance to acquaint himself with all the scholarly disciplines and especially to acquire a firsthand knowledge of the sources of Brazilian historiography. The Biblioteca Nacional was his scientific laboratory. There he participated in the largest bibliographical undertaking ever accomplished in Brazil: the *Catálogo da Exposição de História do Brasil*. His work at the library and his journalism stimulated his intellectual ambitions. Thereafter, Capistrano began to set his heart on a professorial chair at the Colégio Pedro II and election to the Instituto Histórico.

He revealed his ideal for teaching in 1880 in a *Gazeta de Notícias* article in which he commented on and disapproved of the *História do Brasil* by his future examiner, Professor Matoso Maia of the Colégio Pedro II. After revealing the professor's various errors, he observed that Maia had said that he, Capistrano, disliked the Visconde de Pôrto Seguro. Capistrano retorted ironically, "This was so right, because when the Visconde died, my voice was the only one raised to remember his services and to recognize the debt that we owed him." And in conclusion, replying to the professor, who said he was willing to accept a correction, Capistrano stated, "That would not be satisfactory because, among other things, we have not met face to face and we must reserve for then the slightly malicious pleasure of making corrections."

Was writing Capistrano's only historical aspiration? In 1879, after relating that His Majesty once philosophized on Brazilian character by saying that we were limited to two aspirations, to be a senator or a professor at the Colégio Pedro II, he dryly affirmed that he did not aspire at all to the Senate. He wrote,

A professorial chair at the Colégio Pedro II could be what I aspire to, but various conditions are necessary first: the secularization of the Colégio, freedom of opinion, and the prohibition of repeating judgments similar to those given after the examination for the chair of philosophy. This is not to say that I am disinterested. I aspire to a higher position: that of a member of the Instituto Histórico.

His irony and scoffing tone do not succeed in hiding his desire to be admitted as a member of the Instituto Histórico, as he was in 1887, or to teach in the Colégio Pedro II, for which he was a professorial candidate in 1883. A teacher of children when, because of his preparation, he should have been directing seminars, Capistrano became disillusioned. Taken from the active list as a teacher in 1899, he remained, in his own words, "excused from ignorant and absent-minded students."

His articles of 1879, some of which are still not collected or published by the Capistrano de Abreu Society, reveal the decisive influence of the Positivist school on his research as well as on his interpretation of the facts of Brazilian history. In "O Brasil durante o Primeiro Século de Nossa História," he presented Brazil as an inferior type of organism. He stated, "It was small, structurally ill-defined, not functionally differentiated, and its organs were not distinguished." The Positivist lectures that he heard on Sundays at the Positivist Center beginning in 1881 and his friendship with Teixeira Mendes and Miguel Lemos strengthened his theoretical development, begun in Ceará.

His research and study in the Biblioteca Nacional, his constant reading of Varnhagen, and his continuous familiarization with the German authors, whom he could by then read easily, began to show their effect. In the *Gazeta de Notícias* of June 1880, he translated an article from the *Kölnischen Zeitung,* the newspaper which introduced the works of Friedrich Ratzel, the future head of the anthropogeographical school. Beginning in this period, Capistrano started to take a powerful hold on the reality of history, following German ideas rather than Positivist ones, or, as Senhor Barbosa Lima Sobrinho put it so well, he began the determined search for realities, the historian's most important mission.

Capistrano continued to express Positivist theories, but it is evident in his historical articles that he was no longer able to make deductions and generalizations with the same facility he had had before his investigations in the Biblioteca Nacional and his introduction to the German writers. Naturally it is difficult to determine precisely the moment when his thought changed. There was no sudden reversal. The seeds of his new position were present even when he was a militant Positivist in 1881–1882. There were articles in 1879, such as the study on "A Indústria Brasileira no Século XVI," in which reality is strictly represented, without the simple forms with which Positivism manipulates historical facts. In later articles the facts are simplified into natural laws, to which Positivism wanted to reduce historical understanding. The truth is that historical facts are not given to us but are discovered from the documents. He was reoriented by his research in the Biblioteca Nacional and by the influence of anthropogeography and of the methodology of critical historiography of the Germans, who were almost unaffected by Positivism. Various articles from this period already reveal a historical realism instead of historical Positivism. His articles were becoming more objective, stripped of the Positivist terminology and formulations.

Critical historiography, begun by Niebuhr, Ranke, and Humboldt, had created a new instrument of historical knowledge: research and editing of authentic documents. Only this art of interpretation and criticism could give good results in the handling of the old texts. Capistrano no longer sought for laws, or facts subject to laws, but rather an understanding based on reliable data. Proof of this was his publication between 1880 and 1886 of editions of Cardim's *Clima do Brasil,* texts by Anchieta and Nóbrega, Frei Vicente do Salvador's *História do Brasil,* and many more, dependable, trustworthy, authentic, and complete texts. This plan clearly shows the influence of German historical criticism on his collection of facts and his documentary research. One can still discern, however, the influence of Spencer, especially when he deals with the evolution of the family, religion, industry, and the professions, as he did in his thesis for the professorial competition in 1883.

The influence of German historical literature is even more evident around 1900. He sought a basis for investigation and for factual interpretation in Ranke's seminar methods and Ratzel's anthropogeographical doctrines. He wanted to pursue the methodology of critical philology, evaluate testimony, and investigate the authenticity and credibility of the sources. He began to abandon Positivism, which he would later call a "straitjacket." After various trips to São Paulo and Minas Gerais, where he saw man's control over nature, he exclaimed, "This picture hardly supports Buckle's assertions!"

His translations of Wappäus (1884), Sellin (1889), and Kirchhoff (1909), and his reading of Ratzel, Peschel, Ernst Friedrich, Wagner, Semple, and Maull demonstrate his decisive geographical orientation. They led him in a more concrete direction, which neither reduced historical knowledge to a precise knowledge of natural science, nor subjected it to an astonishing oversimplification, as Taine had done with his theory of race, environment, and present moment, or as Buckle, who himself was not a great historian, had done with his theory of man's entire subordination to nature, a tremendous influence on the new generations. Taine wanted to understand the soul and passions that animate humanity and its history in terms of psychological anatomy. He claimed to discover the *faculté maîtresse,* which would perhaps explain everything about a great man except his greatness, because the source of genius escaped all his oversimplifications.

Life's fullness and the mystery of personality sometimes require a more subtle and differentiated treatment. Capistrano de Abreu's studies of intimate history, festivities, and the family indicate a search for the individual traits of our history, an attempt to reduce these significant small facts into something that is typical, regular, and constant.

Did not the logical Positivism of the Vienna Circle, a spurious offspring of Comte, realize that the historian's scientific work consists of this reduction and of the conceptualization of the general judgments upon which it is based? The historian realizes that he cannot reduce human actions to natural laws, because we do not see real life, history's drama, like that. All who understand history realize that factual reconstructions cannot be squeezed into the general causal theory with which Positivism tries to explain humanity's direction.

If we compare the Positivist school, to which Capistrano was linked until he learned German, with the historical realists, which he later joined, we see at once that the results of the former school were notably simplistic and only touched the surface in the collecting of the facts. They do not distinguish between sources as to their credibility, authenticity, and integrity. It was only after the Germanization of his spirit, that Capistrano turned to the investigation of sources based on philological criticism, to the critical editions, to the examination of the faithfulness and interpretation of the sources. Only the text or testimony which has passed the rigorous examination of historical criticism should be used by the historian. In a letter written to the Barão de Studart in 1900, he supported one of the most important theories about critical editing: Interpretation is the basis of this type of editing. In another letter to the Barão de Studart in 1904, he emphatically mentioned Ranke. Speaking of the indispensable necessity to cite exactly what sources were utilized, Capistrano asks Studart,

Why don't you give the origin of the documents that you publish? Why do you rebel against an obligation to which all historians have subjected themselves, especially since the face of history has been altered by archival studies and the criticism of sources instituted by Leopold von Ranke in Germany?

Besides annotating Varnhagen's *História Geral,* Capistrano was preparing to write his excellent book, *Os Capítulos de História Colonial,* which brought factual and theoretical elements together. In 1901 we find him studying economics and psychology as well as history. He said in a letter, "I have been reading different things: two volumes by Wundt which expand his great work on the psychology of people; a book by Breysig about the history of the civilization of modern times from which I hope to learn something applicable to Brazilian history; and a world history by Helmott. . . . I also read Carlyle." In another letter he wrote, "I am reading Schmoller's political economy, which is a monumental work. I am sad when I remember that I have spent many years without acquainting myself with this luminous, superior mind, from whose inspiration I would have gained years." In 1903 he wrote to Studart: "I am up to my neck in political economy. I just discovered a book by a professor of the Polytechnical Institute of Zurich which together with Bücher has been a great help. I strongly recommend it."

Summarizing the stages of his theoretical development, it can be said that his apprenticeship in the Biblioteca Nacional taught him how to research sources and discover the facts; the German historical methodology guided him in the rigorous examination of documents; his understanding of economics and geography focused his vision on the real structure of historical events; the psychology of Wundt, the father of experimental psychology, made him abandon his vague anatomical psychology, and kept him from falling into factualism by giving him an understanding of man's life. These influences made his thinking more realistic. Thereafter his approach was similar to the historical realism of German theory, and his task was to narrate what actually occurred. He had only to overcome the remaining influence of Spencer—who had been so influential even on Schmoller—but without losing his mental organization and logical severity. The important thing was that reality should no longer be molded by preestablished theoretical formulas. Reality is investigated and revealed as it is, rather than being adjusted to preconceived attitudes. He sought a historical realism based on the observation of facts, which were derived from trustworthy sources. He sought the fundamental historical structure from the land and the economy, without comparing them with natural processes. And he tried to understand historical meaning without the hindrance of preconceived values.

Germany provided the intellectual food which nourished the strong spirit of Capistrano. In 1905 he placed his daughter Matilde in the recently established German School, an act which demonstrated his enthusiasm for German knowledge at that moment. A new book about Washington came out in the United States; it was based on historical criticism, with excellent results. Capistrano commented on it to João Lúcio de Azevedo: "It proves that the German methods that are introduced into seminars produce results."

Since learning German from Carlos Jansen in the same group with Ferreira de Araújo and Machado de Assis, Capistrano had translated everything: geography, medicine, natural history, travelogues, and law. According to the autobiography that he wrote for Studart, he translated Kohler's *Introdução à Ciência do Direito*, but the translation was never published. His library reveals the predominance of German influence on him. There were represented not only German historians and geographers, such as Ranke, Mommsen, Meyer, G. Friederici, the writers of the *Dictionary of the Social Sciences*, Sombart, and many others; but also theoreticians, such as Kemmerich and Riess; psychologists, philosophers, and anthropologists, such as Wundt; and jurists, such as Puchta, Litzt, and Kohler. He explained why he had studied German: "I did it because certain German books satisfied my intellectual curiosity, and to wait for their translation meant at best a delay of several years."

Capistrano was careful in selecting his reading. The authors that he studied are still read and have a good reputation. They helped him interpret, with new insight, the history of Brazil, to which he dedicated himself body and soul in 1901. Thus he could counsel Mário de Alencar,

It is possible to give life a new direction in our time, as a cat which, thrown into the air, lands on its feet. Goethe did it after his voyage to Italy. Comte did it after meeting Clotilde. Even earlier, Dante had the idea of a *vita nuova*. There is no lack of precedents. What is lacking is an individual who will be inspired by them and add to the number.

Although he would add that unfortunately he had not succeeded in this and that he had already forsaken such ambitions, it is certain that it also applied to him. His new reading showed that he had recovered from the painful loss of his wife in 1891. He was again moved to communicate to the present the record of the past. Now he began a new work, which was monumental and would give him an extraordinary reputation.

Capistrano had been editing a new edition of Varnhagen's *História Geral do Brasil* since 1900. When the first volume came out in 1907, José Carlos Rodrigues hailed it as an outstanding contribution to Brazilian historiography. "I believe I am not wrong in stating that the editor's work was as good as that of the author." And he correctly added that "Senhor Capistrano de Abreu preferred to give us this third edition of the master, faithfully reproducing his text and notes, rather than trying to write his own history based on new formulas, even though he would like to conquer his own reluctance to write."

This is not the place to acknowledge his special contributions to periodization, historical criticism, and research, which have already been discussed in other books. His role in Brazilian historiography, the significance of his work, and his new departures can be well evaluated by a thorough reading of *Capítulos de História Colonial,* by a study of his ideas and concepts, and by an examination of his contributions to colonial history.

This man, who never attested to anything unless it was rigorously proved by trustworthy documents, nor gave anything more importance than it deserved, since he put the simple truth ahead of elegant lies, had great doubts about republishing his

Capítulos de História Colonial. It was a unique work, a model of composition and synthesis, a book that answered uncertainties and overcame difficulties. He collected, synthesized, and analyzed all the best that he knew of our colonial history. It cannot be compared with any other book, for it is an outstanding work in Brazilian historiography. It is written in a dry, mild, simple language. It has a persuasive doctrine and an understanding that is immediately perceived. This was collected from his vast, endless research. He did not merely accumulate the facts, but with his intuition he understood the men, who came alive in his recounting of their activities.

History is not only fact; it is also the emotion, the sensitivity, and the thought of those who have lived—the most difficult part of human affairs to capture. Did not Capistrano see the disdain that characterized the transoceanic period, the disdain for the land and the disdain for natives? Did he not perceive the psychological revolution that occurred in the third period of our history, in the first years of the eighteenth century? Did he not want to capture the chronicler's personal feelings? Did he not consider our independence as a transference of the Portuguese superiority complex? The peoples' feelings, speculations, thoughts, and aspirations are things that will never repeat themselves. They are just as interesting to the historian as the factual material.

As we have seen in his correspondence, Capistrano appreciated Ranke's methodology. But he was unable to adopt that objective attitude and style which extinguished all mention of "I" in order to be able to see the events just as they happened. Unlike Ranke, Capistrano's critics were never able to compare him with the sphinxes in the second part of Faust:

> Seated in front of the pyramids
> Contemplating the life of the people,
> Floods, wars, and peace,
> Without blinking.

Nobody can read the *Capítulos* without immediately seeing that Capistrano was concerned about "the people castrated and bled, and bled and castrated for three centuries." The work is a well-executed social and economic synthesis, which does not become an erudite lecture, as so many other histories do. Capistrano was well acquainted with that type of history and he knew when and how to use it. But he did not intend his book only to teach the secret of Brazil to Brazilians in a period when, according to José Veríssimo, Brazilian history was so neglected that we had to go to foreigners to learn the history of our country, with the exception of Varnhagen's work, which is only for scholars.

This book was born out of the desire to publicize and modernize the understanding of our history in a simple, nonpedantic form. He wanted it to be more an economic and social history than a political history, as free as possible from the listing of names and dates and from the mere chronology of the viceroys and governors who suffocated or encouraged the aspirations of the Brazilian people in their three-century struggle for independence.

He was not as concerned with the unpublished documents as with the clear, verified truth, sought and collected in libraries and archives, condensed into a few lines and illuminated with his persuasive reasoning. Capistrano was always a man of synthesis, and it is enough to read his correspondence to understand at once that he thought poorly of voluminous studies. In order to compose this synthesis he had to dive into a vast amount of research, as a swimmer plunges into the unknown depths of the ocean. The *Capítulos* were a synthesis of the research that he did to annotate Varnhagen's *História Geral* and to prepare the basic historical texts for publication. The work was the legitimate offspring of a long, careful, and unlimited analysis. Throughout the book one immediately notes the depth of his understanding, which is not a sterile factual description.

Why did he not include in that book the Inconfidência Mineira, which recently has been considered as the most important precursory movement of Brazilian independence? Between 1878, when he criticized Varnhagen for considering the Inconfidência a blundering plot, and 1903, when he complained that the honors given to Tiradentes were detrimental to those who struggled against the Mascates and to the Republicans of 1817, he appears to have become convinced that the Inconfidência really was not as important as it was beginning to be considered. Much more important were the struggles against the *mascates* and the *emboabas,* the awareness of the riches of the country, the *bandeirantes'* deeds, the bloody armed conflicts, and the battles of the Republicans of 1817. In a letter to Mário de Alencar, Capistrano wrote,

Today in Switzerland the teaching of the story of William Tell is prohibited, since historical criticism has demonstrated its invalidity. After I have studied Tiradentes's testimony and the court's sentence, why should I repeat the popular version and place him in the Pantheon? I have never written about him. He was not in the *Capítulos* because he did not fit into its scale. I have given my opinion of him in private conversations.

Capistrano did not give the Inconfidência the same importance that it was beginning to receive in his time. It did not fit into the *Capítulos,* not only because of the proportions of the work, a synthesis, but more because he was not writing a history of ideas and ideological movements. The Inconfidência was not a factual event but rather a thought almost without action and as such belonged to the intellectual history of the Brazilian conscience. Capistrano was never so subjective as to consider history not as it really happened but as an intellectual minority thought or felt when its history was *in statu nascendi.* As a good historian, he wanted to put himself in sympathetic communion with the spirit of the actors of the drama, to reconstruct their thought processes, and to penetrate the conclusions and motives that inspired their actions and made the events occur. But that which was only in the minds of men and later came to influence them, as an example to inspire them, belonged to another history, or at least it did not fit into the history that he wrote for the colonial period.

Tiradentes's execution was a symbolic act. It was an expression of a great character, one of the first protests of the Brazilian republican mind against the outrages of the metropolis.

But in terms of historical realism, the uprising never really happened. Capistrano could never satisfy himself with ideas that never were implemented or were so tenuous that they did not affect the people. It was important to know and understand why the dramatis personae behaved as they did. But he was not concerned with factors that failed to produce results or reactions. What the intellectual minority thought, felt, and did in their small circle affected only intellectual history and not the social and economic history that Capistrano was writing. He was not concerned with ineffectual conspiracy, but with rebellion, revolution, action. In his synthesis there was room only for the influential factors: the *emboabas* and the *mascates,* the battles between the colonists and the Jesuits, the social and economic history of the people, their life and their food, their ethnic types, the geographical conditions, the economic structures of various groups, settlement, roads, fairs, psychological types, the behavior and role of slaves, education, entertainment, customs, religious beliefs, professions, ideologies that are reflected in practice, social differences, the woman's position, commerce and businessmen, conversations, and urban and rural life. The *Capítulos* are the most condensed and most lively colonial history of Brazil. There were no fictional people in his book, only real people who lived and worked. Thus he gave life and blood to his history; as a historian he found the truth more beautiful than fiction.

As ideas change so much from century to century, it was natural that the people were the principal characters in *Capítulos de História Colonial.* Thus we see the people "castrated and bled, and bled and castrated." But to write such an active history, one had to have the intellectual development that Capistrano gave himself, to read what he read—the classics, the liberals, the socialists, and the radicals—and to live free of self-interest and desire for personal profits.

His ideal for Brazilian history and his conception of Brazilian historiography had changed a great deal since his first outline in 1874. In 1890 he wrote his new plans to Rio-Branco: "I have resolved to write a history of Brazil, not the one that I dreamed about in Ceará many years ago, after I had read Buckle and was under the influence of the enthusiasm he imparted, but a modest history with broad outlines up to 1807." He hoped to unite much scattered knowledge, to make a better connection between certain facts, and to call attention to certain disregarded aspects of our national life. "It seems to me that I will be able to say a few new things and at least break Varnhagen's iron grip on our historical thought, which Macedo introduced into the Colégio Pedro II and which still is the basis of our teaching." He was the first to suggest new interpretations that so modified our historical understanding, such as studying the *bandeiras,* the mines, the explorations, and cattle raising, all of which were unrecognized until then.

In 1903 his project acquired a new form. "I intend to accompany each of Varnhagen's volumes (there will be three, the first of which ends in the conquest of Maranhão) with a hundred-page introduction making a synthesis of the corresponding period. If I finish this, it will reduce my ambitions to write a history of Brazil to a volume the size of a French novel." The result was the *Capítulos de História Colonial.*

Like a real historian, Capistrano was sensitive to the spirit of the facts. History is not only facts. It requires a historical imagination that penetrates the motive of the fact, that feels the emotion that has already been felt, that relives the pride or humiliation that has already been experienced. To be detached is to lose some of the vital truth of the fact and prevents the reliving of the emotion and thought of those who have fought, worked, and planned. The historian is interested not only in the conquest of Colônia de Sacramento, not only in the action, but also in the spirit of the action. Therefore, he wrote that "Manuel Lôbo's *Regimento* is one of the documents that gave me the most pleasure in studying our history because it showed me that the regent was in good faith, something that I had doubted."

Capistrano de Abreu achieved an incomparable eminence in his generation because of his theoretical interpretation, tireless research, creative imagination, special qualities, new capabilities, and style. His role in Brazilian historiography between 1878 and 1927 is not limited to the *Capítulos*. Following the line of Varnhagen, Cândido Mendes de Almeida, João Francisco Lisboa, and Joaquim Caetano da Silva, Capistrano de Abreu was a tireless and erudite researcher for new facts and for clarification of old ideas. He published a critical edition of historical texts, conducted profound documentary research, and sought after new facts. Those were the logical first steps for anyone to take who wanted to make a new contribution. It is evident that in research as in interpretation, theoretical preparation plays the same important role. Whoever does not know what to ask and how to ask it will not find the answers in the texts. Did not Capistrano write to João Lúcio de Azevedo, "In your work, the document should confirm your intuition." Yes, it is necessary to bring well-formulated questions that come from a tireless reading and from an extraordinary intuition. The historian does not create, as in fiction, but he re-creates a world which has already lived, suffered, won, or lost. This re-creation is guided by theories, ideological conceptions of the world that vary according to the present interests, while the document is the only permanent thing in this continual change.

Research and the editing of texts are the most important ways to add more facts to the existing fund of facts. That was the way tenaciously followed by Ranke's school of historical criticism. Thereby the study of sixteenth- and seventeenth-century Brazil had been greatly improved by the identification of the "Nono" of the *Gazeta Alemã* as Dom Nuno Manuel, "Antonil" as Andreoni, "Brandônio" as Ambrósio Fernandes Brandão, "Padre de Ouro" as Padre Gouveia; the editions prepared of Anchieta, Frei Vicente do Salvador, Fernão Cardim, the *Diálogos das Grandezas do Brasil,* the *Materiais e Achêgas para a História e Geografia do Brasil;* the studies about the Jesuits, Pero de Magalhães Gândavo, the trials of the Inquisition; and the *Coleção para Melhor Conhecer o Brasil.*

Capistrano made up for many of the deficiencies in Brazilian historiography during Varnhagen's period, which he had pointed out in his article in 1882. In his annotations of Varnhagen and Frei Vicente, Capistrano clarified everything about the conquest of Maranhão and the obscure years between 1590 and 1607 and he explained the little-known period from 1600 to 1630, based on the research of Guilherme Studart. His small but very valuable contributions to the history of the mines and the *bandeiras* were very helpful in orienting the thought of his successors. In *Capítulos de História Colonial* he pointed out that there were not enough documents to write the history of the *bandeiras*. Afonso de Taunay's documentary research and publications are the results of Capistrano de Abreu's suggestions.

The edition of the Jesuit letters—those of Anchieta were edited by Capistrano and those of Nóbrega were edited with his aid—illuminated the history of the first years in Brazil. The edition of Frei Vicente clarified history up to 1627. His [Capistrano's] preface to the *Diálogos das Grandezas do Brasil,* as well as the text itself, brought attention to economic and social history and the customs of the period, which no book had given in such orderly detail as this. The publishing of the records of the trials of the Inquisition of 1591–1595 made a definite contribution to the knowledge of social history and the history of the Jews in the sixteenth century. His preface to *Denunciações da Bahia* relates, in the best synthesis I know, the social and familial life of sixteenth-century Brazil. It was in this synthesis that he defined Brazilian family life as "a taciturn father, a submissive wife, and terrified children." In his preface to *Confessões da Bahia,* he clarified the relations between Bahia and Pernambuco and the São Francisco River. Capistrano's factual and interpretative contribution to the knowledge of the sixteenth and seventeenth centuries is not as small as it seemed at first glance. As nobody before, he shed light on our social history, so ignored before his works.

There is still one more aspect of Capistrano that emphasizes his honored position in Brazilian historiography. In an earlier work I stressed that like all great historians Capistrano periodized but did not divide the historical material, which flowed smoothly. In his books and essays, he tried to unite the events and the spiritual motivations that defined a characteristic phase of Brazilian history. He did not deform the reality of events by emphasizing only economic, political, administrative, or biographical history. He used all types of history in order to learn about the whole of human life. He never mutilated the unity of history, the complex continuity of facts, even though he restricted himself to the colonial period. The historian of a period re-creates the whole of life, although he creates the finite within the infinite of history. The economic, administrative, political, religious, or biographical historian writes one aspect of history and is incapable of realizing the proper mission of the historian, which is to create a total understanding of the course of history. Capistrano was not guilty of this sin. He saw the whole of man.

He paid his debt to the soil with his translations of Wappäus and Sellin, to the Western element with his study of its history, and to the natives with his study of the Caxinauás and Bacaeris. In 1882, when he was only twenty-nine, he pointed out to the students of history a list of obscure problems that indicate his profound knowledge of the state of Brazilian historiography in the last century. It was one of the decisive factors in the radical transformation of our historical knowledge. The problems that he indicated needed greater study were the history of the *sesmarias,* municipalities, *bandeirantes,* Jesuits, and the mines. They all have since experienced a great expansion of perspective and understanding.

Thanks to his development of new concepts, the historiography of Brazil has been enriched. He substituted the concept of culture for that of race. His studies of the Brazilian natives renovated our ethnography. The importance of social history and the history of customs appeared for the first time in the *Capítulos.* In 1910 he understood the significance of the system of the *casa grande* and the *senzala* and its importance in the North. In a letter to Pandiá Calógeras on February 22, 1910, he wrote,

The situation in the North appears to be thus: a very sparse population; abundance in the *casa grande,* thanks to the domestic or natural economy, in which the production and consumption are together in the same limited area; little money. The object of commerce is livestock, either cattle or horses. When they are sold in Recife or in Bahia, they are paid for almost exclusively in provisions. Money is immobilized in jewels, trinkets, and purely ornamental slaves. By the mid-1700s, there was the sudden development of cotton culture which should have modified things; I do not know the particulars.

To summarize, in Capistrano de Abreu's work there are four outstanding studies: *Os Capítulos de História Colonial, Os Caminhos Antigos e o Povoamento do Brasil,* and his critical editions of Frei Vicente do Salvador's *História do Brasil* and Varnhagen's *História Geral do Brasil.*

Os Capítulos de História Colonial is the most perfect synthesis ever achieved in Brazilian historiography. It is a book for everyone, and all can and should read it more than once.

Os Caminhos Antigos e o Povoamento defined the major themes of the colonial period, explained the meaning of the various captaincies, and indicated a new direction for Brazilian historiography. Until the end of the century nobody, except Capistrano, attributed such importance to the conquest and settlement of the *sertão,* and nobody had studied this aspect of our history with such perseverance and thoroughness. *Os Caminhos* was not a jumble of historical, geographical, and anthropological data and contemporary facts as was Euclides da Cunha's *Os Sertões* (1902). It was a terse, readable development of a chapter of his 1883 thesis and of the *Caminhos* of 1889, with a historical, geographical, and anthropological basis that no one knew, either separately or together, as he did in that period. *Os Caminhos Antigos e o Povoamento* is for Brazilian historiography what Frederick Jackson Turner's *The Frontier in American History* is for American historiography.

When Capistrano de Abreu made his appearance in Brazilian historiography, its interest was focused on the coastal communities. He saw the *sertão* and the inland trails as the process of incorporation and expansion of the western frontier. It was a new approach and presented an original interpretation of the colonial development of Brazil. The *sertão* and the roads were

vital factors in the creation of Brazilian life. He was dissatisfied
with the mutilation of human unity by strictly political history,
and he did not divide the historical events with his knowledge
of economics and geography, which he learned from the Germans. In studying the Westernization of Brazil, he was particularly interested in discovering what distinguished Brazil
from the old European civilization. The *sertão* and the trails
into it contributed to the development of a distinctive Brazilian
history. A true understanding of Brazilian history cannot be
gained by a study of the civilization along the coast, but only
by a study of the *sertão* and the trails that led into it and connected it with the central government. In the transformaion
of the *sertão,* the colonists were at first barbarous, but they
changed as the *sertão* changed. This transformation created a
new, distinctly Brazilian personality. His [Capistrano's] pioneer
research in the role of the *sertão* and the roads profoundly
changed the writing and methodology of history in Brazil. The
history of colonial Brazil was not only the colonization of the
Atlantic coast but also the expansion into the interior, either
occupied by or free of barbarians.

Capistrano was never a regional historian. On the contrary,
he always knew how to evaluate the contributions of each region to the whole development of Brazil. He soon understood
that our history is an art of expansion and incorporation. In
his criticism (1894) of Oliveira Lima's *Pernambuco: Seu Desenvolvimento Histórico,* after some observations and judgments,
he agreed with the author that Pernambuco exercised hegemony
over Brazil in the sixteenth century, and continued, "If we want
to assign an epithet to each century of our history, it would be
'Pernambuco' in the sixteenth century, 'Bahia and São Paulo'
in the seventeenth, 'Minas Gerais' in the eighteenth, and 'Rio
de Janeiro' in the period that will soon end."

Os Caminhos Antigos e o Povoamento do Brasil dates from
1889, and *The Frontier in American History* from 1893. With
one essay, Capistrano, like Turner, completely changed the
method and spirit of Brazilian historiography. While the *Caminhos Antigos* was a book for scholars, his critical editions of

Varnhagen's *História Geral do Brasil* and Frei Vicente do Salvador's *História do Brasil* were conversations for erudite men. They were the most perfect examples of historical criticism, with all the rigor of German methodology. In 1907, when he had already published *Caminhos Antigos,* the *Capítulos de História Colonial,* and the first volume of the third edition of Varnhagen's *História Geral,* Capistrano de Abreu had a reputation as the greatest authority on Brazilian history.

Is his literary legacy really so modest, when he left so many definitive contributions, methodological and factual innovations, very original essays, and perspectives for Brazilian historiography? He could have done more, but I do not think that he has made such a small contribution. We are satisfied with what he left us, but he himself wrote, "I conceived many other things, but I could not do them. It was partly my fault and partly due to circumstances. I believed in longevity of life and brevity of art, and I was punished." This historian, who selected for his examination thesis the inscription from Goethe "Minutia obscures vision," clarified Brazilian historiography more than anybody else. He never lacked projects, ideas, and understanding. His correspondence, which will soon be published, reveals his many plans, the extent to which he guided and oriented his friends, and the solutions he sought for the problems of Brazilian historiography.

When the legacy of his correspondence and unpublished essays is studied, we will find the new problems and theses that he suggested to his friends. He said that it is necessary to write a history of Brazilian land tenure, the history of law and legislation, the history of the constitutional Côrtes, and the history of political parties. He suggested the compilation of a historical dictionary. He definitely recommended looking for documentation existing in Europe and the publication of more historical texts. He felt that a historical atlas was indispensible and he worked a great deal on this project from 1916 to 1920. Like Goethe, who expressed the idea in a verse in the prologue to *Faust,* Capistrano made the mistake of thinking that his books would not be read by those whom he most wanted to read them.

However, *Os Capítulos de História Colonial* has been read and reread for fifty years by those who study Brazil. They admire Capistrano de Abreu's devotion to discovering Brazil's secret for Brazilians.

Clarity and discretion, moderation and competence, and honesty and erudition were the qualities of his work and spirit. Thick volumes are not important. We should focus not only on what Capistrano accomplished as a historian, but on what he hoped to accomplish, what he wanted to do, and what he postulated. His essential and incomparable merit resides in his originality and his extraordinary powers of knowing how to sustain it.

In spite of all this, we are again impelled to ask, Where is the permanent value of Capistrano? It is in interpretation. He was a great interpreter because he was a great humanist. What does this mean? As a historian, he prepared himself to know everything that man and human destiny could accomplish in the world, in this world that is Brazil. He was interested in everything that was human, just because it was human: the good and the bad, the noble and the common, joy or disgust for life, the exhilaration of youth and the despair of maturity, life's beauties and the fear of death, God's nearness and estrangement—all this falls within human experience.

There is an obvious contrast between the esteem he is given and the lesson that he taught. Capistrano de Abreu became a legend in the field of historiography, where everybody pays homage to the master. It was fashionable to praise him but to disregard his advice. It is easy to find the reason for this contrast. He is disagreeable company for anybody who seeks immediate success, for he combined a kind of Socratic irony with a puritan intolerance of pride.

Edward Spangler recently noted, in an article published last year in the *Historische Zeitschrift* in the volume dedicated to the ninetieth anniversary of the best European historian, Friedrich Meinecke, that historical conscience belongs to the highest form of genius. History is the most valuable creation of the European spirit.

We would not recognize its power if we considered it only as imitative power. It is much more than this. A great historian constructs the spiritual world, which begins within him in an indissoluble way. His understanding of life rapidly becomes a present force and a future power. For only by understanding and explanation can man become free. Thus, the true historian liberates his contemporaries from the pressure of a past that simply weighs them down.

Thus history is a catharsis. It is also a remembrance of the eternal spiritual legacy, which is the only thing that cannot be stolen from us, for it belongs to everyone, each human being and humanity. So the historical process involves two ambivalent sentiments: the desire to free ourselves from the evil that we endure and that threatens us, and the desire to attain the good or to conserve that good which we already possess—two objectives and only one process. History tells us about the spiritual treasure we have; and, by understanding the past, we can participate in the creation of the future.

Animated by patriotism—"I love and admire Brazil and expect great things for her"—Capistrano was the most lucid conscience of Brazilian historiography.

SÉRGIO BUARQUE DE HOLANDA

Historical Thought in Twentieth-Century Brazil

SÉRGIO BUARQUE DE HOLANDA, a professor of history at the University of São Paulo, is one of Brazil's most stimulating contemporary historians. He has written some valuable interpretive studies, such as *Raízes do Brasil* (Rio de Janeiro, 1936), *Monções* (Rio de Janeiro, 1945), and *Visão do Paraíso* (Rio de Janeiro, 1959), which show a thoughtful insight into his country's history. He is now editing a ten-volume *História Geral da Civilização Brasileira,* which promises to be a major contribution to Brazilian historiography.

Buarque de Holanda credits Capistrano de Abreu with setting the course of twentieth-century Brazilian historiography. He comments in this essay on some of the general tendencies of modern Brazilian historiography and discerns a movement away from expository to interpretive history. Brazilians are applying a new methodology to solving old historical problems. The outlook for the future, according to this historian, is favorable.

The state of historical thought in Brazil during the last half-century is not easy to understand unless we recognize the prominent role of Capistrano de Abreu, the man who took the first step toward expanding its perspectives. In the work of Capistrano de Abreu scholarship completely prevails over speculation. By indirect means it is possible to determine the historical

This essay is translated from the essay "O Pensamento Histórico no Brasil," which appeared in the *Correio da Manhã,* "Cultura Brasileira" (Rio de Janeiro), June 15, 1951, pp. 3 and 12.

thought represented in his work. In distinct contrast to the work of all his predecessors (I refer in this case to the most illustrious), raw fact and undigested documentary evidence do not dominate his work. Even less do they form the malleable clay for creating imaginary structures to please passing personal whims, passions, or interests.

The work of Capistrano de Abreu was kept admirably free from these extreme hazards, to which the majority of the scholars of our past succumbed. He was a constant researcher, who was never entirely satisfied. More than any other since Varnhagen, he worked to discover, evaluate, and utilize the written testimonies of our national formation. He knew that these documents spoke truthfully only to those who dared to formulate precise, well-thought-out questions. In other words, he knew the dictum of the great modern master Marc Bloch—that all historical research presupposes that the inquiry has a definite direction from the start. In the beginning is the spirit. Never has passive observation led to fruitful results in any science.

What are the spirit and the informative thought of Capistrano's work, which would indicate the point of departure for a new direction in our historical studies? We know that in his youth he was not unfriendly to Comtian Positivism and that he later adhered to the doctrines of Spencer with more fervor and firmness. From the rudiments of Positivism and evolutionism he kept only the sense of measure, precision, and rigor of reasoning that retains imagination within plausible limits. He had an especially acute sensitivity to the importance of the influence on human institutions of the natural factors of land, environment, and climate.

References to contemporary historians are very rare in his writings. On the other hand, he emphasized and translated not only some geographers and anthropologists who were concerned with Brazil, such as Wappäus and Sellin, but also those who analyzed the general reciprocal relations between man and land, such as Kirchhoff. Commenting on one of the chapters of Sellin's book, Capistrano wrote that geography should predominate in studies of human development. These words clearly portray the value he attributed to the natural landscape in the formation and evolution of human settlements.

In his characterization of Sellin's book there is an outline of a work that evolved into his small masterpiece, *Os Capítulos de História Colonial,* first published in 1907. His plan is fundamentally different from all previous efforts. The more political aspects, and those that depend on purely individual action, which are difficult to reduce to any order, give way to other considerations, apparently plain and ordinary, which scarcely find shelter in the traditional concept of history.

For example, Capistrano devotes slightly more than thirty pages to the Dutch Wars, a favorite topic of the older historians, while he dedicates more than a hundred pages to the settling of the *sertão.* This is almost the inverse proportion of the space given to the same material in the first edition of Varnhagen's *História Geral.* Capistrano differentiates between the colonizing expeditions, which were an enduring influence in the settling of the *sertão,* and the other expeditions, which appeared to him to be merely depopulating and devastating. He was interested only in the colonizing expeditions. He clearly disliked to study the warlike, revolutionary, and "heroic" phases of the history of the extreme south. His symptomatically silent reaction toward the Inconfidência was certainly deliberate. He regarded the plot as a political movement explicable in terms of the influence of foreign ideas, which were not deeply rooted in our colonial tradition.

The real consequences of this attitude were not immediately understood, even by his disciples and closest colleagues. For example, [João Pandiá] Calógeras's *Formação Histórico do Brasil,* which was directly inspired by and an extension of the first sections of Capistrano's *Capítulos,* reflects little of the same spirit. Seldom do we find a more patient and well-informed investigator than Calógeras, who examined principally political and diplomatic questions in *Política Exterior do Império.* It would be unfair to deny that in his long study about the *Minas do Brasil e Sua Legislação* (1904–1905) and especially in the short and admirable synthesis contained in his lecture in the Biblioteca Nacional in 1912, *O Brasil e Seu Desenvolvimento Econômico,* Calógeras pointed out the ample prospects offered by the exploration of that almost virgin domain: our economic history.

The examples of Capistrano and the Barão de Rio-Branco were more fruitful for scholarly investigation. Capistrano's outstanding introduction to Frei Vicente do Salvador's *História* and Rio-Branco's annotation of [Louis] Schneider's *Guerra da Tríplice Aliança* continue to be models for their successors, such as Rodolfo Garcia—who commented on a large part of the Visconde de Pôrto Seguro's *História Geral* (Capistrano had already annotated the first volume) in addition to such colonial chronicles as the treatises of Fernão Cardim, the *Diálogos das Grandezas do Brasil,* and the *Viagem de Claude d'Abbeville;* and Eugênio de Castro, the editor and annotator of the 1928 edition of *Diário de Navegação de Pero Lopes de Souza,* reprinted in 1940 on the occasion of the Portuguese centennial.

The most important indication of the greater emphasis placed on geographical and social history was the publication of documents which opened up new paths for the study of social and economic history in addition to the more conventional studies of political, military, and genealogical history. A significant result of the new interest in documentation was the publication (due to the initiative of the historian Washington Luiz, who was alert to the value of manuscript sources) of the series of *Actas de Câmara* of Santo André (1914) and of São Paulo (begun also in 1914 and still being published), as well as of the *Registro Geral da Câmara de São Paulo* (begun in 1917), *Inventários e Testamentos* (begun in 1920) and *Sesmarias* (begun in 1921).

Due to the printing of these valuable documents, there was an outburst of studies of the Paulista past, especially the geographic expansion of colonial Brazil. A work such as that of Alcântara Machado's *Vida e Morte do Bandeirante* (1930) would not have been possible without *Inventários e Testamentos.* Without the municipal records, it would be hard to imagine the valuable study of Afonso de Taunay, *São Paulo no Seculo XVI,* later expanded in his history of the town and city of São Paulo. Easier access to these documents permitted the undertaking of numerous works of revision and reconstruction of Paulista and *bandeirante* history by Washington Luiz, Basílio de Magalhães, Paulo Prado, Alfredo Ellis Junior, Américo de Moura, Carvalho Franco, Cassiano Ricardo, Aureliano Leite, Nuto Sant'Ana, and especially Afonso de Taunay, whose opulent *História Geral das Bandeiras Paulistas* was begun in 1924, its eleventh and last volume completed in 1951.

The systematic elaboration of Paulista *bandeirante* history became a reality only in this century, thanks to the texts exhumed from the Paulista archives and also to foreign publications, such as the documents on the Jesuits in Paraguay published in Spain by Padre Pablo Pastells, S.J., and the manuscripts of Seville's archives published, as a result of the initiative of Taunay, in several volumes of the *Anais do Museu Paulista*. In the future this movement promises to expand with the contemporary works of Portuguese historian Jaime Cortesão and his preparation of the abundant manuscript material in the Angelis Collection, which will soon be published by the Biblioteca Nacional.

Another problem of our colonial history that has been explored and further illuminated in the last fifty years is the activities of the Company of Jesus. The renaissance of Jesuit studies dates from the third centennial [1897] of the death of Anchieta. In 1900 a volume was printed of the collected commemorative addresses by Eduardo Prado, Joaquim Nabuco, Teodoro Sampaio, Couto de Magalhães, and Brasílio Machado, among others. Without doubt, this was a considerable contribution. Although they did not use any new documents, these authors contributed to the information already known about the colonial activities of the Jesuits. The effect of this lack of documentation is noticeable even in some later works, such as that of Padre Luiz Gonzaga Cabral and the extensive work about the liberty of the Indians and the Company of Jesus that J. M. Madereira, S.J., presented at the International Congress of the History of America and published in 1929.

Since the publication of the tricentennial commemorations of Anchieta, the bibliography on the Jesuits in Brazil certainly has not ceased to grow. The majority of the documents published do not refer exclusively to the province of Brazil. For example, the previously cited compilation of Padre Pastells and the numerous articles collected by Padre Carlos Teschauer in the third volume of *História do Rio Grande do Sul* (1922) both refer to the extreme south of Brazil. Concerning the extreme north, there has existed since 1901 the important work on the Jesuits in Grão Pará by the Portuguese historian João Lúcio de Azevedo. We owe to him also the *História de Padre Vieira* (1918) and a new, enlarged edition of the *Cartas de Vieira* that has considerably enriched our knowledge of the life and works of that well-known preacher.

In the following years, the Academia de Letras revived interest in the study of the participation of Jesuits in Brazil's colonization with a copiously annotated collection of the previously known letters of the Jesuits describing Brazil. Since the 1930s, the most important step toward a comprehensive history of the work of the Company in Brazil was taken by Padre Serafim Leite. In 1937 his studies and lectures were collected in *Páginas da História do Brasil* and in 1940 expanded in *Novas Cartas Jesuíticas*. They constitute just a sample of the richness of the documentary materials that the author was able to collect, not only from the Archives of the Society of Jesus in Rome, but also from other European archives. The principal result of these researches was the *História da Companhia de Jesus no Brasil*, of which the first volume appeared in 1938 and the tenth and last in 1950. One could not hope for a better climax for the half-century of investigation by numerous historians about the work of indoctrination and colonization undertaken by the army of St. Ignatius.

Another aspect of Brazilian history that was clarified largely in the last half-century relates to the Platine questions during the empire, especially the Paraguayan War. The basis for a good understanding of the different episodes of the campaigns of the Triple Alliance is provided by the long studies of Tasso

Fragoso (1934) and Ramón Cárcano (1939–1942), written from a Brazilian and an Argentine point of view, respectively. Other aspects have been clarified by the printing, in 1925, of the journals of the army commanded by Caxias; in 1935, of Conde d'Eu's diary; and in 1910, of the reminiscences of Dionísio Cerqueira. The publication in 1924 of several volumes of the Visconde de Taunay's scattered works, including some entirely unpublished material, made additional contributions of the author of *Retirada da Laguna* accessible.

Most of the works written about the Paraguayan War are either partially or predominantly polemical. A recent work by Ambassador Cárcano, who tries to be perfectly impartial, contains many propositions that have not been well received in Brazil, or even in Argentina. Senhor Júlio de Mesquita Filho recently defended the Brazilian point of view on some of these propositions in one of his *Ensaios Sulamericanos*.

As would be expected, similar disagreement exists about the Platine war of the First Empire. One of the episodes of those battles gave rise to Ambassador José Carlos de Macedo Soares's work on the "Falsos Troféus de Ituzaingó" and later to Tasso Frangoso's study of the "Batalha de Passo do Rosário." Regarding the events following the Cisplatine campaigns and preceding the War of the Triple Alliance, there is abundant material and documentation in the books of Souza Docca (1919) and Pelham Horton Box (1927); the latter is in English and is devoted to the antecedents of the conflict. The results of Hélio Lôbo's investigation in diplomatic archives about the events immediately preceding the hostilities were published in *As Portas da Guerra* (1916). In *A Invasão Paraguaia no Brasil* (1940), Walter Spaulding presented us with largely unknown material about the development of the war. Recently our Ministério de Relações Exteriores offered students of our military history a rich source with its accurate *Catálogo da Coleção Rio Branco,* containing 5,122 entries from the Paraguayan archives.

During this progress of the last half-century toward a better understanding of our past, one cannot forget the extensive publication of more accurate texts about the initial phase of the occupation of the land. The publication [in Portugal] of the monumental three-volume *História da Colonização Portuguêsa* commemorates the first centennial of independence and includes numerous texts generally transcribed with dedication and preceded by scholarly commentaries. Following this example, there were those who endowed us with documentaries that were more lucidly and capably interpreted. It suffices to remember the previously cited *Diário* of Pero Lopes with commentary by Eugénio de Castro; the new Portuguese text of *Nova Gazeta de 1514,* organized and exhaustively annotated by Clémente Brandenburger; and Jaime Cortesão's valuable commentary in his excellent edition of Pero Vaz de Caminha's letter. In the same spirit, the Cortés Society published a facsimile edition of the *História* of Gândavo (New York, 1922) which was enriched with the important notes and commentary by John B. Stetson, Jr.

Capistrano de Abreu stimulated much of the interest about the problems which have been well explained during this last half-century, such as the activity of the Jesuits, the discovery and occupation of the land, and the conquest of the *sertão,* but not including the southern campaign of the empire. His opinion concerning the activity of the Company of Jesus is especially well known. Capistrano said that anyone would be presumptuous to write the history of Brazil before writing a history of the Jesuits' activity. If this was true, it is now appropriate to say that one can write the history of Brazil without being presumptuous.

Despite Capistrano's advice, there has been no shortage of attempts to write a history of Brazil based on a cumulative and often laborious presentation of historical facts, as in the considerable *História do Brasil* of Rocha Pombo. The very condensed, didactic volume of João Ribeiro is a significant, though isolated, contribution and an important methodological addition to the study of our past. Ribeiro adopted a structure and an expository system which separate him from the general tendencies of his Brazilian contemporaries and predecessors. His characteristic division of the country into well-defined historic regions at least appears to closely resemble the program outlined by Martius and also by H. Handelmann, whose *História do Brasil,* published in German more than a century ago, was translated into Portuguese only in 1931.

Beginning in this century, the emphasis on the development of regional studies became possible because of the already existing nucleus of scholars gathered around provincial institutions patterned after the Instituto Histórico e Geográfico Brasileiro. For example, the Barão de Studart lead the Instituto de Ceará until his death in 1927 and contributed considerably to the development of research on the settlement of the coast and the *sertão* of the Northeast. Equally important in Pernambuco was the influence of José Higino, Alfredo de Carvalho, Pereira da Costa, and Rudolfo Garcia; or in Bahia of Borges de Barros, Braz do Amaral, Teodoro Sampaio, Orville Derby, Toledo Piza, and Eduardo Prado. Publications such as the *Revista do Arquivo Público Mineiro* and the *Revista do Instituto Histórico do Rio Grande do Sul* extended a similar effort, though sometimes disorganized, to other areas.

If it is possible to say that the work of Capistrano de Abreu stressed the role of determinism (especially geographic determinism, as well as anthropological determinism as it related to the Indian influence) in Brazilian life, there has been no lack in this half-century of those who have made the stress again fall on the role of the individual in certain phases of our past. A good example of this genre, Joaquim Nabuco's *Um Estadista do Império* (1889), offers us an opulent tableau of the Second Empire; the warmth of filial devotion does not cloud his clear vision of history.

Written in another spirit and with the principal advantages and disadvantages of a greater distance in time, Oliveira Lima's *Dom João VI no Brasil* (1908) continues to be the most comprehensive source of information about the kingdom. It has not lost its importance because of the publication of Tobias Monteiro's *Elaboração da Independência,* which stresses the anecdotes and intimate aspects of Brazilian life in the time of that king.

The series of studies on the life and works of Mauá by Alberto Faria, Castro Rebelo, Lídia Besouchet and Cláudio Ganns merit a place of distinction among the biographies that have made a considerable contribution to the knowledge of the Brazilian past. The artificial, modern, romantic biographies which have been appearing have not succeeded in detracting from the authors of recent works that demonstrate the best qualities of biographical studies. These biographers are Heitor Lira, on Pedro II; Alberto Rangel, on Dom Pedro I and the Marqueza de Santos; Wanderley Pinho, on Cotegipe (only the first volume was published); Marcos de Mendoça on the Intendente Câmara; and Álvaro Lins on the Barão de Rio-Branco. Senhor Octávio Tarquino de Souza's series of biographies are an irreplaceable contribution to our intellectual history. While not dealing as completely with the First Empire, they greatly enlarge our knowledge of the Regency through the studies of some of its central figures: Evaristo da Veiga, Bernardo de Vasconcelos, Feijó and José Bonifácio.

While not speaking of the history of art and literature, which does not fit into this account, we should mention some of the peripheral works which have come to enrich the strictly historical studies. Many people have begun to be excited about the essays of social investigation and interpretation. I refer to the works of Couto de Magalhães, Batista Caetano, Macedo Soares, Rebouças, Sílvio Romero, José Veríssimo, Teodoro Sampaio, Orville Derby, Euclides da Cunha, Manuel Bonfim, Alberto Tôrres, among others. They opened paths for a type of research that our historians have hitherto scarcely used.

The first sociological study by Oliveira Viana, *As Populações Meridionais do Brasil,* is a historian's work as well. In his examination of the population of south-central Brazil, he sought to apply Le Play's method of indirect investigation. Oliveira Viana expanded this by resorting to predominantly racial doctrines in his later works. Departing from the geographical determinism of his first works, he substituted a type of biological determinism. At the same time, he wrote essays of social and psychological history inspired by the events and personalities of the Second Empire. Oliveira Viana thus popularized the genre of the interpretative essay already successfully undertaken by Euclides da Cunha in his *Contrastes e Confrontos* and *A Margem da História.*

Beginning with the publication of his *Casa Grande e Senzala* in 1933, Senhor Gilberto Freyre gave new strength to interpretative studies based on historical materials. Freyre had an ideal perspective from which to approach our historical formation because of his extensive knowledge of the Northeast's rural past and his methodological orientation, which was influenced by the methods of Franz Boas and his American disciples and by many North American and European studies on social contacts and miscegenation. Starting with the triangle created by the patriarchial family, plantation agriculture, and slave labor, Freyre analyzed their social repercussions in a series of studies. The final volume is still in preparation.

While not disregarding the biological factor in the formation of Brazilian society, Freyre—in contrast to Oliveira Viana— emphasized the cultural element in his studies. He understood the word "culture" in its anthropological meaning as a whole complex of beliefs, customs, ideals, living standards, values, technical processes, products, and artifacts, which the individual receives as a traditional legacy from society rather than as the result of the individual's own creative efforts.

In his later work, *Nordeste,* this type of inquiry naturally led Freyre to an examination of the relations between man and land in the sugar-producing areas extending along the coastal region between Bahia and Maranhão. He associated them with patterns of ecology which had only the name in common with the theories of human ecology developed by Park and Burgess in Chicago after 1921.

The historiography of the 1930s contains largely interpretive writings which simultaneously clarify and distort the facts by characterizing them in a particularly nationalistic manner. The importance of these works, stimulated by an epoch of crisis and transformation, would require a separate study. Although they have helped to give a new direction to historical studies, it would not be possible to go further than to make an incomplete list of them without overexpanding this study.

For example, there is the *Retrato do Brasil* by Paulo Prado, a Paulista historian intimately linked with the "school" of Capistrano de Abreu. Supported by copious historical evidence, he proposes to show that the country is still sleeping in "its colonial dream." Two years before the Movement of 1930, Prado stated the necessity of "making a *tabula rasa* before thinking of a total revision." The opposite attitude was adopted by José Mária dos Santos in his interpretative essay, *Política Geral do Brasil*. It is an alluring, though necessarily partial, synthesis of the history of the Second Empire and the First Republic. Santos tries to reveal the evils of the present as the fruit of an involuntary process born of "republican deformation." Without hesitating, he alludes to the remedies of the past. Balancing the advantages of parliamentarianism against presidentialism, Santos believed that the Revolution of 1930 would not halt the evils of presidentialism but rather would aggravate them, thus preparing for the advent of *caudilhismo* and the "era of the man on horseback."

In numerous studies on [national] formation published in the 1930s there is a persistent appeal to that which an American essayist called the "utilizable past," the presentation of alluring remedies offered as the perfect panacea for all our ailments. These imagined reconstructions are scarcely based on historical investigation, and in their extreme form lead to manifestations of totalitarianism, especially fascist doctrines.

The attempts at regional analysis are more interesting. Although they are sometimes overly laudatory, this does not prevent them from clarifying some of the neglected historical problems. In his book about the *Formação do Rio Grande do Sul*, which revives the theme of Rubén de Barcelos's short essay, Jorge Salis Goulart attempts to characterize the *sulina* population, past and present, with the help of historical geography, social psychology, sociology, etc. Employing similar criteria, Alfredo Ellis Junior had previously tackled the problems of Paulista de-

velopment in his studies. In *Marcha para o Oeste,* Cassiano
Ricardo attempts something like the approach Gilberto Freyre
had developed for the Northeast, by separating regional from
national and past from present.

In addition to the regional interpretations, the social and
psychological interpretations of Brazilian life provided us during the same period with other significant works. The most outstanding was *O Conceito de Civilização Brasileira* (1936), by
Afonso Arinos de Melo Franco. This interest in interpretative
studies continued into the next decade. In *A Cultura Brasileira*
(1943), sociologist Fernando de Azevedo used Durkheim's social
research methods to analyze our social, cultural, and political
evolution. In *Formação de Sociedade Brasileira* (1944), Nelson
Werneck Sodré desires, through an inquiry of the past, to serve
the present and "to furnish a guide for future paths."

Although these works deserve little consideration in the
strictly historiographical literature of the epoch, they reflect a
vigorous tendency toward goal-oriented, personal interpretation
which is moving away from the usual expository presentations.
Now, in addition to his already numerous works, including
studies of the Bahian expansion and the Casa da Torre and his
vast *História do Brasil,* Pedro Calmon is publishing a *História
Social do Brasil,* which has reached the Republican era in its
third volume. In the historical studies by Afonso Arinos de
Melo Franco, one also finds this interest in economics and society. He is principally interested in our material civilization
and its economic evolution. His *História do Banco do Brasil*
was suspended after its first volume.

Beginning with *Primeiros Povadores do Brasil* and now having completed an eight-volume series, J. F. de Almeida Prado
has utilized a large number of foreign travelers' accounts for his
interpretation and revision of the social, economic, and historical facts of the initial centuries of Brazil's colonization.

Even in this brief account, one should not overlook certain
works dedicated to regional history: Aurélio Pôrto and Borges
Fontes on the colonization of the extreme south; Arthur César

Ferreira Reis on the extreme north; Albert Lamego on the region of Campos dos Goitacazes; Tavares de Lira on Rio Grande do Norte; Oswaldo Cabral on Santa Catarina; Alúzio de Almeida on the south of São Paulo; Noronha Santos, Luiz Edmundo, Vivaldo Coaracy, and Gastão Cruz on Rio de Janeiro; Estévão de Mendonça and Virgílio Correia Filho on Mato Grosso; Romario Martins on Paraná; Cônego Raimundo Trinadade on the Archdiocese of Mariana; Rego Monteiro on Colônia do Sacramento; and José Honório Rodrigues and José António Gonçalves de Melo on the Dutch rule in the Northeast. Of Gonçalves de Melo's work, which was directly influenced by Freyre's own ideas and writings, the Pernambucan sociologist Gilberto Freyre writes that it is "the most complete, detailed, and comprehensive work that exists in any language" on the period of Dutch control.

These studies of Brazil's development were followed in 1942 by Caio Prado's studies of the historical evolution of modern Brazil since the eve of independence. His ambitiously large volume is merely the first of a long series that should take its place among the important sociological-historical studies by Oliveira Viana, Gilberto Freyre, and Fernando de Azevedo. Although his historical approach is based upon the doctrines of historical materialism, Caio Prado Junior concentrates mainly on the study of economic problems, which he feels are decisive for understanding the past and the present. This increased emphasis on economics is rapidly opening up unexplored territory for historical research.

The most important impetus for this type of research was provided by the publication of the first two volumes of Roberto Simonsen's *História Econômica do Brasil*, which was drawn mostly from the course that he gave in São Paulo's School of Sociology and Politics. These two volumes cover only the colonial period, but the next ones should cover the most puzzling problems of the empire and the republic. I expect that these economic questions will be grappled with only after a great deal of groundwork has been laid by many different specialists studying specific problems of defined periods, rather than by a broad synthesis in which these particulars would vanish and be lost for the benefit of some illusory vision of the whole.

Some aspects of our economic and financial history have been tackled in exhaustive monographic studies. The most important of these is Afonso de Taunay's fourteen-volume *História do Café no Brasil,* which is full of detailed information. This monumental work is worthy of the author of *História Geral das Bandeiras.* There exist many valuable studies of our financial history, beginning in the time of the monarchy with those by Sebastião Ferreira Soares, followed by Amaro Cavalcanti, Pandiá Calógeras, Severino Sombra, and most recently by Dorival Teixeira Viera. Concerning the history of extractive industry in the Amazon, there is Arthur César Ferreira Reis's modern work, which merits being expanded. Aided by modern historiographic resources, São Paulo's Alice P. Canabrava has attacked various questions related to colonial commerce, especially the contraband trade with the Plata and the sugar plantations in the north of Brazil and in the Antilles.

The complexity of these matters requires increased use of the methods developed in the countries with a long tradition of specialized historical study. I believe that the most auspicious aspect of our current historical thought is the concern to incorporate some of these methods and to apply them to Brazilian problems. Referring to the creation of our first faculties of philosophy and letters in São Paulo and the Distrito Federal in 1933 and 1934, respectively, Fernando de Azevedo in his *A Cultura Brasileira* noted our lack of really eminent personalities in the various intellectual and scientific specializations.

One cannot overemphasize the influence on the whole Brazilian teaching profession of the recent missions to our universities of foreign professors from France, Italy, Germany, the United States, and England. The activity of these foreign teachers, such as Jean Gagé and Fernand Braudel in São Paulo, Henri Hauser and Eugène Albertini in the former Universidade do Distrito Federal, was and continues to be a decisive influence on the new generations interested in Brazilian history. What has been achieved up till now suggests new types of research, and also creates new problems, such as the difficulty of making certain types of study (special courses, seminars, and thesis programs) available to the general public. It is not unreasonable to believe that these are the seeds of promise for a future flowering of Brazilian historical study.

E. BRADFORD BURNS

A Bibliographical Essay
on Brazilian Historiography

A large number of Brazilians have dedicated themselves to a study of their national past, some as professionals, but most as dilettantes. Despite their ever-growing interest in history, Brazilians have shown little inclination toward historiographical studies, and virtually no one has faced in print the philosophical problems of history. A notable exception to that generality would be José Honório Rodrigues, who has written much and well on historiographical topics. It is not mere chance that so many of the essays translated in this collection come from his pen. An essential starting point for any study of Brazilian historiography would be his *Teoria da História do Brasil*, 2 vols. (São Paulo: Companhia Editôra Nacional, 1957). This excellent work treats historiography in general and Brazilian historiography in particular. In the same year, his article "La Historiografía Brasileña y el Atual Proceso Histórico" appeared in the *Anuario de Estudios Americanos*, Vol. XIV (1957). This excellent essay is concerned with the trends in contemporary Brazilian historiography. Professor Rodrigues is afraid that Brazilian historians are not playing a useful role in society. He believes that they have valuable services, which they should give to the nation. These works were preceded by a less important but still highly informative study by him of the research undertaken by some of Brazil's foremost historians, especially during the archival missions to Europe which they headed: *A Pesquisa Histórica no Brasil: Sua Evolução e Problemas Atuais* (Rio de Janeiro: Instituto Nacional do Livro, 1952). Rodrigues has himself made a study of the European sources of Brazilian history in *As Fontes da História do Brasil na Europa* (Rio de Janeiro: Imprensa Nacional, 1950). The Livraria São José in Rio de Janeiro published a collection of his essays in 1951 under the title *Notícia de Vária História.* Among the essays were six related to historiography: "Historiografia Brasileira em 1945"; "Historiografia Brasileira em 1946"; "Historiografia Pernambucana"; "Historiografia Cearense"; "Rudolfo Garcia e Afonso Taunay"; and "Rudolfo Garcia." The number of articles and essays of a historiographical nature which Professor Rodrigues has published over the years and the number of lectures he has given on the subject are impressive. Recently those widely dispersed lectures, articles, and essays have been brought together and published in two volumes: *História e Historiadores do Brasil* (São Paulo: Editôra Fulgor, 1965) and *Vida e História* (Rio de Janeiro: Civilização Brasileira, 1966). Both are convenient and useful collections.

The French scholar Jean Glénisson offered a course in historical studies at the University of São Paulo, and in 1961 his book on the subject, *Iniciação aos Estudos Históricos* (São Paulo: Difusão Européia do Livro), was published. The general article on Brazilian historiography by Pedro Moacyr Campos included in this collection appeared as an appendage to Glénisson's general historiographical study. Ribeiro Manoel is an example of the scant Brazilian interest in historical problems. He wrote a brief, general, and unoriginal discussion entitled *Do Método na História* on the objective of history and the use of scientific methodology (Aracajú, Sergipe: Livraria Regina, 1945). The prolific Pedro Calmon also gave his attention to the study of historiography. In his *Introdução à História do Brasil* (Rio de Janeiro: Ministério de Educação, 1960), he first discussed the subject in universal terms, penning in very broad strokes a general essay. Then in a second essay he focused on the development of Brazilian historiography from the letter of Pero Vaz de Caminha to the present.

There have been a number of general interpretive treatises. The first, and one of the most important, was the essay by Martius which forms a part of this collection. Another one of the period, although of lesser significance, was "Dissertações acêrca do Sistema de Escrever a História Antiga e Moderna do Brasil" by Cunha Matos and Silvestre Rebêlo. It appeared in Volume XXVI (1863) of the *Revista do Instituto Histórico e Geográfico Brasileiro*. The Comisión de Historia of the Instituto Panamericano de Geografía e Historia in Mexico City has published three invaluable studies of Brazilian history: Emílio Willems, *Brasil: Período Indígena* (1953); José Honório Rodrigues, *Brasil: Período Colonial* (1953); and Américo Jacobina Lacombe, *Brasil: Período Nacional* (1956). They are perfect guides for an understanding of the broader meanings in Brazilian history. The contributions of João Capistrano de Abreu have been discussed elsewhere in the book, but in this particular context, one cannot refrain from reemphasizing the importance of his *Capítulos de História Colonial (1500–1800)*, 2d ed. (Rio de Janeiro: Leuzinger, 1928) and *Caminhos Antigos e o Povoamento do Brasil* (Rio de Janeiro: Briguiet, 1930). A unique work which should be included here is Nelson Werneck Sodré's *O Que se Deve Ler para Conhecer o Brasil* (Rio de Janeiro: Ministério da Educação, 1960). Particularly germane is the chapter entitled "Estudos Históricos," which is a brief historiographic and bibliographic guide. Two Americans have written interpretative essays of historiographic value which deserve consultation for a fuller understanding of Brazil: Richard M. Morse, "Some Themes of Brazilian History," *South Atlantic Quarterly*, LXI (1962); and Alexander Marchant, "The Unity of Brazilian History," in T. Lynn Smith and Alexander Marchant (eds.), *Brazil: Portrait of Half a Continent* (New York: Dryden Press, 1951). Another article of some interest in this category is by William R. Shepherd, "Brazil as a Field for Historical Study," *Hispanic American Historical Review*, XIII (November, 1933).

The studies devoted exclusively to the colonial historians and chroniclers are few, but they are generally of high quality. Thus far, literary histories have been the best sources for information on and critiques of colonial historiography. Sílvio Romero, in his classic *História da Literatura Brasileira*, 2d ed. (Rio de

Janeiro: Garnier, 1902), gave a full and perceptive account. A more recent evaluation can be found in Volume I of *A Literatura Brasileira* by José Aderaldo Castello, entitled *Manifestações Literárias da Era Colonial* (Sao Paulo: Editôra Cultrix, 1962). A critical resume of colonial historiography was the subject of the lecture of José Carlos de Macedo Soares entitled "Curso de Historiografia na Academia Brasileira de Letras," which was published in the *Revista do Instituto Histórico e Geográfico Brasileiro,* CCXL (July-September, 1958). Alan K. Manchester presented for the first time in English an introduction to two eighteenth-century historians, Pedro Taques de Almeida Paes Leme and Gaspar de Madre de Deus, in the two-part article "Some Brazilian Colonial Historians," *Bulletin of the Pan American Union,* September and October, 1934. E. Bradford Burns discussed the contents and importance of the Jesuit letters in "The Sixteenth-Century Jesuit Letters of Brazil," *Historical Records and Studies,* XLIX (1962). The most valuable treatment of colonial historiography has been made by José Honório Rodrigues. Indispensable are his studies of the sixteenth and seventeenth centuries: *Historiografía del Brasil (Siglo XVI)* (Mexico: Instituto Panamericano de Geografía e Historia, 1957) and *Historiografía del Brasil (Siglo XVII)* (Mexico City: Instituto Panamericano de Geografía e Historia, 1963). Also important is his historiographic account of one of the most crucial events in colonial history, the Dutch invasion and occupation of the Northeast and their expulsion in 1654: *Historiografia e Bibliografia do Domínio Holandês no Brasil* (Rio de Janeiro: Instituto Nacional do Livro, 1949).

Both national and foreign historians have given greater emphasis to a study of historiographic developments in the nineteenth and twentieth centuries. The essays in this collection represent some of the best of these efforts. Luís Lisanti recently published in Italy a general survey of national historiography, "La Storiografia Brasiliana tra il XIX e il XX Secolo," *Rivista Storica Italiana,* LXXVII (September, 1965), which is not dissimilar to the Moacyr Campos article included in this book. An indication of the volume and directions of contemporary historical output was given by Hélio Vianna in his "Atuais Tendências da Historiografia Brasileira," *Inter-American Review of Bibliography*, No. 21 (January–March, 1963). American and French historians have also investigated this subject. The careful study of Stanley J. Stein is a model: "The Historiography of Brazil, 1809–1889," *Hispanic American Historical Review*, XL (May, 1960). Professor Stein also made some useful observations on Brazilian historiography in another, broader article, "Latin American Historiography: Status and Research Opportunities," in Charles Wagley (ed.), *Social Science Research on Latin America* (New York: Columbia University Press, 1964). George C. A. Boehrer discussed "Brazilian Historical Bibliography: Some Lacunae and Suggestions" in the *Inter-American Review of Bibliography*, No. 14 (April–June, 1961). The two French studies on Brazilian historiography are very general in nature: Emile Coornaert, "Aperçu de la production historique au Brésil," *Revue d'Histoire Moderne*, XI (January–February, 1936), and Henri Hauser, "Notes et réflexions sur le travail historique au Brésil," *Revue Historique*, CLXXXI (January–March, 1937).

One promising source for historiographic studies which needs to be investigated—and a challenging investigation it will be!—is the *Revista do Instituto Histórico e Geográfico Brasileiro*. Hidden away in the pages of its many volumes must be treasures waiting to be uncovered. Quite probably the examination of articles dealing directly or indirectly with historiography would produce a significant profile of the subject for the century during which that venerable institution dominated historical studies. J. M. Pereira da Silva's biographical essay "Sebastião da Rocha Pita" in Volume XII (1849), pp. 258–76, serves as an example of the type of rewarding article which can be found. Primarily, of course, it treats the revered Bahian historian of the eighteenth century. But at the same time, the author took the opportunity to express his historical philosophy, thereby giving an insight about one of the most active historians of the mid-nineteenth century. He informed his colleagues—and posterity as well—how he thought history should be written and what he considered to be the qualities of the historian. History, he laudably emphasized, must be more than "simple narrations." It must be a synthesis solidly based on facts. After finding and understanding the truth, the historian must be able to express himself well in order to communicate his discoveries and insights, for style is "the secret of intelligence, the mystery of the writer." In the words of Pereira da Silva (pp. 265–66), the task of the historian requires much:

The true and only historical school demands extremely high moral and intellectual qualities. Love of the truth and only of the truth ought to characterize the historian. To find such truth requires both zeal of exactitude and scrupulous patience. Tombs, monuments, epitaphs, everything in short, can be of service to him. He must decipher with constant care old and faded papers and tortured documents, as well as consult new books. He must search for truth amidst the dust of manuscripts and at the cost of constant vigilance and redoubled efforts. Once the truth is found he will need cold-blooded judgment to do justice to it and to analyze it impartially.

It sounds quaint. It was, after all, the language of mid–nineteenth-century Romanticism. The style in itself gives a historiographical lesson. Aside from that, the ideas on methodology expressed were in complete accord with the most advanced European thought at that moment on historiography. The Brazilian scholar knew at least by name all the major continental historians. Much can be deduced about historical thought in Brazil in 1849 from this essay. I strongly suspect even more rewarding insights await the historiographical researcher in the *Revista*.

Regional historiographic studies are more difficult to locate. Most of the states have historical institutes which publish journals, and a search of those periodicals probably would turn up a few such studies. The strictly regional distribution of books in Brazil further compounds the difficulty in finding local works. For example, the Oiliam José book *Historiografia Mineira* (Belo Horizonte: Itatiaía, 1959) cannot be found easily outside of the capital of Minas Gerais. Two other examples of local historiographic studies are José Antônio Gonsalves de Melo's

Estudos Pernambucanos: Crítica e Problemas de Algumas Fontes da História de Pernambuco (Recife, 1960) and David Carneiro's *História da História do Paraná* (Curitiba: Centro Paranaense, 1952). After a general consideration of the philosophy of history, Professor Carneiro discussed historians who have written about Paraná, and gave a critique of their works.

Another category of studies are those which give a critique or analysis of the major Brazilian historians. Clado Ribeiro de Lessa has written what is probably the best biographical study of the foremost historian during the empire, Francisco Adolfo de Varnhagen. Entitled "Vida e Obra de Varnhagen," the biography appeared in the *Revista do Instituto Histórico e Geográfico Brasileiro,* CCXXIII–CCXXVII (1954–1955). Ribeiro de Lessa also edited a volume of Varnhagen's correspondence, *Francisco Adolfo de Varnhagen: Correspondência Ativa* (Rio de Janeiro: Instituto Nacional do Livro, 1961). A shorter study of Varnhagen is Celso Vieira's *Varnhagen: O Homen e a Obra* (Rio de Janeiro: Álvaro Pinto, 1923). João Capistrano de Abreu made two analyses of his predecessor; one is included in this book, the other is "Necrológio de Francisco Adolfo de Varnhagen, Visconde de Pôrto Seguro," found in the third edition of Varnhagen's *História Geral do Brasil* (São Paulo: Companhia Melhoramentos, n.d.) I, 502–8.

The Brazilians have written more on Capistrano de Abreu than on any other historian, a further indication of his significance for their historiography. Unfortunately he is little known or appreciated outside his own country. There are no studies of him except in Portuguese, and none of his major works is translated. In general, alas, even the Brazilian studies tend to be superficial. The essay by José Honório Rodrigues included herein is a laudable exception. That essay appeared in the introduction to the useful *Correspondência de Capistrano de Abreu,* 3 vols. (Rio de Janeiro: Instituto Nacional do Livro, 1954), which Rodrigues edited, as well as in Volume CCXXI (October–December, 1953) of the *Revista do Instituto Histórico e Geográfico Brasileiro.* That issue of the *Revista* contained a number of worthwhile essays on the historian from Ceará, un-

der the title "Curso Capistrano de Abreu." Some of the articles
are "A Vida de Capistrano de Abreu," by Rodrigo Otávio Filho;
"Capistrano de Abreu e a Interpretação do Brasil," by Gustavo
Barroso; "Capistrano e a Cultura Nacional," by Múcio Leão;
"Capistrano Geógrafo," by Arthur César Ferreira Reis; "Con-
siderações sôbre Capistrano de Abreu," by Mozart Monteiro;
and "Recordando Meu Avo," by Honorina de Abreu Monteiro.
Of the many biographical studies of the man and discussions
of his works, two merit special attention: Hélio Vianna's *Capistrano de Abreu* (Rio de Janeiro: Ministério da Educação,
1955) and Pedro Gomes de Matos's *Capistrano de Abreu: Vida
e Obra do Grande Historiador* (Fortaleza: A. Batista Fontenelle
Editôra, 1953). The latter is especially well illustrated. The
shorter studies tend to repeat the material found in the above
sources. Illustrative of these are Barbosa Lima Sobrinho, *Capistrano de Abreu: Historiador* (Recife: Editôra Nordeste, 1954);
Raimundo de Menezes, *Capistrano de Abreu: Um Homem
que Estudou* (São Paulo: Edições Melhoramentos, n.d.); Alba
Canizares, *Capistrano de Abreu: O Homen e a Obra* (Rio de
Janeiro: Briguiet, 1931); E. de Castro Rebello, *Capistrano de
Abreu e a Síntese Histórica* (Rio de Janeiro: Livraria São José,
1956); and Hélio Vianna, "João Capistrano de Abreu (1853–
1927): Síntese Biobibliográfica," *Inter-American Review of Bibliography,* No. 3 (July–September, 1954).

Contrary to the fate of Capistrano de Abreu, the contemporary social historian Gilberto Freyre has attracted considerable
attention abroad as well as at home. An anthology of friendly
Brazilian opinion is contained in the mammoth *Gilberto Freyre:
Sua Ciência, Sua Filosofia, Sua Arte* (Rio de Janeiro: José
Olympio, 1962). Lewis Hanke was one of the first to call at-
tention to the author of *The Masters and the Slaves,* in an
article entitled "Gilberto Freyre: Brazilian Social Historian,"
Quarterly Journal of Inter-American Relations, I (July, 1939).
Ordem e Progresso, another important contribution of Freyre,
was the subject of an excellent critique in Thomas Skidmore's
"Gilberto Freyre and the Early Brazilian Republic: Some Notes

on Methodology," *Comparative Studies in Society and History,* VI (July, 1964).

Three recent articles discuss the contributions of other Brazilians to national historiography. The first is by Joaquim Ribeiro, "Joaquim Caetano Fernandes Pinheiro e a Historiografia do Brasil," *Revista do Instituto Histórico e Geográfico Brasileiro,* CCXL (July–September, 1958). Ribeiro credited Fernandes Pinheiro with being a pioneer of literary criticism and of the historical essay in Brazil, and discussed his role as both professor and writer of history. The second, "Alfredo do Vale Cabral, 1851–1894," by José Honório Rodrigues, *Inter-American Review of Bibliography,* VIII (1958), commented on the importance of a scholar who greatly facilitated the task of historical research by preparing lists of primary sources, bibliographies, and critical texts. The third is a valuable study of Afonso de Taunay by José Honório Rodrigues, "Afonso de Taunay e o Revisionismo Histórico," *Revista de História de America,* LXI (June, 1961). Rodrigues pointed out that Taunay, as a disciple of Capistrano de Abreu, ably and amply provided the facts for his mentor's thesis that the conquest of the *sertão* was the most important event in colonial history. The revisionism mentioned in the title is the turning away from the usual history of the coastal area to a study of the conquest of the interior. It was that conquest which brought about "the creation of a distinctly Brazilian historical personality."

The study of that "distinctly Brazilian historical personality" (if it does exist, or to what extent it does exist) is certainly one of the major challenges in contemporary Brazilian historiography. A knowledge of the facts of the past is the first step toward defining that personality, but the second and more demanding step is to know which facts are significant and how they relate to the broader sweep of Brazilian development. By comparison, the facts of Brazilian history have been examined and are known. There is a need to find meaning in them, to synthesize them, to understand them. The new generation of Brazilian historians—that is, those who followed

Capistrano de Abreu—have tended to be more interpretive
in their approach to the past, but nonetheless the movement
away from expository history has been extremely slow. It is
significant in this respect to note that Brazil has produced not
one philosopher of history and only one historian of truly international stature, Gilberto Freyre. He is a master of interpretive history. He, by the way, has done more than anyone
else to define the "distinctly Brazilian historical personality."

This brief essay gives a general indication of the paucity of
material on Brazilian historiography. There is a need for an
interpretive history of Brazil—several of them—or at least a
synthesis of the national period which will compare to Capistrano de Abreu's masterpiece for the colonial period. There
is a need for a sharp but constructive criticism of the colonial
and national historians, most particularly of the contemporary
historians. No one has yet properly pointed out the major
significance of the contributions which Sebastião da Rocha
Pita, Sílvio Romero, Euclides da Cunha, Sérgio Buarque de
Holanda or José Honório Rodrigues, to mention just a few,
have made to Brazilian historiography. Regional historiography
seems to be a virgin field for future work. The questions of
periodization and thematic cohesion are by no means solved.
The great challenge is the amount of work still to be done.

NOTES

INTRODUCTION

1. There are numerous Portuguese editions of that letter. An excellent English translation of it can be found in Charles David Ley (ed.), *Portuguese Voyages, 1498–1663* (New York, 1947), pp. 39–59.

2. For a study of their letters see E. Bradford Burns, "The Sixteenth-Century Jesuit Letters of Brazil," *Historical Records and Studies,* XLIX (1962), 57–76.

3. Serafim Leite (ed.), *Cartas do Brasil e Mais Escritos do P. Manuel da Nóbrega* (Coimbra, 1955).

4. *Cartas Jesuíticas II: Cartas Avulsas* (Rio de Janeiro, 1931).

5. José de Anchieta, *Cartas Jesuíticas III: Cartas, Informações, Fragmentos Históricos, e Sermões* (Rio de Janeiro, 1933).

6. *Cartas Jesuíticas* II, p. 17.

7. *Ibid.,* pp. 263–65.

8. The two works of Pero de Magalhães de Gândavo have been translated into English by John B. Stetson, Jr., and published in two volumes under the title *Histories of Brazil* (New York, 1922).

9. *Ibid.,* I, 127.   10. *Ibid.,* I, 41.   11. *Ibid.,* I, 84.

12. José Honório Rodrigues, *Historiografía del Brasil, Siglo XVI* (Mexico City, 1957), p. 47.

13. Gabriel Soares de Sousa, *Tratado Descritivo do Brasil em 1587* (São Paulo, 1938), p. 2.

14. For a fascinating study of the European reaction to the New World see Sérgio Buarque de Holanda, *Visão do Paraíso: Os Motivos Edênicos no Descobrimento e Colonização do Brasil* (Rio de Janeiro, 1959).

15. Bertil Maier (ed.), *Orto do Esposo* (Rio de Janeiro, 1956), I, 14.

16. *Cartas Jesuíticas II,* p. 264.

17. Ambrósio Fernandes Brandão, *Os Diálogos das Grandezas do Brasil,* ed. by Rodolfo Garcia (Rio de Janeiro, 1943), p. 298.

18. Rodrigues, *Historiografía del Brasil, Siglo XVII* (Mexico City, 1963), p. 177.

19. João Antônio Andreoni (André João Antonil), *Cultura e Opulência do Brasil* (Bahia, 1955), p. 252.

20. Samuel Putnam, *Marvelous Journey: A Survey of Four Centuries of Brazilian Writing* (New York, 1948), p. 59.

21. Frei Vicente do Salvador, *História do Brasil* (São Paulo, 1931), p. 153.

22. See J. C. Fernandes Pinheiro, "A Academia Brasílica dos Esquecidos," *Revista do Instituto Histórico e Geográfico Brasileiro,* Vol. XXXI, Part 2 (1868), pp. 5-32.

23. For a brief introduction in English to a study of the academies see the essay "Aspects of the Enlightenment in Brazil," by Alexander Marchant, in Arthur P. Whitaker (ed.), *Latin America and the Enlightenment,* 2d ed. (Ithaca, N.Y., 1961), pp. 95–118. Essays in Portuguese are more numerous but still scarce. As examples see Fidelino de Figueiredo, *Estudos de História Americana* (São Paulo, 1927?); Alberto Lamego de Campos, *A Academia dos Renacidos: Sua Fundação e Trabalhos Inéditos* (Paris, 1923); Moreira de Azevedo, "Sociedades Fundadas no Brazil desde os Tempos Coloniaes até o Começo do Actual Reinado," *Revista do Instituto Histórico e Geográfico Brasileiro,* Vol. XLVIII, Part 2 (1885), pp. 265–322.

24. Figueiredo, *Estudos,* p. 117.

25. Sílvio Romero, *História da Literatura Brasileira,* 2d ed. (Paris, 1902), I, 169.

26. Quoted in Manuel Bandeira, *A Brief History of Brazilian Literature* (New York, 1964), pp. 42–43.

27. Nativism as the precursor of nationalism has been frequently mentioned in a variety of studies, but apparently there has not yet been a full treatment of this subject. Almost all Brazilian writers credit the victory over the Dutch as the first impetus to patriotic feeling in the colony. Afrânio Coutinho asserts, "In Brazil, there is perhaps no other line of thought more coherent, more constant, and older than nationalism." *Conceito de Literatura Brasileira* (Rio de Janeiro, 1960), p. 42. Manoel de Oliveira Lima believes that "manifestations of Brazilian national sentiment" began with the eighteenth-century writers. *Aspectos da Literatura Colonial Brasileira* (Leipzig, 1896), pp. 1, 240–42.

28. Hans Kohn, *Nationalism: Its Meaning and History* (New York, 1955), p. 30.

29. Alan K. Manchester, "Some Brazilian Colonial Historians," *Bulletin of the Pan American Union,* Part I, Sept., 1934, pp. 636–37.

30. Romero, *História,* I, 373.

31. Péricles da Silva Pinheiro, *Manifestações Literárias em São Paulo na Época Colonial* (São Paulo, 1961), p. 103.

32. The influence of the interior or frontier on the development of the

Brazilian and as a force in history was neglected until João Capistrano de Abreu pointed out its importance in his excellent essay *Os Caminhos Antigos e o Povoamento do Brasil*. José Honório Rodrigues stated that this essay was to Brazilian historiography what Turner's *The Frontier in American History* was to American historiography. (See "Capistrano de Abreu and Brazilian Historiography," p. 176, in this volume.) In another essay, Rodrigues stated that the conquest of the interior resulted in the "creation of a distinctly Brazilian historical personality." ("Afonso de Taunay e o Revisionismo Histórico," *Revista de História de América*, No. 51 [June, 1961], p. 126.)

33. Romero, *História*, I, 373.

HOW THE HISTORY
OF BRAZIL SHOULD BE WRITTEN

1. Martius was referring to the *Revista do Instituto Histórico e Geográfico Brasileiro*.

2. The Indian population of Brazil at the time of the Portuguese arrival was small, perhaps not more than half a million. The Indians were divided into five major linguistic families. For Portuguese purposes the two most important groups were the friendly Tupi and the hostile Tapuya. The nomadic Tupi generally inhabited the coastal region; the Tapuya were found widely dispersed in the *sertão*. The Brazilian Indians had a rudimentary civilization in no way comparable to the grandeur of the Incan, Aztec, or Mayan.

3. This was the original name with which the official discoverer, Pedro Álvares Cabral, christened the Portuguese domains in the New World in 1500.

4. Catherine II, "Catherine the Great," Empress of Russia, who ruled from 1762 to 1796.

5. It is interesting to note that a century later the distinguished French anthropologist Claude Levi-Strauss made a similar observation. He remarked: "Today, in the light of recent discoveries, and thanks, as far as I myself am concerned, to years spent in the study of North American ethnography, I realize that the western hemisphere must be considered as a whole. The social organization and religious beliefs of the Gé correspond curiously to those found in the forests and prairies of North America, just as the analogies between the tribes of the Chaco, such as the Guaicuru, and those of the plains of Canada and the USA have long been evident,

even if no conclusion was drawn from them. The civilizations of Mexico and Peru were certainly in touch with one another, at many moments in their history, through the intermediary of rafts plying along the Pacific coast." (*A World on the Wane* [London, 1961], pp. 239–40.)

6. Joseph François Lafitau (1670–1740) was a French Jesuit missionary among the Iroquois in Canada.

7. The Portuguese discovered Brazil in 1500. Martim Afonso de Sousa made the first permanent settlement at São Vicente (near the present-day Santos) in 1532. The crown did not send a governor-general until 1549, and the coast was not completely conquered until 1614.

8. In 1532 the crown divided Brazil into fifteen captaincies and granted them with broad powers to twelve court favorites.

9. King Diniz of Portugal ruled from 1279 to 1325. He is remembered for the salutary laws he gave the kingdom.

10. The Jesuits arrived in Brazil in 1549 and transferred European church-centered culture to Portuguese America until their expulsion in 1759.

11. Since then Serafim Leite has published his monumental ten-volume study of the Jesuits in Brazil: *História da Companhia de Jesus no Brasil* (Rio de Janeiro–Lisbon, 1938–1950).

12. The first Negro slaves brought directly from Africa may have arrived in Brazil as early as 1538. By 1585 there were 14,000 Negro slaves out of a total population of 57,000. The slave trade, and consequently the Negro proportion of the population, increased rapidly thereafter until the slave trade was effectively abolished in 1850. It is estimated that between 1538 and 1850 some 3,600,000 Africans were imported into Brazil. The preponderant number of Negro slaves present in the seventeenth century made the Jesuit Antônio Vieira comment, "Brazil has the body of America and the soul of Africa." Slavery was not abolished until 1888. The census of 1872 classified the population as 38 percent white, 20 percent black, and 42 percent mixed.

13. The first Negro slaves were imported into Lisbon about the year 1442.

AN OUTLINE OF BRAZILIAN HISTORIOGRAPHY IN THE NINETEENTH AND TWENTIETH CENTURIES

1. Not all think in this way; see V. M. Dean, *The Nature of the Non-Western World* (New York, 1957), in which all Latin America is excluded from the Western world.

2. Karl H. Oberacker, Jr., *Der deutsche Beitrag zum Aufbau der brasilianischen Nation* (São Paulo, 1955), p. 2.

3. R. G. Collingwood, *The Idea of History* (Oxford, 1946), p. 215.

4. See L. Weckmann, "The Middle Age in the Conquest of America," in *Seculum*, XXVI (1951), 130–41; also Sérgio Buarque de Holanda, *Visão do Paraíso* (Rio de Janeiro, 1959), pp. 78 and *passim*.

5. Y. Belaval, in *Diógene*, No. 28 (Oct.–Dec. 1959), inside cover.

6. See Sílvio Romero, *História da Literatura Brasileira*, 3d ed. (Rio de Janeiro, 1943), II, 238 ff., for other chroniclers of the period. J. M. Pereira da Silva, in "Sebastião da Rocha Pita," *Revista do Instituto Histórico e Geográfico Brasileiro* (cited hereafter in the notes to this essay as *RIHGB*), XII (1849), 261, wrote: "Brazil is in need of a history that is the combination or fusion of all the published and unpublished writings on its discovery, colonization, indigenous peoples, important explorations, and great events, because it had to spend its first days as the object of envy by so many nations who coveted the innumerable riches of its happy soil and the majesty of its geographical position. Brazil's greatest glory would be if this history were written by one of her sons, rather than by any other foreigner, devoted though he may be to Brazil."

7. See Ronald de Carvalho, *Pequena História da Literatura Brasileira*, 5th ed. (Rio de Janeiro, 1935), p. 133; also Romero, *História*, II, 62.

8. João Capistrano de Abreu, *Ensaios e Estudos* (Rio de Janeiro, 1931), III, 174.

9. Another academy, the Academia dos Renacidos ("the reborn") had planned to compose a general history of Brazil; see *RIHGB*, Vol. XLV, Part 1 (1882), pp. 49 and *passim*.

10. Capistrano de Abreu, in *Gazeta de Notícias*, March 23, 1880; quoted by Romero, *História*, II, 65.

11. Robert Southey, *History of Brazil*, 2d ed. (London, 1822), I, v.

12. Southey, in a letter of May 27, 1815, to Thomas and Henry Koster; in *RIHGB*, CLXXVIII (1943), 45.

13. See Southey's letter to Grovenor Bedford, with notes by Oliveira Lima, in "Retrato de Southey," *RIHGB*, Vol. XLVIII, Part 2 (1907), pp. 233–52. See also Capistrano de Abreu, *Ensaios*, I, 139.

14. Southey, *History of Brazil*, I, 27.

15. See Sérgio Buarque de Holanda, *Visão do Paraíso*, pp. 325–26.

16. Southey's interest in America, in general, is also reflected in his plans to found a literary-agricultural colony in North America, together with Coleridge and others. See Jack Simmons, *Robert Southey* (London, 1945), p. 44; also O. Lima, "Retrato de Southey," *RIHGB*, Vol. XLVIII, Part 2 (1907), p. 237.

17. Southey, *History of Brazil*, I, 1–2.

18. J. M. Pereira da Silva, "Sebastião da Rocha Pita," *RIHGB*, XII (1849), p. 271.

19. Southey, *History of Brazil*, I, vi.

20. Lima, "Retrato de Southey," *RIHGB*, Vol. XLVIII, Part 2 (1907), p. 246.

21. Southey, *History of Brazil*, I, 1.

22. See Southey's letter to C. H. Townshend, with notes by O. Lima, in "Retrato de Southey," *RIHGB*, Vol. XLVIII, Part 2 (1907), p. 247: "It would betray the sincerity which I owe you, to hide that my work, a long time from now, will be found among those that are not destined to perish; that it will assure me of being remembered in countries other than my own; that it will be read in the heart of South America and will transmit to the Brazilians, when they will have become a powerful nation, much of their history which otherwise would have disappeared, leaving for them what the work of Herodotus is for Europe."

23. R. A. Humphreys, *Latin American History: A Guide to the Literature in English* (London, 1958), p. 65. Oliveira Lima's judgment of Southey can be condensed into the following words: "the most conscientious, detailed, and exact [work] before Varnhagen, [and] the most literary, handsome, and captivating even after Varnhagen." ("Retrato de Southey," *RIHGB*, Vol. XLVIII, Part 2 [1907], p. 233.) Varnhagen himself said: "We will not say that he made a complete work; he himself acknowledged that he did not when, in December of 1821, he estimated how much his *History of Brazil* could be added to by someone who would scrutinize the Lisbon archives; but he did what he could and no one of his time could do better." ("Primeiro Juízo," *RIHGB*, VI [1844], 63.) In England, the reception to his work was not entirely favorable; one critic considered the *History* "the most unreadable production of our time. Two or three elephant folios about a single Portuguese colony! Every little colonel, captain, bishop, friar discussed at as much length as if they were so many Cromwells or Loyolas." (From *Blackwood's Edinburgh Magazine*, February, 1824, noted in C. R. Boxer, *The Dutch in Brazil, 1624–1654* [Oxford, 1957], pp. vii–viii.)

24. This despite his being an honorary member of the Instituto Histórico. Southey's death was remembered by Manuel de Araújo Pôrto Alegre in the usual address about the deaths during the year; see "Elógio dos Sócios do Instituto," *RIHGB*, Supplement to Vol. VI (1844), pp. 40–41.

25. Januário da Cunha Barbosa, "Discurso," *RIHGB*, I (1839), 13.

26. *Ibid.*, pp. 18–19.

27. Romero, *História*, II, 65: "The idea of independence did not please him; when he dealt with any separatist symptom, his sympathy was never with the Brazilians."

28. Visconde de São Leopoldo, "O Instituto Histórico e Geográfico é o Representante da Idéias de Illustração," *RIHGB*, I (1839), 77.

29. "Tome o Brasil a França por Madrinha." See Romero, *História*, II, 91.

30. In the lecture of Cunha Barbosa, moreover, reference is made to another romantic French historian, Barante.

31. The pro-Indian and anti-Portuguese position is clear. See "Dissertação Histórica, Etnográfica e Política pelo Coronel Inácio Accioli de Cerqueira e Silva," *RIHGB*, XII (1849), 233: "The heart shudders with horror upon remembering the cannibalistic acts employed against the Indians . . ."

32. See Romero, *História*, II, 47–48.

33. See Pereira da Silva, "Sebastião da Rocha Pita," *RIHGB*, XII (1849), 273.

34. Barão Homem de Melo, "O Brasil Intelectual em 1801," *RIHGB*, LXIV (1901), v.

35. Among the objectives of the Instituto was cited "the cooperation of many Brazilians . . . in order that they may serve as members of the body [dedicated to the preparation of] a general and philosophical history of Brazil." ("Breve Notícia," *RIHGB*, I [1839], 4.)

36. G. Lefebvre, "Notions d'historiographie moderne," Centre de Documentation Universitaire (Paris), pp. 123–24.

37. Cunha Barbosa, "Discurso," *RIHGB*, I (1839), 17–18.

38. Among the honorary members of the Instituto, besides several other French personalities, was the president of the historical institute of Paris, Count Le Peletier d'Aunay; in turn, Cunha Matos and Cunha Barbosa were members of the Paris institute.

39. See "Os Estatutos do Instituto Histórico," Art. No. 1, in the opening pages of the first issue of the *RIHGB*, 1839.

40. Cunha Barbosa, "A Lembrança do Que Devem Procurar nas Províncias os Sócios do Instituto Histórico e Geográfico Brasileiro," *RIHGB*, I (1839), 141–42.

41. *Ibid.*, pp. 272–73.

42. For the request of the Instituto, see *RIHGB*, Supplement to Vol. II (1840), p. 72. Martius's essay is translated in this collection under the title "How the History of Brazil Should Be Written."

43. Among the authors that can be referred to here, outstanding are

214   *Notes: Outline of Brazilian Historiography*

Pedro Taques de Almeida Paes Leme, Frei Gaspar Madre de Deus, José de Sousa Azevedo Pizarro e Araújo, Luiz Gonçalves dos Santos, Baltasar da Silva Lisboa, José Feliciano Fernandes Pinheiro, Inácio Accioli de Cerqueira e Silva, and Manuel Aires do Casal.

44. See "168ª Sessão em 10 de Junho de 1847," *RIHGB*, IX (1847), 279–80.

45. See Romero, *História*, V, 133–62.

46. "The plan for writing the history of Brazil which seems the wisest is surely that which Livy, João de Barros, and Diego do Couto followed; that is, relating the events of certain periods by decades. . . ." (Júlio de Wallenstein, "Memória sôbre o Melhor Plano de se Escrever a História Antiga e Moderna do Brasil," *RIHGB*, XLV [1882], 159.)

47. This summary of nineteenth-century research is dependent on J. H. Rodrigues, *A Pesquisa Histórica no Brasil* (Rio de Janeiro, 1952). See also Virgílio Correia Filho, "Missões Brasileiras nos Arquivos Europeus," *RIHGB*, CCXIII (1951), 133–75.

48. "1º Sessão de 1 de Dezembre de 1838," *RIHGB*, I (1839), 48.

49. "203ª Sessão em 19 de Abril de 1849," *RIHGB*, XII (1849), 280.

50. "8ª Sessão em 11 de Setembre de 1874," *RIHGB*, Vol. XXXVII, Part 2 (1874), pp. 424–31.

51. According to Rodrigues, *A Pesquisa*, p. 40.

52. Quoted in Rodrigues, p. 43.

53. Hermann J. E. Vätjen puts Varnhagen's use of Dutch archives in doubt: "On one hand, he had at his disposal the results of Netscher's investigations; on the other hand, he could rely on Caetano da Silva's copies of Dutch documents. This saved him the inconvenience of doing his own research in The Hague. It seems that he had no knowledge whatsoever of the existence of the West Indies Company archives." (*O Domínio Colonial Holandês no Brasil* [São Paulo, 1938], p. 42.)

54. Rodrigues, *A Pesquisa*, p. 50. See Varnhagen, *História Geral do Brasil*, 3d ed. (São Paulo, n.d.), I, x.

55. According to Rodrigues, *A Pesquisa*, p. 56.

56. *Ibid.*, p. 63.

57. See letter of A. H. Leal (April 12, 1857), in *ibid.*, p. 82.

58. "Joaquim Caetano da Silva, the most scholarly man that Brazil has had. . . ." (Capistrano de Abreu, *Ensaios e Estudos*, I, 198.)

59. Rodrigues, *A Pesquisa*, p. 97.

60. See Varnhagen, *História Geral*, I, xix. The best work on Varnhagen which we know of is Clado Ribeiro de Lessa's "Vida e Obra de Varnhagen," *RIHGB*, CCXXIII (April–June, 1954), 82–297; CCXXIV (July–

Sept., 1954), 109–315; CCXXV (Oct.–Dec., 1954), 120–293; CCXXVI (Jan.–Mar., 1955), 3–168; and CCXXVII (April–June, 1955), 85–236.

61. Varnhagen, *História Geral*, I, p. xxii.

62. *Ibid.*, p. xviii.

63. *Ibid.*, p. xxi.

64. *Ibid.*, p. xiv. As an example of one of the studies of the period on the Indians see Francisco Adolfo de Varnhagen, "Ethnografia Indígena: Língua, Emigrações, e Arqueologia," *RIHGB*, XII (1849) 366–76.

65. Varnhagen, *História Geral*, I, 54; after considering the Indians he concluded: "The picture that we have of these people . . . is truthfully not very flattering." On Varnhagen in comparison with Southey, see Capistrano de Abreu, *Ensaios e Estudos*, I, 213–15.

66. *Ibid.*, p. 196.

67. Varnhagen, *História Geral*, I, xii.

68. *Ibid.*, p. ix.   69. *Ibid.*, p. 5.   70. *Ibid.*, p. xiii.

71. See Romero, *História*, V, 164–66.

72. Reprinted in 1940 by the same journal.

73. Romero, *História*, V, 163–64.

74. Capistrano de Abreu, *Ensaios e Estudos*, I, 136.

75. *Ibid.*, I, 199.   76. *Ibid.*, I, 201.   77. *Ibid.*, I, 215.

78. See Romero, *História*, V, 177.

79. "Elógio dos Sócios Falecidos: Pereira da Silva," *RIHGB*, LXI (1899), 762–65. See Capistrano de Abreu, *Ensaios e Estudos*, I, 215.

80. "Sebastião de Rocha Pita," *RIHGB*, XII (1849), 266.

81. *Ibid.*, pp. 264–65.

82. Carvalho, *Pequena História*, p. 268.

83. An example of the importance of works on local history is found in the prologue by Capistrano de Abreu to *Notas sôbre a Paraíba* by I. Joffily, in *Ensaios e Estudos*, I, 221 and *passim*.

84. Romero, *História*, V, 187, 189.

85. See Nazareth Menezes, "Joaquim Felício dos Santos e Sua Obra" in *Memórias do Distrito Diamantino* (Rio de Janeiro, 1924), p. xxiii.

86. *Ibid.*, p. xxx.

87. *Ibid.*, pp. 200–1.

88. Romero, *História*, V, 193.

89. *Memórias do Distrito Diamantino*, pp. 272–82. See Capistrano de Abreu, *Ensaios e Estudos*, I, 212.

90. Joaquim Norberto de Sousa Silva, *História da Conjuração Mineira*, 2 vols. (Rio de Janeiro, 1948).

91. *RIHGB*, XII (1849), pp. 550 and *passim*.

92. Joaquim M. de Macedo, furthermore, composed works on Brazilian history, *Lições de História do Brasil* (1861) and *Efemérides da História do Brasil* (1877), and was the first secretary and orator of the Instituto Histórico e Geográfico Brasileiro.

93. See A. J. Lacombe, *Brasil: Período Nacional* (Mexico City, 1956), p. 104.

94. See Varnhagen, *História Geral*, I, xv, xviii; also "Actas das Sessões de 1890," *RIHGB*, Vol. LIII, Part 2, pp. 474–77.

95. Marie Armand Pascal d'Avezac, author of *Considérations géographiques sur l'histoire du Brésil* (Paris, 1857).

96. See Humphreys, *Latin American History*, p. 90: "His information was generally exact and the high reputation which his history enjoys is well deserved."

97. See Oberacker, *Der deutsche Beitrag*, pp. 313–15, where there is a list of German contributions to Brazilian historiography of the nineteenth century.

98. See p. vii of H. Handelmann, *História do Brasil*, published in *RIHGB*, CVIII (1931).

99. *Ibid.,* p. 996.

100. See J. Cruz Costa, *O Desenvolvimento da Filosofia no Brasil no Seculo XIX e a Evolução Histórica Nacional* (Rio de Janeiro, 1956), pp. 107 and *passim*.

101. *Ibid.,* pp. 125 and *passim*.

102. See Carlos Suessekind de Mendonça, *Silvio Romero* (São Paulo, 1938), p. 293.

103. Romero, *História*, V, 259.

104. See Capistrano de Abreu, *Ensaios e Estudos*, I, 208.

105. *Ibid.,* pp. 114–15.

106. *Ibid.,* p. 116.   107. *Ibid.,* p. 121.   108. *Ibid.,* p. 123.

109. For a suitable example of the results of these readings see *ibid.,* pp. 61–107, compiled when Capistrano was 21 years old. See also the words of Araripe Junior, noted by Castro Rebelo in *Capistrano de Abreu e a Sintese Histórica* (Rio de Janeiro, 1956), pp. 9–10.

110. See A. Pinto do Carmo, *Bibliografia de Capistrano de Abreu* (Rio de Janeiro, 1942/43), p. 22; and Castro Rebelo, *Capistrano de Abreu,* pp. 13–14.

111. "The Spencerian theory furnished the historical philosophy of the author." (Romero, in *Lucros e Perdas*, No. 2 [July, 1883]; quoted by Pinto do Carmo, *Bibliografia,* p. 42.)

112. *Correspondência de Capistrano de Abreu,* ed. by Rodrigues, 3 vols. (Rio de Janeiro, 1954–1956).

113. *Ibid.,* I, 203, 204, 150.

114. *Ibid.,* II, 220, 244, 290.

115. *Ibid.,* II, 334, 369.

116. See as an example, *ibid.,* I, 203. But he was also interested in non-Western history; *ibid.,* p. 205.

117. See Capistrano de Abreu, *Os Caminhos Antigos e o Povoamento do Brasil* (Rio de Janeiro, 1930), p. 219.

118. *Correspondência de Capistrano,* I, xliv.

119. Castro Rebelo, *Capistrano de Abreu,* p. 15.

120. *Correspondência de Capistrano,* I, 29.

121. *Ibid.,* p. 240.

122. This did not stop Capistrano from being attracted personally to Germany. See his letter to Mário de Alencar in *Correspondência de Capistrano,* I, 235–39, as decisive proof in this respect.

123. *Ibid.,* I, 268.   124. *Ibid.,* 165–66.

125. Capistrano de Abreu, *Ensaios e Estudos,* I, 138, 139–40.

126. From a letter to Guilherme Studart, in *Correspondência de Capistrano,* I, 162.

127. *Ibid.,* II, 165.   128. *Ibid.,* I, 284.

129. Rodrigues, *A Pesquisa,* p. 130; *Correspondência de Capistrano,* I, 118.

130. *Ibid.,* pp. 112–13.

131. Capistrano de Abreu, *Ensaios e Estudos,* II, 176–79.

132. *Ibid.,* pp. 193–98.

133. Rodrigues, "Capistrano de Abreu and Brazilian Historiography," pp. 168, 169, 176, and 177 in this volume. J. H. Rodrigues is also the author of the Introduction to *Capítulos de História Colonial,* 4th ed. (Rio de Janeiro, 1954).

134. Capistrano de Abreu, *Ensaios e Estudos,* I, 70, n. 9.

135. *Ibid.,* III, 155.

136. Furthermore, the desire to penetrate into the deep strata of these relations is frequently felt in Capistrano: "The ideal history of Brazil would be one in which the place occupied by the Dutch and Spanish wars would move beyond foreign successes in such events. Perhaps our grandsons will see this." (*Correspondência de Capistrano,* II, 16.)

137. Capistrano de Abreu, "A Critique of Francisco Adolfo de Varnhagen," pp. 154–55 in this volume.

138. See Rodrigues, *A Pesquisa,* pp. 127, 129; *Teoria da História do Brasil,* 2d ed. (São Paulo, 1952), pp. 463–68, 470–73.

139. See Carolina Nabuco, *A Vida de Joaquim Nabuco,* 2d ed. (São Paulo, 1929), pp. 297–98.

140. See Romero, *História,* V, 378–80.

141. Published in the *RIHGB,* Vol. XXXI, Part 2 (1868), pp. 62–135.

142. *Correspondência de Capistrano,* I, 133.

143. See his "Relação dos Manuscritos Portuguêses e Estrangeiros de Intêresse para o Brasil Existentes no Museu Britânico de Londres," *RIHGB,* Vol. LXV, Part 2 (1902), pp. 1–139; see Rodrigues, *A Pesquisa,* pp. 104–11.

144. Sérgio Buarque de Holanda, "Historical Thought in Twentieth-Century Brazil," p. 189 in this volume.

145. *Correspondência de Capistrano,* I, 350–417.

146. Buarque de Holanda, "Historical Thought . . . ," p. 184 in this volume.

147. Rodrigues, *Teoria,* pp. 173–74; *Correspondência de Capistrano,* II, 80, 226.

148. The 16th edition was published in Rio de Janeiro in 1957.

149. Buarque de Holanda, "Historical Thought . . . ," p. 184 in this volume.

150. See Rodrigues, *Notícia de Vária História* (Rio de Janeiro, 1951), pp. 210–23.

151. *Correspondência de Capistrano,* I, 63.

152. *Ibid.,* II, 234, 420. The change in attitude toward nature among the Brazilian intellectuals of the beginning of the twentieth century was a phenomenon of very rich significance. See Carvalho, *Pequena História,* pp. 365–66.

153. *Correspondência de Capistrano,* I, 416; II, 420.

154. One among many examples: *ibid.,* I, 233.

155. *Ibid.,* II, 21.

156. Humberto de Campos, *Crítica: Primeira Série* (Rio de Janeiro, 1940), p. 60. See Rodrigues in *Capítulos de História Colonial,* p. 26.

157. *Correspondência de Capistrano,* I, 228.

158. Hélios [Menotti del Picchia], "Nacionalismo Perigoso," *Correio Paulistano,* May 4, 1920, in Mário da Silva Brito, *História do Modernismo Brasileiro: Antecedentes da Semana de Arte Moderna* (São Paulo, 1958), p. 125.

159. Carvalho, *Pequena História,* p. 371.

160. See Mário da Silva Brito, "Os Patrocinadores da Semana," in *Estado de São Paulo*, Suplemento Literário, No. 121 (Feb. 21, 1959), p. 4.

161. Paulo Prado, *Retrato do Brasil*, 3d ed. (São Paulo, 1929), pp. 200, 214–15.

162. *Ibid.*, pp. 183–84.

163. *Correspondência de Capistrano*, I, 272–350. See also Buarque de Holanda, "El Pensamiento," *Ficción*, No. 11 (Jan.–Feb., 1958), p. 144.

164. Fernando de Azevedo, *A Cultura Brasileira*, 2d ed. (Rio de Janeiro, 1943), pp. 405–6.

165. Concerning the teaching of history in the Faculty of Philosophy at the University of São Paulo, see Pedro Moacyr Campos, "O Estudo da História na Faculdade de Filosofia, Ciências e Letras da Universidade de São Paulo," published in *O Estado de São Paulo*, Jan. 25, 1954, and reprinted in *Revista de História*, No. 18 (1954) and in *Ensaios Paulistas* (São Paulo, 1958).

166. See George P. Gooch, *History and Historians in the Nineteenth Century* (New York, 1959), p. 405.

167. Only in 1955 was the publication of a large French collection begun: the *História Geral das Civilizações*, under the direction of M. Crouzet, published by Difusão Européia do Livro, São Paulo, (1955–1958).

168. Concerning news of the *Revista de História* abroad, see Mauro, "Au Brésil: la Revista de História," in *Annales*, Vol. XII, No. 1 (Jan.–March, 1957), pp. 103–6; *Revue Historique*, Vol. CCVI, No. 422 (1953), pp. 362–63; *Bulletin Hispanique*, Vol. LIII, No. 1 (1951), pp. 106 and *passim*.

169. The situation was much the same in Portugal. As V. M. Godinho informs us, there is no Portuguese library sufficiently large to afford research in depth in the history of other European countries. ("Le problème des découvertes," *Annales*, Vol. III, No. 4 [Oct.–Dec., 1948], p. 523.)

170. *Ibid.*, pp. 541–50.

171. Myriam Ellis, *O Monopólio do Sal no Estado do Brasil, 1631–1801*, (São Paulo, 1955); and *Aspectos da Pesca da Baleia no Brasil Colonial* (São Paulo, 1958). Nícia Vilela Luz, *A Luta pela Industrialização do Brasil, 1808 a 1930* (São Paulo, 1961).

172. Rodrigues, *Teoria*, p. 324.

173. The Instituto de Açúcar e Alcool, for example, planned a service specialized in historical documentation. It began in 1954 to publish documents on the history of sugar.

174. In spite of everything, the over-all historical research in Brazil leaves much to be desired. See Rodrigues, *A Pesquisa*, p. 155.

175. See F. Braudel, "Deux livres de Caio Prado," *Annales,* No. 1 (1948), pp. 99–103.

176. Octávio Tarquínio de Souza, *Introdução à História dos Fundadores do Império do Brasil* (Rio de Janeiro, 1957), pp. 8–9.

177. See Pedro Calmon, "Arquivos Portuguêses e História Brasileira," *RIHGB,* CXCII (July–Sept., 1946), 134–36.

178. See Buarque de Holanda, "Historical Thought . . . ," pp. 192–94 in this volume.

179. See also the guides published in Mexico by the Pan American Institute of Geography and History, in 3 vols., 1953–1956, under the direction of Emílio Willems, José Honório Rodrigues, and Américo Jocabina Lacombe. Full data on these three works are given in the bibliographic essay at the end of this book.

180. Buarque de Holanda, "Historical Thought . . . ," p. 191 in this volume.

181. *Ibid.,* p. 151.

182. On the ignorance about Brazil in Europe, see C. R. Boxer, *Salvador de Sá and the Struggle for Brazil and Angola* (London, 1952), pp. vii–viii, or H. Hauser, "Notes et réflexions sur le travail historique au Brésil," *Revue historique,* CLXXXI (Jan.–March 1937), p. 86.

183. Particularly pertinent is the work published by Stanley J. Stein: "The Historiography of Brazil, 1808–1889," *Hispanic American Historical Review,* XL (May 1960), 234–78.

PROBLEMS IN
BRAZILIAN HISTORY AND HISTORIOGRAPHY

1. Pierre Denis, *Le Brésil au XXe. siècle,* 6th ed. (Paris, 1921); Jacques Lambert, *Le Brésil: Structure sociale et institutions politiques* (Paris, 1953).

2. David Riesman, *The Lonely Crowd* (New Haven, 1950).

3. Rollie E. Poppino, "A Century of the *Revista do Instituto Histórico e Geográfico Brasileiro,*" *Hispanic American Historical Review,* XXXIII (May, 1953), 313–15.

4. Of the 36 publications of the Arquivo Nacional, 17 are devoted to the colonial period; of the 108 volumes of the *Documentos Históricos* of the Biblioteca Nacional, 100 are related to the colonial period; and of the 75 volumes of the *Anais da Biblioteca Nacional,* the majority are on

the colonial period; the series of Paulista and Bahian historical documents are colonial, as are most of the journals of the historical societies of the other states.

5. Vianna Moog, *Bandeirantes e Pioneiros* (Rio de Janeiro, 1954).

6. Emílio Willems, "Luso-Brazilian Character," *Atas do Colóquio Internacional de Estudos Luso-Brasileiros* (Nashville, Tenn., 1953), pp. 77–78.

7. Poppino, "A Century . . . ," *Hispanic American Historical Review*, XXXIII (May, 1953), 316–17.

8. Capistrano de Abreu, "A Literatura Brasileira Contemporânea," *Ensaios e Estudos*, 1st series (Rio de Janeiro, 1931), pp. 75–76.

9. Sérgio Buarque de Holanda, "Historical Thought in Twentieth-Century Brazil," p. 191 in this collection.

10. Henri Hauser, "Notes et réflexions sur le travail historique au Brésil," *Revue Historique*, CLXXXI (Jan.–March, 1937), pp. 93–94.

11. *Sinopse Estadística do Ensino Superior*, 1955, published by the Ministério de Educação.

12. Fidelino de Figueiredo, "Historiografia Portuguêsa do Século XX," *Revista de História*, XX (Oct.–Dec., 1954), 348.

13. J. R. M. Butler, *The Present Need for History* (Cambridge, 1948), p. 19.

14. See José Honório Rodrigues, *As Fontes para a História do Brasil na Europa* (Rio de Janeiro, 1950).

15. B. Groethuysen, *La formación de la conciencia burguesa en Francia durante el siglo XVIII* (Mexico City, 1927; rev. ed., 1943).

16. Professor Rodrigues has published his own study of Brazilian character, *Aspirações Nacionais* (São Paulo, 1963), translated as *The Brazilians: Their Character and Aspirations* (Austin, Texas, 1967). The American bibliography is immense. A. L. Sidorov, *Les problèmes fondamentaux de la science historique soviétique et certains résultats de son developpement* (Travaux des historiens soviétiques préparés pour le Xe. Congrès International des Sciences Historiques à Rome [Moscow, 1955]) several times refers to "especially national traits" of different countries (p. 81) and of the ancient Russian culture (p. 101). The same thing is done by the contemporary Polish historians. See B. Lesnodorski, "Les Sciences Historiques en Pologne au cours des années 1945–1955," *Relazioni*, Vol. VI, X Congresso Internazionale di Scienze Storiche (Florence, 1955), pp. 463, 487.

17. Charles Boxer, "Some Notes on Portuguese Historiography, 1930–1950," *History*, XXXIX (Feb.–June, 1954), 1–14.

THE PERIODIZATION OF BRAZILIAN HISTORY

1. *Revista do Instituto Histórico e Geográfico Brasileiro* (hereafter cited in the notes to this essay as *RIHGB*), I (1839), 57.

2. In the second session of the Instituto Histórico, those who offered suggestions on the periodization of Brazilian history, were Brigadier General Raimundo José da Cunha Matos, José Lino de Moura, and José Silvestre Rebêlo; they also read papers on the subject. Those taking part in the discussion were Pedro da Alcântara Bellegarde, Januário da Cunha Barbosa, Cunha Matos, Emílio Joaquim da Silva Maia, José Feliciano Fernandes Pinheiro (Visconde de São Leopoldo) and José Marcelino Rocha Cabral.

3. Raimundo José da Cunha Matos, "Dissertações acêrca do Sistema de Escrever a História Antiga e Moderna do Brasil," *RIHGB*, XXVI (1863), 121–44.

4. In the sixth session of the Instituto Histórico, it was discussed by Silvestre Rebêlo, Januário da Barbosa, Judge Rodrigo de Sousa da Silva Pontes, and Dr. Emílio Joaquim da Silva Maia.

5. José Inácio de Abreu e Lima, *Compêndio da História do Brasil* (Rio de Janeiro, 1843). It came out in a second edition "continued till our days by a suitable liberal" (Rio de Janeiro, 1882), which does not merit any confidence because of the disrespect for the original text, and many printing errors. (José Honório Rodrigues, "Abreu e Lima: O general das Massas," *Digesto Econômico*, No. 25 [Dec., 1951], pp. 97–106). The study of Portuguese periodization began with the work of Alexandre Herculano: "Cartas sôbre a História de Portugal," *Opúsculos*, V (Lisbon, 1886), 33–155, especially 120–21.

6. Letter of Abreu e Lima to Januário da Cunha Barbosa, n.d., read in the 112th session of the Instituto on September 14, 1843: *RIHGB*, V (1843), 370.

7. *Ibid.*, pp. 369–71.

8. Francisco Adolfo de Varnhagen, "Primeiro Juízo: Submetido ao Instituto Histórico e Geográfico Brasileiro pelo Seu Sócio Francisco Adolfo de Varnhagen, acêrca do *Compêndio da História do Brasil pelo Sr. José Inácio de Abreu e Lima*," *RIHGB*, VI (1844), pp. 60–83.

9. José Inácio de Abreu e Lima, *Resposta do General J. I. de Abreu e Lima ao Cônego Januário da Cunha Barbosa ou Análise do Primeiro Juizo de Francisco Adolfo Varnhagen acêrca do Compêndio de História do Brasil* (Pernambuco, 1844).

10. *Ibid.*, p. 39.

11. The 138th session of the Instituto on August 7, 1845; see *RIHGB*, VII (1845), 421.

12. Varnhagen, *Réplica Apologética de um Escritor Caluniado e Juízo Final de um Plagiário Difamador que se Intitula General* (Madrid, 1846).

13. Abreu e Lima, *Resposta*, p. 39.

14. Opinion of the *Comissão de Redação*, signed by Januário da Cunha Barbosa and Antônio José de Paiva Guedes de Andrade on January 11, 1844; *RIHGB*, VI (1844), 125.

15. *Resumo da História do Brasil até 1828*, translated from M. [Jean Ferdinand] Denis and corrected and enlarged by H. L. de Niemeyer Bellegarde (Rio de Janeiro, 1831). There was a second edition (Rio de Janeiro, 1834). In it Bellegarde stated that he abandoned the first edition and composed another with less data from Denis; thus it no longer said "translated from M. Denis." This second edition was adopted by the Brazilian government to use in the schools and was approved by the *Circular às Câmaras Municipais* of April 26, 1834.

16. A flagrant example of the use of scissors and glue is in the section referring to the invasion of Bahia in 1624, written in the same words. It does not appear that Abreu e Lima had copied Bellegarde. In any case, they both repeated the same "authority." Compare Bellegarde, 1831 ed., p. 85 (1834 ed., p. 39) with Abreu e Lima, 1843 ed., pp. 112–13 (1882 ed., p. 75).

17. Antônio Ladislau Monteiro Baena, *Compêndio das Eras da Província do Pará* (Pará, 1838).

18. "Compêndio das Épocas da Capitania de Minas Gerais desde o Ano de 1694 até 1780," *RIHGB*, VIII (1846), 53–64.

19. José da Silva Lisboa, *História dos Principais Sucessos Políticos do Brasil*, 4 vols. (Rio de Janeiro, 1826–1830).

20. Karl Friedrich Philipp von Martius, "How the History of Brazil Should Be Written," appears on pages 21–41 of this collection.

21. Report delivered by Dr. Francisco Freire Alemão, Monsenhor Joaquim da Silveira, and Dr. Tomás Gomes dos Santos at the 168th session on June 10, 1847. For the text of their report see *RIHGB*, IX (1847), 279–87.

22. Henrique Júlio de Wallenstein, "Sôbre o Melhor Plano de se Escrever a História Antiga e Moderna do Brasil," dated September 30, 1843, Rio de Janeiro, and reprinted in *RIHGB*, XLV (1882), 159–60.

23. It should be noted that Varnhagen greatly varied his division of material from the first to the second edition of his *História Geral do Brasil*. Both editions had the same purely chronological criteria, and the sections were very unsuccessfully and, at times, vaguely titled: "Sucessos Imediatos

à Criação do Arcebispado" (1st ed., sec. 37), or "Outros Fatos e Providências durante 1750" (1st ed., sec. 40), "Ouro e Diamantes" (1st ed., sec. 42), or "Fatos e Sucessos de 1703 a 1715 Estranhos à Luta" (2d ed., sec. 39). Besides, his first edition contained 58 sections, while his second had only 54. In spite of this deficiency, the second edition was more precise and had a better division. The third edition followed the second in leaving out the whole part of the first edition that covered the period from 1817 to 1831. It is curious to see that Varnhagen put the whole part referring to the land and the people in the very front of the book in the second edition, reacting to d'Avezac's criticism. The first edition began with the discovery of America and the first explorations, and began to describe Brazil and its people only in section 7.

24. Varnhagen, *História Geral do Brasil*, 4th ed. (São Paulo, n.d.), I, xiii.

25. João Capistrano de Abreu, "Necrológio de Francisco Adolfo de Varnhagen," in Varnhagen, *História Geral do Brasil*, 4th ed., I, 507.

26. Justiniano José da Rocha, *Ação, Reação, Transação: Duas Palavras acêrca da Atualidade Política do Brasil* (Rio de Janeiro, 1855), p. 5.

27. *Suplemento ao Catálogo de Exposição da História do Brasil* (Rio de Janeiro, 1883), "Chave de Clasificação, II: História do Brasil."

28. On the theories of Capistrano de Abreu see José Honório Rodrigues, "Capistrano de Abreu and Brazilian Historiography," pp. 156–80 in this collection.

29. Capistrano de Abreu, articles in the *Gazeta do Rio de Janeiro*, November 21, 22, and 23, 1882, reproduced in Varnhagen's *História Geral do Brasil*, 3d ed., III, 440–44.

30. Capistrano de Abreu, Introduction to the *Informações e Fragmentos Históricos de Padre José de Anchieta (Materiais e Achegas para a História da Geografia do Brasil)* (Rio de Janeiro, 1886), p. 1.

31. The first edition of *Capítulos de História Colonial* by João Capistrano de Abreu was published in *O Brasil: Suas Riquezas Naturais* (Rio de Janeiro, 1907) under the auspices of the *Centro Industrial do Brasil*, and bore the title of "Breves Traços da História: Colônia, Império e República." The offprint had the definitive title; 1928 is the date of the edition by the *Sociedade Capistrano de Abreu* (Rio de Janeiro), now in a 4th ed., rev., annot., and pref. by José Honório Rodrigues (Rio de Janeiro, 1954).

32. Wilhelm Bauer, *Introducción al estudio de la historia* (Barcelona, 1944), p. 157.

33. [Marie Armand Pascal] d'Avezac, *Considerations géographiques sur l'histoire du Brésil* (Paris, 1857), pp. 9–10.

34. Varnhagen, *Examen de quelques points de l'histoire géographique du Brésil* (Paris, 1858), pp. 12–13.

35. Joaquim Nabuco, *Um Estadista do Império*, 2d ed. (Rio de Janeiro, 1936), 30n.

36. *Ibid.*, p. 428.   37. *Ibid.*, II, 374n.

38. José Honório Rodrigues is preparing a "História da História do Brasil" wherein there will be a special chapter on didactic history.

39. These are the subjects of the chapters of João Ribeiro's *História do Brasil*, 12th ed. (Rio de Janeiro, 1929): 1) Discovery. 2) Attempt to unify and defensive organization. 3) Battle of free trade against monopoly: the French and the Dutch. 4) Preliminaries: Spanish rule. 5) Dutch invasion. 6) The formation of Brazil: universal history. 7) The formation of Brazil: local history. 8) Territorial definition of the country. 9) Autonomous spirit. 10) Absolutism and the republican constitutionalist revolution. 11) The empire: progress of democracy. 12) The republic.

40. Bauer, *Introducción*, p. 154.

41. Oliveira Lima, *Formation historique da la nationalité* (Paris, 1911), translated into Portuguese by Aurélio Domingues as *Formação Histórica da Nacionalidade Brasileira* (Rio de Janeiro, 1944).

42. Lima, *Aspectos da História e da Cultura do Brasil* (Rio de Janeiro, 1923).

43. Lima, *Dom João VI no Brasil*, 1st ed. (Rio de Janeiro, 1909), 2 vols; 2d ed. (Rio de Janeiro, 1945), 3 vols.

44. Lima, *História Diplomática do Brasil: O Reconhecimento do Império* (Rio de Janeiro, 1901).

45. Lima, *O Império do Brasil, 1822–1889* (São Paulo, 1927).

46. João Pandiá Calógeras, *Formação Histórica do Brasil*, 1st ed. (Rio de Janeiro, n.d.); 3d ed. (São Paulo, 1938 [Coleção Brasiliana]). This book was translated into English and edited by Percy Alvin Martin under the title *A History of Brazil* (Chapel Hill, N. C., 1939); this edition was reprinted in 1963 in New York.

47. Calógeras, *As Minas do Brasil e Sua Legislação* (Rio de Janeiro, 1904–1905), 3 vols.; *La politique monétaire du Brésil* (Rio de Janeiro, 1910); *A Política Exterior do Império* (Rio de Janeiro, 1927–1928), 2 vols.

48. Calógeras, *As Minas*, I, 149–50; II, 523.

49. *Ibid.*, I, 175.

50. Capistrano de Abreu, "As Minas Nacionais," *Jornal do Comércio*, October 26 and 27, 1904, reprinted in *Calógeras na Opinião de seus Contemporâneos* by António Gontijo de Carvalho (São Paulo, 1934), pp. 31–32.

51. Oliveira Viana, *A Evolução do Povo Brasileiro* (1st ed., São Paulo, 1923; 2d ed., 1933).

52. Gilberto Freyre, *Casa Grande e Senzala,* 1st ed. (Rio de Janeiro, 1934). The work has been translated into English under the title *The Masters and the Slaves* (New York, 1948). An abridged paperback edition appeared in 1964.

53. Freyre, *Sobrados e Mucambos: Decadência do Patriarcado Rural no Brasil* (São Paulo, 1936). The work has been translated into English under the title *The Mansions and the Shanties* (New York, 1963).

54. Freyre, *Ordem e Progresso* (Rio de Janeiro, 1959).

55. Sérgio Buarque de Holanda, *Raízes do Brasil* (1st ed., Rio de Janeiro, 1936; 2d ed., revised and expanded, Rio de Janeiro, 1948).

A CRITIQUE OF FRANCISCO ADOLFO DE VARNHAGEN

1. Pero Lopes de Sousa, brother of Martim Afonso, kept a diary of their expedition along the east coast of South America, 1530–1532. *Diário de Navegação de Pero Lopes de Sousa,* preface by Capistrano de Abreu (Rio de Janeiro, 1927).

2. Written anonymously in 1511, this report spoke of early trade along the coast of Brazil. This report can be found in volume two of the *História da Colonização Portuguêsa do Brasil,* Carlos Malheiro Dias (ed.) (Oporto, Portugal, 1923), pp. 343–47.

3. Gabriel Soares de Sousa arrived in Brazil in 1569 and remained there until 1586 as a sugar plantation owner. He is noted principally for his *Tratado Descritivo do Brasil em 1587* (São Paulo, 1938).

4. Fernão Cardim went to Brazil in 1583 and died there in 1625. His three works, *Do Clima e Terra do Brasil, Do Princípio e Origem dos Índios do Brasil,* and the *Narrativa Epistolar,* are usually treated under the single title *Tratados da Terra e Gente do Brasil,* 2d ed. (São Paulo, 1939).

5. Both Cândido Mendes de Almeida and João Capistrano de Abreu have proved that this extremely informative report was written by the Jesuit José de Anchieta. It describes the religious, economic, and political life of the colony. José de Anchieta, *Cartas, Informações, Fragmentos Históricos e Sermões do Padre Joseph de Anchieta* (Rio de Janeiro, 1933).

6. Brazil as it is known today was composed of two separate colonies throughout most of the period of Portuguese domination: the State of Brazil and the State of Maranhão. The latter was created in 1621 and lasted until the Marquês de Pombal centralized and unified Portuguese

America in 1774. The State of Maranhão was formed by the present-day states of Ceará, Maranhão, Pará, and Amazonas.

7. The full title is *A Descripção do Estado do Maranhão, Pará, Corupá, e Rio das Amazonas* (Vienna, 1874).

8. Ambrósio Fernandes Brandão is considered as author of the *Diálogos das Grandezas,* written in 1618. An edition with an introduction by Capistrano de Abreu was published in Rio de Janeiro in 1930.

9. The struggle between the Portuguese merchants of Recife and the Brazilian planters of Olinda took a physical form in 1710–1711.

10. Varnhagen's *História da Independência* was published in the *Revista do Instituto Histórico e Geográfico Brasileiro,* Vol. LXXIX, Part 1 (1916). It was published in book form in Rio de Janeiro in 1938.

11. This correspondence was published by Dr. Jeronymo de Avellar Figueira de Mello in the *Revista do Instituto Histórico e Geográfico Brasileiro,* Vol. LXXVII (1914) and Vol. LXXX (1916).

12. September 7, 1822, is the date of Brazilian independence.

13. The eighteenth-century academies in Brazil set the precedent of dividing the study of history into a variety of topics, such as military, religious, administrative, etc., and assigning one topic to each member.

14. The author is referring to Minas Gerais in the colonial period.

15. The Franco-Brazilian dispute over the territory north of the Amazon River, comprising most of the area known today as Amapá, was settled favorably for Brazil by arbitration in 1900.

16. The Portuguese founded Belém in 1616.

17. Teixeira, in command of a Portuguese party of exploration (1637–1639), ascended the Amazon, Solimões, and Napo to visit Quito. On his return he founded Tabatinga (1639), the farthest westward claim of Portugal in the heartland of South America.

18. Reference here is made to Joaquim Felício dos Santos's *Memórias do Distrito Diamantino* (Rio de Janeiro, 1924).

19. José de Sousa Azevedo Pizarro e Araújo, *Memórias Históricas da Capitania do Rio de Janeiro, e das Demais Capitanias do Brasil,* 9 vols. (Rio de Janeiro, 1820–1822).

20. The Torre do Tombo is the national archive of Portugal.

21. João Manuel Pereira da Silva wrote principally on the First Empire and the years immediately thereafter.

22. José Maria da Silva Paranhos, the Barão de Rio-Branco, was a specialist in the history of the Prata area.

23. José Inácio de Abreu e Lima, *Compêndio da História do Brasil* (Rio de Janeiro, 1843).

A Glossary
of Portuguese Words Used in the Text

aldeia   A village. It frequently refers to the Indian settlements administered by the religious orders in the colonial period.

baiano   A citizen of the state of Bahia.

bandeirante   One who participated in the *bandeiras*.

bandeiras   Armed expeditions in the colonial period that penetrated the interior to explore, to capture Indian slaves, or to search for gold. The dispatch of these expeditions from the coastal settlements and particularly from São Paulo was a chief characteristic of colonial activity from 1650 to 1750.

caboclo   Either a pure-blooded Indian who has been Europeanized, or a Brazilian half-breed of white and Indian blood.

câmara   This word is used in the text as a shortened form of *senado da câmara*, the Portuguese term for town councils.

casa grande   The large plantation house, residence of the rural aristocracy.

caudilhismo   A highly personal and authoritative government rigidly controlled by an omnipotent political leader known as the *caudilho*.

emboaba   A pejorative term used by the native of an area to refer to an outsider. In eighteenth-century Minas Gerais, the local inhabitants used this term for the adventurers who came from Portugal or the coast in search of gold and diamonds.

entrada   A penetration by a band of explorers from the coast into the hinterlands.

fazenda   A plantation, ranch, or farm; the word is also used to refer to the governmental department of the treasury: Ministério da Fazenda.

230 *Glossary*

garimpeiro   A prospector for gold or diamonds.

Inconfidência Mineira   The conspiracy in Minas Gerais in 1789 to declare Brazil's independence from Portugal. It was discovered by the Portuguese officials, and the principal leader, Tiradentes, was executed.

Integralista   A right-wing, neo-Fascist organization in Brazil during the 1930s.

língua geral   Literally, "universal language"; usually the term refers to the Tupi Indian language, the Indian tongue most commonly spoken or understood in Brazil.

mameluco   The offspring of white and Indian parents.

mascate   Literally, "peddler of wares"; the term was used, sometimes pejoratively, in the eighteenth century to refer to the incipient merchant class.

mazombismo   Dedication to things Brazilian rather than Portuguese.

mazombo   A Brazilian born in the New World of white, European parents.

mineiro   Of or pertaining to the state of Minas Gerais, or its inhabitants.

paulista   Of or pertaining to the city or the state of São Paulo, or their inhabitants.

quilombo   A colony of runaway slaves; such colonies existed in the Brazilian interior until 1888, when slavery was abolished.

regimento   Any royal ordinance or set of rules or laws.

reinóis   A Portuguese born in the Old World who resided temporarily or permanently in Brazil during the colonial period. The term can be contrasted with *mazombo*.

senzala   Plantation slave-quarters.

sergipano   A citizen of the state of Sergipe.

sertanejo   A native of the *sertão*.

sertanista   One who studies or knows a great deal about the *sertão*.

sertão   The interior, backlands, or hinterlands of Brazil. The term refers particularly to the hinterland region of northeastern Brazil.

sesmaria   A land grant in colonial Brazil.

sulino   Of or pertaining to the state of Rio Grande do Sul, or its inhabitants.

Index

Abreu, João Capistrano de, *see* Capistrano de Abreu

Abreu e Lima, José Inácio de, 154; on periodization of history, 116–20, 129, 135

Academies in colonial Brazil, 15–16, 17, 45

Alencar Araripe, Tristão de, 157

Almeida, Cândido Mendes de, *see* Mendes de Almeida

Anchieta, José de, biography of, 14–15; *see also* Jesuit letters

Antonil, André João, 12, 17

Azevedo, Fernando de, on university teaching, 82, 195; contributions to sociology, 88–89, 193

Barbosa, Januário da Cunha, *see* Cunha Barbosa

Bellegarde, Henrique Luís de Niemeyer, 119–20

Belo, José Maria, 88

Borges de Fonseca, Antônio José Vitorino, 17

Boxer, C. R., 89

Brandão, Ambrósio Fernandes, 10–11, 144, 173

Buarque de Holanda, Sérgio, 88, 106, 107, 108, 134, 181, 206; on periodization of history, 136, 138

Cabral, Alfredo do Vale, *see* Vale Cabral

Cairu, Visconde de, 37; on periodization of history, 120

Calmon, Pedro, 88, 193; on historiography, 198

Calógeras, João Pandiá, 77, 79, 131; *A History of Brazil*, 1; *Formação Histórica do Brasil*, 78, 133; studies of economic history, 133–34, 183–84, 195

Caminha, Pero Vaz de, 4, 7, 188, 198

Caminhos Antigos e o Povoamento do Brasil, Os (Capistrano), 74–75, 105–6, 156–57, 176–77, 178

Canabrava, Alice P., 85, 195

Capistrano de Abreu, João, 42, 56, 59, 114, 131, 134, 192, 205, 206; on Varnhagen, 61, 62, 73, 124, 142–55, 157–58, 160–61; biographical data, 67–68, 160; influences on, 68–71, 159, 161–66; works of, 70–76, 167–74, 176–78; compared to Frederick Jackson Turner, 75, 157, 176, 177; correspondence, 79–80, 82; and new historiography, 105–6, 107, 108; on periodization of history, 125–30, 137, 138, 149–51; J. H. Rodrigues's critique of, 156–80; and documentation, 181–82; approach to history, 182–83, 188, 189; contributions to historiography, 199; historiographical studies about, 203–4

Capítulos de História Colonial (Capistrano), 71, 74, 75, 106, 128–29, 133, 156, 165, 167–72, 176, 178, 179, 183

Cardim, Fernão, 7, 8, 144, 163, 173, 184

Carneiro, David, 203

Carvalho, Ronald de, clarification of *modernismo*, 81

Casa Grande e Senzala (Freyre), 22

Chronicles: definition of, 3; style of, 8–9; nativism in, 9–10; contrast with histories, 20, 38, 147

Conto, Domingos do Loreto, *see* Loreto Conto

Costa, João Cruz, 86

Cultura e Opulência do Brasil (Antonil), 12–13

Cunha, Euclides da, 78, 191, 206; *Os Sertões* compared to Capistrano's *Os Caminhos*, 176

Cunha Barbosa, Januário da, 57, 118; in praise of Brazil, 48; on writing of Brazilian history, 49, 51, 52; questions put before the Instituto Histórico, 115–16, 121

Cunha Matos, José da, suggestions for periodization of history, 115–16, 135

Deus, Gaspar da Madre de, *see* Madre de Deus

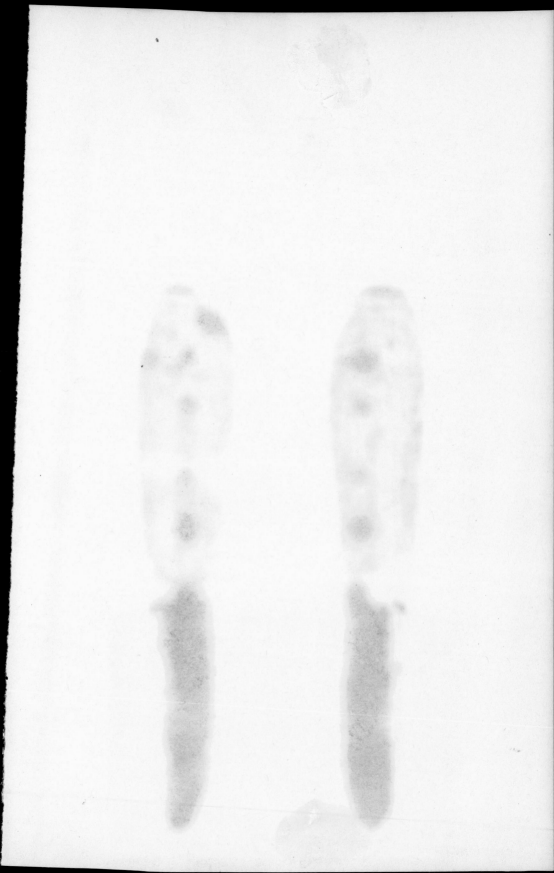

DATE DUE	
DEC 03 1996	